# SATIR FAMILY THERAPY IN ACTION

To Chris & Jasmine:
I wish you many moments
of joy in your beautiful family.
Love from
Val
July, 2015

# Satir Family Therapy in Action

MARIA GOMORI

The Haven Institute Press 2015

THE HAVEN INSTITUTE PRESS

240 Davis Rd
Gabriola Island, BC
V0R 1X1 Canada

www.haven.ca

ISBN 978-0-9784618-9-8

Designed and typeset by Toby Macklin
www.tobymacklin.com

# CONTENTS

*To my family
and the families who participated in this project,
with thanks and appreciation.*

M.G.

By Sun Yafang

This book is an English version of material that was first published in two volumes in Taiwan in Mandarin and then in China in Simplified Chinese. I personally encouraged Maria to have this book published in English, in order to share with a wider audience the benefits that Chinese families and therapists have received from working with her. I believe that families, therapists and other professionals around the world have much to learn from it. It is a book about real families and real life, written by one of the most humane, wise, and energetic individuals I have ever met.

Maria Gomori, now ninety-four years old, has devoted herself for five decades to the creation of healthy family life. Over the last ten years, I have been honoured to keep in close contact with her. She is one of my most treasured teachers and confidantes.

During the time I have known her, Maria has taught with special enthusiasm in China. She says that she has developed a connection with Chinese people, who she experiences as humble, eager to learn, unashamed to ask questions, and willing to practice what they learn. Chinese families have had the courage to participate in open workshops and have agreed to have their sessions published for the benefit of others, as they are in this book. At the same time, psychologists and professionals in China have been willing to put aside their preconceptions in order meticulously to study Satir family therapy, and have begun to apply it in their practice of medicine and education.

Maria has held over one hundred workshops in mainland China, Hong Kong, Taiwan, Thailand and Singapore during the past 27 years. She now has students all over the world. This book is a partial record of her efforts to train psychologists and counsellors in China in family therapy.

In Maria's training, many professionals in the field discovered that their patients' symptoms were often cries for help, or ways of coping with the real problem, which lay within their family system. Hospitalizing patients and prescribing drugs do not address this underlying problem. In this respect, family therapy is much like traditional

Chinese medicine, which seeks to understand and ease the overall system rather than specific symptoms. Only when problems in the family system are resolved can patients find relief.

For me, attending Maria's workshops has been a kind of spiritual experience. Maria once said, "Humans are miracles. I believe people have the ability to change. I can see miracles happen when I connect with them at a spiritual level and connect with them in Satir's process."

I have seen for myself the respect and inclusion Maria shows for the people she works with. She is able to build trust with families within a very short period of time. During each interview, her remarks are full of positive energy, wisdom, humour, and sharp wit. At the end of a two-hour session, members of a rigid and dysfunctional family are attempting congruent communication and will commit to one another around the changes they intend to make and the goals they have decided on. After the interview, the heartfelt words of the family members are very touching. People make changes they never thought possible.

At each workshop, Maria takes on multiple tasks, training students and assistants as well as interviewing and working with families and individuals. She works ten hours or more a day and often holds meetings over lunch. At the close of each workshop, everyone is exhausted. Maria, however, still has energy to answer emails and plan her next workshop.

People ask her, "Maria, where do you get your energy?" She often jokingly replies, "I get my energy from being with you." I think what she says is true. For Maria, people are exciting puzzles to know. She feels most gratified when working with people and seeing individuals and their families change.

I have also discovered that the same principles can be effective in business and leadership contexts. In 2006, I invited Maria to give leadership training sessions to executives in the company for which I work. After a few days, Maria told me excitedly that she found our executives open and receptive and that they easily understood the new concepts she was presenting. She creatively applied the principles of family systems to team systems. Together with Ben Wong and Jock McKeen, Maria designed for us questionnaires and course material in pressure management. To date, approximately 80,000 of our employees have found great benefit in them. Other companies in China have now invited Maria to give training sessions to their teams.

Together with her colleagues, Maria has developed a well-organized, widely applicable and easy-to-study process that is deeply faithful to the work of Virginia Satir. Her work, however, is not narrow or confined. She has creatively integrated into it what she learned from Milton Erickson, Carl Whitaker, Ben Wong, Jock McKeen, Jeff Zeig, and many others.

Maria is the most congruent person I have ever met. She never wastes energy flattering others or defending herself, either in work or life; instead, she always presents her most real and natural self to others. She has a strong, almost child-like desire for new learning. She is a leader in family therapy, yet she never acts like an authority, and has never stopped learning. She is forever young at heart.

It seems to me that as Maria gets older, and in spite of recent health challenges that have included surgery for lung cancer, her work has become even more focused and effective than before. How remarkable!

***

Recently I was invited to stay at Maria's home for three days. Seeing her daily life has allowed me to better understand her love for her family, her spirit of independence, and her interpretation of freedom. I have also learned more about how she appreciates the events of her past and lives very much in the present.

Maria's life has been dramatic: her autobiography, *Passion for Freedom* (published in 2014 by The Haven Institute Press), spans the fervour and romance of 1930s Paris, escape from a Nazi death march, a daring flight from the Soviet invasion of revolutionary Hungary, and a new life of freedom in Canada.

Her home in Winnipeg is filled with mementos of the past, which contribute to her enjoyment of the present. Her walls are covered with photographs of people who had a significant influence on her, in her childhood and adult life. Through all that she has experienced, Maria has remained optimistic, and this spirit shines out from many photographs of herself.

During my stay, I was honoured to hear about the important people in Maria's life as she shared with me the stories behind the pictures. She has a very good memory and described in vivid detail the time, background and events of each photo. Her refrigerator is covered with photos of her family: her son, grandsons and, most prominently, her three great granddaughters. She said that her family gathers at her house every holiday, during which time she prepares simple Hungarian dishes for them. She says this is the only way she knows to cook. Although she dislikes the winter in Winnipeg, she says the cold weather is warmed up by her family and the joy of being with them.

There are also many pictures of Maria with Virginia Satir; seeing them and hearing Maria talk, I felt the depth of their friendship and appreciated Virginia's profound influence on her. Alongside such artifacts from the past, Maria is also surrounded by the latest high-tech products. She uses an iPod, iPhone, iPad, iCloud, so that she can watch movies, show photos, and keep in touch with people via Internet.

She also has lots of sports equipment at her home, including a whole-body and foot vibration machine. She collects this kind of equipment during her travels to different countries. She was excited to tell me recently that she had bought a new stationary bicycle from New York. She rides the bike for half an hour a day and swims at the gym downstairs in her building.

Each year until recently, Maria and her friends spent one week in New York, enjoying movies, musicals, opera, and ballet, and visiting museums and galleries. I was very happy to attend this New York gathering in 2011. Every morning, the group had breakfast in a café, during which time they would share their experiences from the previous evening.

Maria is very punctual. In fact, she likes to be early. She always arrives at the airport terminal three or four hours before her flight. She is usually early for her workshop engagements too, and sometimes she even starts her classes five minutes early. If her trainees are not there, when they arrive (at the appointed time) she lectures them for being late! When she is reminded that they are actually on time, she pokes fun at herself. When traveling together, she and I both need to make adjustments. For example, if we agree to have breakfast at 7:30, she will arrive at the restaurant at 7:00. She is used to doing things ahead of the time. In order not to make her anxious, I try my best to keep in sync with her. In her eyes, I am on time.

Maria enjoys tropical weather and all her life hoped to live near the ocean in a warm climate. She jokingly explains that she and her husband Paul didn't choose Winnipeg for its weather when they came to Canada. Paul got his veterinary licence in the province of Manitoba, so it was the opportunity for him to practice that brought them there.

Knowing this, in February 2013, after Maria's workshops in China were over, we took a four-day vacation on Hainan Island, a trip we had been planning for two years. I knew she loved swimming, so I booked a room with direct access to the pool from the veranda. We were in the water enjoying the sunshine almost every day.

During a business trip to Europe in June 2014, Maria and our friend Jock McKeen joined me in visiting three European cities: Paris, Budapest, and Berlin. These three cities are all especially meaningful to Maria.

Paris is where Maria first enjoyed freedom, and she took us to places there where she studied and went on dates with her first boyfriend. Budapest is where she was born and raised, as well as where she endured World War II and the Hungarian Revolution. We accompanied Maria to her father's grave there. She told us how he had always trusted her and supported her, raising her in such a way that she learned to believe in herself. She was pleased to see the beautiful poppies that graced her father's resting place.

I felt privileged to have Maria share her experiences with us as we visited these cities. In Berlin and Budapest especially what impressed me most was her positive attitude as she recounted the historical tragedies that took place there. As someone who narrowly escaped death on multiple occasions, she harbours no hatred, nor does she think of herself as a victim. Instead, she intently looks beyond herself, her family, and her country, and digs deep into what really happened during the war, arriving at penetrating reflections on what each country should learn from history.

There are many museums in Berlin to show what really happened during the war and remind Germans and people all over the world of the atrocities committed at that time. For Maria, these actions in facing past mistakes demonstrate the confidence and courage of the country and its people. She believes other countries could learn from this example. Although Maria experienced so many hardships and threats to her life, she is able to recount what she suffered in an optimistic and sometimes humorous manner and embrace what history has to teach us. As Virginia Satir taught, it is as if she keeps these memories in a large museum. She can visit them if she wishes, but she does not re-live or make herself victim to them. Because she can let go of these hurts, she can move forward optimistically and resolutely, using them as resources to survive and thrive. As an advocate of Satir's family therapy model, Maria practices what she teaches.

It has been my privilege and pleasure to know Maria and my hope that this book will further spread the ideas and spirit that she has devoted her life to demonstrating and teaching.

In this brief preface, I want to offer my personal reflections on the family therapy teaching project recorded in this book, which took place in Shanghai and Nanjing, China, in 2011 and 2012. I wish also to thank the many people who have contributed to the publication of this book.

The teaching experiences that I describe have brought many gifts into my life. The greatest of these has been to meet such hard-working and motivated people. It was my joy to share myself with them and to experience their loving support and curiosity. It has been a privilege to learn more about Chinese culture and family life. I also consider it a gift to discover that there were changes, as reported by the various therapists, in the lives of each family we worked with.

Another gift arrived on the last day of this 18-day journey, when I asked each small group to present their learnings, using humour. I think humour gives people the freedom to say what they want without fear of judgment. I also believe we can only really use humour around something that we know about and have integrated. The last afternoon of the workshop was full of laughter as participants role played what they had learned about family therapy. Each group created a sculpt to represent the various theories and concepts. I found it most gratifying, as it confirmed that they had understood and learned what I had set out to teach.

Finally, there is the gift that came in the form of a decision by the participants to record and transcribe the entire workshop experience, eventually turning it into a two-volume publication in Chinese, so that other families and therapists could share in the learning.

For these Chinese books, we chose sessions with seven families who had given us permission to include their interviews. Many of the group leaders and participants were involved in translating and transcribing the videotapes, verbatim, into English. They then sent the written document to me for review and editing. All this then had to be translated back into Chinese! Knowing that this would be a complicated process, and because I wanted to know exactly what was going to be in the books, I suggested to the publisher that she take on one of my long-time students as the sole translator. I knew that Grace, who was a small-group leader and is currently writing a book on the similarities between the Satir Model and Buddhism, was committed to the precise translation of what I had written.

When the Chinese transcripts were ready, Grace sent them to the relevant therapists to review and to discuss with the families involved. Finally, the publisher edited the material, which ended up being 800 pages long, divided into two volumes. The title of the first volume is *The Elephant in The Room*, while the second volume is called *Crossing The River*. These were published in Traditional Chinese in Taiwan in November 2013 and in Simplified Chinese in Shanghai in March of 2014. An official book signing in Taiwan in November 2013 drew an audience of 900 people. It was a heartwarming experience, at which my students gave me an embroidered gift, which is hard to describe; suffice it to say, it is very beautiful.

An additional gift that came from this book project is that I learned how to trust and manage my anxiety, knowing that in the end I can never really know exactly what is contained in those books!

Originally, I had no intention of publishing this material in English. There are already many wonderful English language books on family therapy and I didn't think we needed another one. In my nineties as I am, I did not want to spend the money and energy that would be needed; nor did my ego need another title bearing my name on the shelf. That all changed, however, when Sun Yafang, one of my closest friends, who was also a participant in this group, began to encourage and support me to publish an English version. When I asked her why she felt so strongly about it, she said she believed the material contained a lot of important teachings and she wanted people outside of China to read it.

I think Yafang's mission in life is similar to that of Virginia: to help people become more human. So the reason I agreed to invest my time and energy in this project was as a tribute to Virginia and an expression of my passion for the Satir Model. I also wanted to share my experience, my learning, and my love for the families and the students who shared the 18-day journey of discovery that inspired the book.

I hope that we all learn from the families that appear in this book. Every family and student I have ever worked with has been a gift to me. While each is unique, we share so many similarities. I'm sure some of the stories here will seem familiar to you, the reader. My hope is that they will provide inspiration and guidance in your life and in the lives of your loved ones.

## Acknowledgements

I am grateful to Yafang for her consistent support of this book. I also want to appreciate my friend Val Monk. When I mentioned to her that I was looking for someone to help me to produce this book, she generously offered her time and help. Val teaches the Satir Model herself and integrates it into her practice as a family business advisor and family therapist. She offered to be my English advisor, since my native tongue is Hungarian. For the editing of the book I am grateful to Carolin Vesely, and to Toby Macklin at The Haven Institute Press, who also designed the book. Toby also edited and designed two of my previous books: *Personal Alchemy: The Art of Satir Family Reconstruction* (2008) and *Passion for Freedom* (2014).

I am also thankful to the Chinese families I worked with for granting me their trust to work with and learn from them, to track their changes and their growth. Their issues are not different from my own family issues, or that of any ordinary family in the West. Virginia knew this. Her dream was to demonstrate how we could work with families in any part of the world and see that the foundation of the family system is similar, regardless of race, colour, culture or religion. That was certainly my experience working with Chinese families. Fundamental issues and family processes are similar across cultures. I am grateful to everyone involved for showing me that this is so.

My thanks go also to the many students and participants who devoted countless hours to the transcription and translation that brought this text into existence.

## Overview

The book is divided into two parts. Part One contains two personal essays. In Chapter One, I give a brief account of the life and career of Virginia Satir. This material represents my own understanding, drawing on my personal experience, and has not been available in book form until now. In Chapter Two, I tell something of my own story. I describe how I first met Virginia and became involved in her work. I write too about how I came to be teaching her processes not only in Canada, where I have lived for the last 60 years, but also in China and many countries around the world, including Hungary, where I was born.*

Part Two focuses on the family therapy teaching project itself. In Chapter Three, I explain the background and purpose of the project, and outline various elements of the Satir Model which were presented as guidelines for participants.

Chapter Four offers brief synopses of the cases transcribed in the book. Chapters Five to Nine are the transcripts themselves and include commentaries, participant feedback and my own evaluations of the processes, with reference to the guidelines outlined in Chapter Three. My hope is that these elements will be especially valuable to students and other readers of this book.

---

* If you would like to read more about my sometimes dramatic life, my autobiography *Passion for Freedom* is available from The Haven Institute Press.

# PART ONE

## *Personal Essays*

## Chapter One
### VIRGINIA SATIR: A VISIONARY LIFE

Virginia Satir was born the eldest of five children on a farm in Wisconsin in 1916. A bright and curious child, she taught herself to read at the age of three, and by the time she was nine, she had devoured all of the books in the library of her one-room schoolhouse. Her family was dysfunctional. Her parents had a turbulent relationship, and she struggled to make sense of their erratic behaviour – hating each other one day and dancing together the next. So, when she was five, Virginia vowed that when she grew up she would become "a children's detective on parents" to help youngsters solve puzzles like this one. As she later explained in her book *The New Peoplemaking* (1988): "I didn't quite know what I would look for, but I realized a lot went on in families that didn't meet the eye."

Having reached her full height of 5 feet 10 inches by the age of 10, Virginia always felt different from her peers. She couldn't go shoe shopping with the other girls, as she usually had to buy her footwear in men's stores. There were no "tall girl" shops at the time. Virginia's high school years coincided with the Great Depression, during which the family lost all their belongings and moved from the farm into the city of Milwaukee. There, at age 16, she enrolled in teachers' college. She worked in a department store and babysat to pay her tuition, and graduated with her teaching degree at age 20. A year later, she was a school principal.

It soon became apparent to her that the education system had little interest in the lives of its students outside the school walls. Virginia, however, was very interested, so she took the unusual step of going home with her students to meet their families. One day, she accompanied a little boy to his house, only to be greeted at the door by his mother, who took one look at her and said: "Oh my God, what has he done?" The woman had assumed that only her child's bad behaviour would motivate someone charged with his education and well being to show an interest in his home life. But the woman didn't know who she was dealing with. By intuitively seeking to know and understand individuals in the larger context of their lives, Virginia had already begun to recognize and to value the family as a force for healing and transformation.

In the late 1930s, Virginia started graduate studies at the University of Chicago's School of Social Services Administration. She didn't exactly do things by the book, which was not surprising given her emerging unorthodox approach to helping people. After awarding her a D grade in field work, one professor told her she was "obviously not cut out to be a social worker."

In 1976, that same university would award her a gold medal for "outstanding and consistent service to humankind." She accepted the award on the condition that she be allowed to address the audience, which included many of her teachers. During her speech, she graciously shared how it felt to encounter such a lack of acceptance. She said:

"I came to this university with stars in my eyes when I was a student and I found that it offered the same old things I had received in other institutions. And I told myself that when I grew up, I was going to do things differently." The crowd gave her a standing ovation.

After graduate school, Virginia entered private practice, drawing on her training in social work and psychoanalytic theory. But nothing could prepare her for what she encountered. Many people who came to her office had been deemed hopeless cases. No one wanted to work with them, and they had fallen through the cracks. Virginia was drawn to these haunted outcasts and found she was able to help many of them, without really knowing what it was she was doing that was proving effective. There were no role models, no one to learn from or mentors to follow. She had the will and the courage to follow her intuition and to break the mold that did not fit her. She started from scratch, inventing every step of her work.

Virginia entered the therapy world at a time when there was no women's movement, and no private insurance for psychotherapy. She was not only working in a male-dominated field, but one that was firmly grounded in the medical model. Prevailing psychoanalytic techniques focused on intra-psychic processes; on this model problems originated within an individual's psyche or mind, not with interactions between people. But Virginia knew the interpersonal realm was fertile ground for helping people to address the issues that were preventing them from living healthy and satisfying lives. And she had the courage and will to break rules and sidestep norms that didn't fit with her philosophy. Including entire families in the therapy room in the early 1950s was a radical move. But the woman who described herself as "an evolutionary freak" forged ahead, unknowingly planting the seeds for what would eventually come to be known as the Satir Model of therapy.

Although her model has been described primarily as a communications approach or experiential, Virginia's therapy defies categorization. Some criticized her as being too atheoretical and therefore too difficult to emulate. Indeed, she worked so intuitively and so fluidly that she probably seemed more an artist than a clinician. She built her theory from the ground up, by observing people and how they interacted with one another. She was a doer, a practitioner, an observer; like an artist she innovated her theory and her models from her practice observations. Her ideas were based on life itself.

Virginia grew up on a farm, and was connected to nature. She observed very early in her life that there is an order in the universe. We are all part of a vast Universal Life Force, providing the energy for all growth. We do not create life. We do not create ourselves, but we activate and co-direct how our lives unfold.

Virginia searched for the universal patterns that sustain life in living things and how these apply to human beings. She observed the basic nature and components of growth: she saw that growth results from nurturing, removing obstacles from the path of growth, as opposed to the dominance and submission model on which most human systems are based. Each new experience with a family lead to a new discovery about human nature and being fully human.

In a paper titled "The Growing Edge of Myself as a Family Therapist" (1976), Virginia recalls her shift away from the psychoanalytic approach of the day toward a more humanistic, transpersonal one:

In January 1951, I inadvertently saw my first family with intent to "cure." I had literally stumbled into what later came to be called family therapy. I had eight years of experience as a psychoanalytic-oriented psychotherapist working with individuals. It took a long time for the patient to make changes, but on the whole, the results were good – so much so that I dared to enter private practice. I had six years of elementary and secondary teaching experience and eight additional years struggling to help people by working with them individually.

At that time, I was working with a 24-year-old woman who had come to me with the diagnosis of "ambulatory schizophrenia." After about six months of bi-weekly sessions and much improvement, I got a call from her mother threatening to sue me for alienation of affection. For whatever reasons that day, although I clearly heard her threat, I heard something else: the plea under the threat, and under that threat was hurt. I responded to that and invited her to join her daughter and me – an invitation she promptly accepted.

Within a matter of minutes after the mother joined the interview, my patient began to behave as she had when I first saw her. All the seeming growth had evaporated before my eyes. I went through many emotions very quickly. Disbelief, anger, and self-criticism, until finally I stopped blaming and became an observer of what was happening. After I collected myself, I stopped listening to the words and started watching the non-verbal clues going back and forth between the two, and began to notice repetitive patterns emerging. It seemed that the daughter had different cues to deal with in her mother than she did with me. It further seemed that the pattern established with her mother was more powerful than with me. Much later I theorized that of course it would be that way because she and her mother had a survival basis for that relationship that was not true for me. Later, I became aware that until somehow the patient became an initiator as well as a responder, she would be hopelessly a victim of other people's initiation.

I didn't know it then, but I was at the beginning of an understanding of how human behaviours take place by a response to the current interactional clues and how eventually this evolves into a predictable pattern. Nor did I understand how this, in turn, weaves itself into a system to serve the needs of survival. I was also aware that I was violating the psychoanalytical rule, "Don't see relatives." Then, somewhere between a period of five or six weeks of seeing mother and daughter together, it occurred to me that there just might be a father somewhere. I inquired, and sure enough, there was a father.

Once more I was violating a cardinal rule because in those days only mothers were seen to be in the pathological picture. Father accepted my invitation to join us. After his entrance, the pattern widened to include more movement and these movements were compatible with what I had seen with the mother and daughter. I didn't realize that at the outset, but I was looking at the double-bind phenomenon that only later was to be named by Gregory Bateson and Don Jackson. This pattern came to be commonly associated with families where there was a schizophrenic member. The picture of this family was completed when the patient's "good" brother came into the interview. When he came in, the same imbalance again occurred. I worked with that until a new balance was reached. Shortly after that treatment was finished, my follow-up information was that the new balance was holding and things were going well.

I cannot tell you now exactly how I did change that situation except that I clung to a deep conviction that all the family members could be in contact with one another and speak congruently with each other. Being convinced that was possible, it was achieved. Then I had to figure out what I did. What I learned from that family I used with other families as I went along.

That early period was an exciting one for those of us beginning to look at families, for we were breaking new ground. It was scary because we were theoretically and sometimes literally putting our professional reputations on the line. Since I was non-medical, I did not get much criticism, nor did I have that much to lose.

At the offset, most of us were working in isolation and were not in touch with what others were doing. Since all of us were dealing with schizophrenia, which was considered more or less untreatable anyway, we were initially on the fringe of the psychiatric community.

Virginia always worked from observation and direct experience to theory. Her work with this schizophrenic woman and her family was essentially the beginning of a transformative journey where she turned those live observations into the theoretical approach that we know today as the Satir Model.

When the young woman's mother threatened to sue for alienation of affection, Virginia heard two messages: a threat (the words) and a plea (in the woman's tone of voice). Rather than react to the threat, Virginia responded to the non-verbal plea, "I am helpless, I am afraid," and invited the mother to join the next session. To her delighted surprise, the woman accepted. During the session, Virginia observed what she later called a non-verbal cueing system, which is part of double-level messages – what is said doesn't match how it is said. In every communication, there are always two parts: the verbal and the non-verbal, which includes body language and affect, or emotions. The verbal part comes from the left brain. The non-verbal, meanwhile, represents the person's internal experience and sends a message from the right brain. Most importantly, according to Virginia, every message also contains a plea for self-validation. This was the foundation of Satir's communication theory.

Later, when Virginia invited the young woman's father to join the therapy session, a new phenomenon occurred. Where mother and daughter had been relating well up to this point, the father's presence somehow triggered a communication breakdown. Virginia would later identify this configuration as the "primary survival triad," and it would become a conceptual focus of her work.

Virginia considered the original triad of mother, father and child the primary unit of human relationship. The primary triad is where we gain support and affection, and also where we learn our basic coping strategies for dealing with stressful situations. Parents form a triadic relationship with each child that comes along, and other triads also form among all family members. Healthy triads create healthy families, Virginia believed. She defined a healthy triad as one where all members feel valued, connected and free to communicate authentically.

As she observed the schizophrenic woman's family, Virginia noticed that when the brother, "the good guy," joined the family, his sister took on the role of the "sick one." It was becoming clear that the family operates as a system. And whenever a new person is introduced, the system changes. When two people become parents, the arrival of a child affects the couple system. An in-law or other relative, or even a therapist, entering the picture will similarly change the entire family system.

Within a system, you find action, reaction and interaction. Individual members affect and are affected by the system. When the brother entered the system, everything changed. It turned out he was the head of the family and controlled everything. Everybody placated him while discounting his sister, who was slapped with the label of "patient."

After that experience in 1951, Virginia knew she was on to something new and ultimately very important. From that point forward, she always invited family members to therapy sessions. In this way she continued to learn about systems theory by observing how family members interacted with one another. Step by step, Virginia developed her own communication theory. Doing so meant she often had to summon the courage and will to swim against the tide. Virginia followed her heart and her intuition into the unknown, pushing against boundaries to blaze trails into a new frontier of family connection. Today Virginia is credited as one of the founders of family therapy, the first woman in a group of pioneers, and has an entire school of therapy named after her.

Under the dominant influence of psychoanalysis, there was at that time a tremendous emphasis on the individual psyche and its internal conflicts. In this climate much was learned about child development, but clinicians often lost sight of the interpersonal context.

Freud knew that psychological disorders in adulthood were often the consequences of unresolved problems in childhood. However, he excluded the family in his approach. Following this tradition, Child Guidance Clinics in the United States focused at first on children's individual symptoms. Gradually, however, clinic workers realized that a child's presenting issue, such as bed-wetting, often had its source in the tensions of the family. In therapy, at the beginning, the mother and child were seen separately. The mother was perceived as the cause of the problem. Fathers were ignored. They were not identified as being part of the emotional life of the family. The usual arrangement was for a psychiatrist to treat the child and a social worker to see the mother. The major purpose of seeing the mother was to reduce the emotional pressure and anxiety and modify her child-rearing attitudes. Although the importance of family attitudes was recognized, mothers and children were treated as separate individuals.

The pioneers of family therapy evolved in the late 40s and 50s in different parts of the United States, separate from each other. Virginia Satir saw her first family in 1951; Salvador Minuchin in 1959. Murray Bowen and Carl Whitaker hospitalized whole families in the early 50s when there was a member diagnosed with schizophrenia. In the 1950s research focusing on the link between family life and the development of schizophrenia led to Gregory Bateson's pioneering "project for the study of schizophrenia," illuminating the relationship between communication, families and treatment.

In 1956, Virginia connected with a group of researchers in Palo Alto, California who were studying schizophrenia and the nature of communication. The Palo Alto Group – included Gregory Bateson, Don Jackson, Jay Hayley and John Weakland – has one of the strongest claims to originating family therapy. Bateson's 1954 research paper on family homeostasis posited the idea that symptomatic behaviour in children serves to restore the family to status quo. His aim was to develop a communication theory that explained the origin and nature of schizophrenic behaviour (symptoms) within the context of the family.

In 1959, Don Jackson founded the Mental Research Institute (MRI) and invited Virginia to join the Palo Alto Group. The institute was dedicated to studying how family members relate to one another, and how these relationships promote the health or illness of individuals. Researchers studied in depth families in which one member was considered schizophrenic. As a course of treatment, they all agreed to use systems theory to identify the patterns and rules, levels of messages, and governing processes in families. Virginia became MRI's Director of Training, in charge of what would be the first formal training program in family therapy, allowing her to focus on the practical application of research being carried out at the institute.

In 1964, Virginia moved to Esalen, a residential personal growth and retreat centre in Big Sur, California, where she became director. There she met and worked with the originators of Gestalt Therapy (Fritz and Laura Perls) and Transactional Analysis (Eric Berne), and discovered psychodrama, body therapies, and a range of other non-traditional forms of therapy. She began to integrate these modalities into her own practice, challenging herself to stay current with the developments and zeitgeist of the period. Virginia never stopped learning. A sponge for information, she continued to develop and deepen her model by absorbing and adapting to her work what she saw, heard and read.

Virginia also published her first book, *Conjoint Family Therapy*, in 1964. Hers was a revolutionary approach in the 1960s, as reflected first in her work at MRI and later in her move to Esalen. While most professional therapeutic training at the time focused on symptoms, making pathology the centre of attention, Virginia disagreed. In her view, equating symptoms with pathology assumed that absence of illness was the same thing as presence of health, which she didn't believe to be true. Virginia saw healing and growth as an ongoing process, one in which we learn to recognize our old patterns of coping and let go of what no longer fits. To her, therapy was an educational process for becoming more fully human.

In the early 60s, Virginia was increasingly invited to consult and teach family therapy in different hospitals in California. As her reputation spread, requests began to come from countries around the world. Virginia's passion, her vision, and her faith in people now fuelled a global journey that saw her move tirelessly from workshop to workshop, from one country to the next.

Not surprisingly, as Virginia's work with people evolved, so did her vision. In Ken Wilbur's words, "Her evolution was spirit in action." Her vision expanded outward from helping people to become more fully human in their relationships and families to promoting peace in the world. She had a gift for being able to think and move in increasingly larger systems and dimensions. As she moved her focus from the individual to the family and beyond, she concluded that if people can connect in their humanness between each other and between families, they could also connect between nations.

Virginia was on a new mission: to plant seeds for growth all over the world. She fully believed that world peace is possible when people become aware of themselves, respect the humanness of others, then connect with each other. She saw people in their interrelatedness — across racial, cultural and religious boundaries, and in their shared spiritual connection to the whole cosmos. Now the woman who had been dubbed the "Columbus of Family Therapy" really was navigating uncharted waters. Looking at the family as a microcosm of the world, she set her sights on helping not just the families of the world, but also the world family itself to connect in love and understanding.

In her broad vision, she saw the possibility for all people to connect. Her wish for humanity was freedom from the burdens and distortions we all carry from our childhood. Her goal was to reconcile people with their own inner experience, and then with each other.

Over and over again, Virginia saw how people were able to connect with each other once they connected with themselves. Her own life reflected this ongoing and ever-growing search for shared humanity. She walked her talk, revealing that her own personal, individual, human and spiritual evolution had a synchronicity with the evolution of her work and practice.

There was no taming this free spirit. She never wanted to be confined to one geographical area. Up until the late 70s, she had no permanent residence nor did she own a car, opting instead to store her belongings with friends. She later rented an apartment in San Francisco, but never really settled in. She bought a house in Menlo Park, California, in the early 80s, but never spent much time there, either. Only after she was diagnosed with terminal cancer did Virginia really settle down. She spent the last few months of her life in her house in Menlo Park, where she eventually died.

Professionally, Virginia was sometimes criticized for not "settling down" at a university to do research and write more books. She did try once, in the 1970s. She moved to Maryland by invitation of Columbia University, rented an apartment and decided to work and teach there. She lasted three weeks. She said she could never be "institutionalized." Her mission called for freedom to move and to teach in the world at large. Virginia logged more than two million miles and interacted with more than 30,000 workshop participants in pursuit of that mission.

In Virginia's presence, people got in touch with their own spirit and life force and experienced personal transformations that were often described as magical. She said that human beings have the light inside themselves. The therapist or educator's job is to help people find their own light. When people experienced Virginia's light, they got in touch with their own. In other words, they accessed their own life force and self-esteem. Her teachings and processes are simply a match to ignite our own light.

Everywhere she travelled, Virginia planted seeds of growth. She did that by reaching people at their core, on the level of their life force, which is the level where people want to connect with themselves and others. On that level, there are no enemies, only human beings. She reached the goodness in people. In her way of thinking, that goodness and connectedness, when expanded person to person, could change the world.

People responded to her message. They described her as charismatic and magical. Within a very short time, they were making new choices in front of hundreds of witnesses. People everywhere understood her teaching, regardless of language or cultural barriers. She taught through interpreters and dwelled on universal themes that connected all people, no matter how diverse they appeared to be.

Virginia often said that what people saw as magical and charismatic in her was merely her absolute belief that every human being is a miracle. That's how she approached everyone – in mind, body and spirit. People felt it, on an energetic level, when they were in her presence. And because of it, they empowered themselves.

Virginia's vision stretched around the globe to include the entire human race. She travelled the world to highlight basic similarities among human beings and families, regardless of their ethnic origin. She taught that the relationship between self-esteem and communication was key to empowering individuals. She touched thousands of people around the world, covering most of the continents. She did training in many countries, including Germany and Israel (I describe my experiences with her in these countries in the next chapter), England, Canada, France, Sweden, Taiwan, Hong Kong, the Soviet Union, Eastern Europe and Venezuela.

Virginia planned to go to Ireland to promote understanding between divided Catholic and Protestant families and communities. She also dreamed of going to the White House during the Cold War to work with the families of both the American and the Russian presidents. She embraced "peace weaving" and learning about and respecting different cultures. In her last trip to the Soviet Union before she died, she videotaped her family sessions. She hoped to have family therapy sessions from all cultures on videotape so that people could see that the foundation is always the same. It was part of her larger mission to plant seeds of growth all over the world and to foster a belief that world peace is possible if people first become aware of themselves so that they can respect and honour the humanness of others.

As she made her way around the world, Virginia shared her vision of peace and her belief that family therapy and world peace have the same starting point. "The more you appreciate yourself," she said, "the less you will have to deprecate anyone else. The more you can appreciate yourself, the more you can appreciate others."

Virginia believed that peace in the world is a real and viable possibility. She understood that the hope for peace lay in the welfare of the individuals who make up the world, "to love and to connect and to use each other's energies to have a better world." In her mind, teaching someone how to live effectively in the world was no different than training them to live effectively in a family. Her life's work essentially provides a road map for peace. The basic universal patterns and principles that formed the heart of her work can be summed up in her universal mantra: "Peace Within, Peace Between, Peace Among Humankind."

At the first Evolution of Psychotherapy conference in California in 1985, Virginia managed to collect 7,000 signatures on a petition to get Presidents Ronald Reagan and Mikhail Gorbachev to end the cold war and start talking about peace.

Virginia died in 1988. After her death, the seeds she had sown really started to germinate and professional training groups using the Satir Model sprang up across the world. In the ensuing decades, people in many parts of the world gathered together regularly to reflect on what they had learned from Virginia, and to figure out how best to share that wisdom with others. As a legacy to Virginia and her teachings, they created Satir Institutes — nearly 30 of which are operating today. Second, and third generations of Satir trainers and trainees are currently continuing her work. It fills my heart with pride to know that hundreds of people in China, Taiwan, Russian, the Czech Republic, Slovakia, Canada and other countries in Europe and South America are spreading Virginia's message and helping others learn how to live it in their daily lives.

THE SATIR MODEL

Virginia believed that "the family is the microcosm of the world," and that "healthy families create a healthy world." The Satir Model as we know it today is based on Virginia's ongoing therapeutic philosophy. Each piece of the Satir Model contains all the other pieces. Every piece is a *holon* — simultaneously a whole and a part. It is not linear. It is a holistic, circular model with processes that are simultaneously woven together for positive change. Virginia's approach is growth and health oriented. The goals are to raise self-esteem, develop congruent communication and improve coping. "The only thing that changes people," she said, "is that they get in contact with their life force. This is the essence of self-worth."

Virginia's main focus was the process between human beings, and she took into account the entire range of human experience. In a therapeutic setting, she emphasized, the first step is for the therapist to centre him or herself. Next, therapists need to get in touch with their own internal experience so they can be fully present and available to the person in front of them. Her metaphors – the iceberg, the mandala, and the communication stances – all feature the self as the essential focal point.

"The use of self" within the therapeutic process is a key contributor to the change process and one of Virginia's biggest legacies to the field of family therapy. She believed that it is through our shared humanity that we, as therapists, can relate to and connect with the people we are trying to help have new experiences and make new choices. But, before a therapist can be an effective guide and companion for someone on this journey of discovery, he or she has to be a whole person. That means that the therapist must first learn about him- or herself and work through any unresolved issues. This is an ongoing process.

Satir Model training addresses the whole person. Virginia expected her trainees to be aware of body, mind and spirit, as well as their own family history. She also expected them be congruent, with themselves and others. She never made decisions for her clients, but rather facilitated processes to empower them to do it for themselves. This evolved into what became known as "concurrent assessment and intervention" – identifying a need and processing it by working with people "on the spot."

Virginia believed it was essential to empower people to act on their own behalf, be in charge of themselves, and develop strengths based on respect for self and others rather than domination over others. She called her interventions "vehicles for change" and she found ways to externalize internal processes. Virginia had special ways of using tools such as sculpting and role playing to create safe opportunities to relive formative experiences that may carry the influence of generations of family members. Her creativity and resourcefulness provided opportunities for people to make new choices and acknowledge, own and access their inner resources. She believed in hope, and spoke the language of hope.

Virginia embraced experiential learning because it provided a well-rounded experience – cognitive, sensory and emotional. She considered it a "spiritual event" when even two people gathered. "Meeting of two manifestations of life is a cause for celebration," she wrote. Likewise, an encounter between a therapist and one other person was nothing less than a spiritual experience. She eschewed the traditional "healer-patient" power imbalance. "When I am completely harmonious with myself, it is like one light reaching out to another," she said. "In a therapeutic session, it is not 'I will help you.' It is life reaching out to life."

Her dream was to create a university where people learned to become more fully human. Becoming more fully human meant increasing access to the sacred realm inside each human being. Respect was a guiding principle in her work: honouring the whole person. Therapy was all about education. An effective therapist was a good teacher.

Virginia wrote her 1972 book *Peoplemaking* for the public, as well as for therapists, to reflect her belief that "learning is equivalent to therapy and therapy is equivalent to learning." Her training methods were based on equality of relationship rather than hierarchical management; the uniqueness of individuals instead of conformist behaviours. She believed that human beings must evolve a new consciousness, one that places value on being human, leads to cooperation, and recognizes our spiritual foundations.

## UNFINISHED WORK: THE THIRD BIRTH

Virginia's work was just a beginning. When she died in 1988, she left us her vision, her books and tools, and students to carry her vision forward. It is up to those of us who share her dreams and goals for humanity to write the next chapter – the Third Birth. Virginia had already referred to this concept in her lectures, and *The Third Birth* was also the title of an unfinished manuscript she left when she died.

She wrote that the first birth is when sperm and egg meet. The second birth is when we come out of the womb. The third birth is when we become our own decision makers, responsible for ourselves, and responsible and accountable for our own choices.

Virginia developed processes to guide people to reach their third birth. Through these processes we can learn to

- connect with our parents as people, understanding and accepting their humanness rather than relating to them merely in their role as father and mother.
- become responsible for living up to our own expectations
- let go of unmet expectations
- no longer depend on our parent's and others' validation
- stand on our own feet, supported by our internal self-validation

Virginia believed that the world itself is in a similar evolutionary process. It will take people who have experienced their own third birth to create a fully evolved world. This book and the training project on which it is based are intended as contributions to the continued evolution of a better world.

## Chapter Two
### MY JOURNEY WITH VIRGINIA, AND BEYOND

The first time I heard of Virginia Satir was in 1968, when a psychiatrist loaned me a book, *Conjoint Family Therapy*. At the time, I was a 48-year-old Hungarian refugee living in Winnipeg, a former economist trying to reinvent herself personally and professionally in a country famous for its regard for freedom and human rights.

When I came to Canada with my husband and teenage son after the 1956 Hungarian Revolution, I knew that I no longer wanted to work in government, or for corporations. I wanted to work directly with people and so I went back to university, where I earned a master's degree in social work. Two years later, I was director of social work at a large teaching hospital in Winnipeg. But something was missing. Reading Virginia's book changed everything.

Having come from a country where oppression and injustice were rampant, I yearned to connect with people who believed in humanity, human dignity and, above all else, personal freedom. And here was Virginia, a fellow social worker whose primary goal in working with people was not to fix or cure them, but to help them "become more fully human."

Virginia's book described a way of doing psychotherapy that included the family in the therapeutic process. This was a revolutionary idea in the early 1960s. It essentially contradicted everything I'd learned in my studies and training up to that point. Satir encouraged therapists to view people's problems as symptoms of dysfunctional patterns learned in the family system, not as individual pathology. As she famously said, "The problem" – the presenting issue – "is not the problem. Coping is the problem."

I was intrigued and excited. Although I didn't fully understand it yet, Virginia's book had awakened in me a yearning for a new, bold and authentic way of relating to myself and to others. Later that same year, I found myself in Brandon, a city two hours from Winnipeg, at my first Satir workshop. Over the course of five days, I learned about such therapeutic tools as communication stances, the iceberg, sculpting and family reconstruction. I participated in role plays of births, weddings and funerals that externalized family dynamics. Even people's feelings and inner resources were acted out in these small family dramas. There were laughter and tears. I saw people transform before my eyes.

I was transfixed by this tall, warm and charismatic woman who seemed intuitively and effortlessly to understand people's emotional experiences and attend to their needs. It was magical. In fact, at the end of the workshop, I told Virginia that I thought that her talents were so unique that she was basically performing magic. She laughed. "I hope that isn't true," she told me, "because I am teaching my process. The magic is in you and in everybody. My work is to help people find their own magic."

I became Virginia's student that day and would be involved in many of her workshops over the next 20 years. She also became my colleague and dear friend. In 1973 I invited her to come to Winnipeg for a three-month program, in which her teaching had a profound impact on many levels, from families to professionals to university and government teams. This project was just one step on a transformational journey that took her around the world, working to help people connect deeply with themselves and with each other, and to realize their full human potential. In the process, her mission became my mission.

To give this some context, let's travel back in time to 1939, in Paris, France. The whole world was upside down and hurting. In the Luxembourg Gardens, French existentialist philosophers Jean-Paul Sartre, Albert Camus and their contemporaries were talking to students. Amid the danger and the horror, they spoke of their passion for a just and free world for all of humanity. They said a better world was possible, and I, a 19-year-old university student, listened intently to every word.

I believe that the seeds for my curiosity and my passion for learning, and existentialism, were planted at that time when I was a student living in Paris. Only much later would I appreciate how great an influence that time would have on my entire life.

Virginia dreamed about a world in which people are connected and united by their similarities and learn from their differences. This was my dream when I was a student in Paris before the war. I was yearning to find freedom and security again in my life. It was her belief system that connected me most strongly to her. She not only taught it, she practiced it in her own life. With her I found my faith again, I found hope. Her dream became my dream, and I discovered that it works for people universally.

In 1972, I accompanied Virginia to Israel. She wanted to establish a laboratory situation in which both Israelis and Palestinians could experience the innate similarities between human beings. Again, the magic happened. Participating in role plays, people discovered there is no difference between a Palestinian mother and an Israeli one. They experienced the humanness that connects a parent from an Arab background and a parent from an Israeli background. By the end of Virginia's workshop, differences related to ethnicity, race, colour and geography had disappeared and people were connected in a beautiful, collective human spirit. This experience only fuelled her interest in working with people from different religious and cultural backgrounds.

She invited me to be her intern in Germany in 1979, an experience that challenged my earlier beliefs, as well as my belief in myself. I was reluctant to go after my World War II experience. I eventually accepted her invitation after a year of hesitation. I had unresolved judgments, fears and prejudices to be in that environment. It was a challenge to work in that context. During the workshop I discovered that this is a new generation and it became clear to me that I would not want my son and his children to be judged for my sins. I was also surprised to hear that the participants of this new generation were carrying shame about their previous generation and were concerned that I would judge them with the "crimes of their fathers". By the end of the month we shared our mutual fears and concerns. It was an important learning that Virginia provided for me. This experience was a turning point in my life.

As a teacher and a mentor, Virginia was an inspiration for me. She was tough and had high expectations. We, her students, were often in the "doghouse" when we did not live up to her expectations. When we did well, she gave us cookies she baked herself! She gave me plenty of opportunity to learn, to grow, to trust myself and to start doing, not only learning. She encouraged me to practice what I learned at a time when I did not believe I could. She supported me in every step of early practice.

The most important thing I learned from Virginia, beyond her processes and models, is that healing begins inside us. To help another, I must first start with myself. I learned to trust and value myself, to appreciate my resources and my ability to survive, to believe in my strength, and to become my own friend. Virginia constantly reminded me that to be a good therapist I first needed to become the best possible "Maria" I can be.

As Virginia said in that very first workshop, the "magic" is inside everybody. We only have to help people to uncover their own magic. This is also the basic message that I heard as a teenager in Paris.

Through Virginia's work around the world, I learned, at a theoretical level, about the universality of being human. I now know it at a deep level, from my own experience. As I have grown older, I have been able to connect more and more with the basis of my passion, my work, and the never-ending learning about myself.

I have been fortunate to find other people whose ideals and teachings were grounded in those same principles and philosophy and I have had many wonderful teachers on my journey. Somehow, the combination of working with Virginia and experiencing renowned American psychiatrist and hypnotherapist Milton Erickson and other great teachers, was all part of getting to understand people, the world and myself. I was blessed to meet and become a student and friend of Drs Ben Wong and Jock McKeen, who founded The Haven, a personal and professional growth centre on Gabriola Island, B.C. Their theoretical and spiritual workshops added to what I was learning from Virginia. It was most enriching for me to develop a deep friendship with Ben and Jock and to connect Virginia with them at The Haven. Virginia used to conduct her three-week workshop there twice a year. It was a valuable learning experience for me. Although Ben has now passed, he continues to be a major influence in my learning and growth.

I think it was my natural curiosity that led me to these teachers. Once I started living in Canada, I took every opportunity I could to attend workshops and conferences and to hear inspiring people. Hungry for knowledge, I was always ready to learn more and was particularly drawn to people who were concerned with existential issues. I see now that that this is a common thread among all the teachers I chose instinctively to study with.

Today, at the age of 94, I feel overwhelmed as I reflect on the countless individuals and families who have shared their vulnerability, curiosity and openness and contributed to Virginia's dream of healing the world, one person, one family, at a time.

Although Virginia focused at first on helping individuals, she soon broadened her vision to apply her concepts and methods to working with families, couples, groups and in international relations. The family is a microcosm of the world, she said. "By knowing how to heal the family, I know how to heal the world. Healthy families create a healthy world."

## The Avanta Network/The Satir Global Network

Virginia's dream was to have a training organization. In 1978 she invited a group of us who had participated in many of her workshops to join in a training process. The invitation read: "I invite you to make a commitment, and I am not sure yet what the commitment is." I made the commitment. Forty-two of us met with Virginia in the San Francisco area. She had made arrangements for us to do two three-day workshops at different agencies, organizations and hospitals under her supervision; places whose requirements she never had time to fulfill. This was a very exciting, frustrating and anxiety-inducing learning experience. We had to work in triads and Virginia supervised our work every day. It was the first opportunity to have feedback from Virginia and from my triad members. It was also the beginning and the foundation of the Avanta Network.

Although Virginia died in 1988, her legacy lives on. Today, her training organization is called The Virginia Satir Global Network, which currently has 250 members in more than 18 countries around the world, as well as nearly 30 training institutes. Second and even third generations of Satir trainers and trainees are now working to nurture and grow the seeds of hope and transformation that Virginia planted.

Virginia once said: "There are 4.5 billion people on earth. There is no way to connect with so many people. Twenty per cent can get it going; six per cent will work to start it off and then another 14 per cent will make it go. These are the movers and shakers in the world. If one-fifth of the world mobilizes in the human connectedness direction, new things can happen."

My wish was to be part of the six per cent. When I accepted Virginia's invitation to participate in training, I wasn't completely clear what I was committing myself to. I now know I was making a commitment to be one of the six per cent who would pursue a mission to share Virgina's teachings with the world.

## Process community, training and growth

Once a year from 1981 to 1988, Virginia led a month-long workshop for 90 people from across the world. We lived in condominiums in a beautiful setting in the mountains of Crested Butte, Colorado — the site Virginia would choose for her grave. The structure for Process Community was as follows: Virginia led the group of 90 people in the morning. In the afternoon, the group was divided into three groups of 30. Trainers, in training triads, led each of these groups, under Virginia's supervision. Participants had an opportunity to learn in the large group of 90 and in small groups of 30, as well as in their own triads and condo groups. John Banmen, Jane Gerber and I formed a triad, and continued our work together for more than ten years, including a later stint in Hong Kong.

In the second year of Process Community training, Virginia suggested we needed to add Module Two, which would be a higher level of training. This would be the training component to integrate theory into practice and application, for those who had already finished Module One. My triad volunteered, and since no one else came forward, Virginia gave us the opportunity to develop the new module. It was a scary, exciting and very rewarding experience. We felt we were not ready, but we took the risk.

At the beginning of Module Two, there was a level of resistance from the participants, who were now in a position where they would be learning from my triad – their peers – instead of from Virginia, their mentor. We actually felt the same way about this – and I attribute our success to our being congruent with ourselves and with the group. We acknowledged our fear and anxiety, shared our reservations with the group members and invited them to contribute their learning and experience to the process. Being congruent supported us in designing and delivering Module Two, then and for many years to follow. The Avanta trainers continued Process Community until 1990, two years after Virginia's death.

## My journey in Asia

Virginia first travelled in Asia in 1983 when she taught in Hong Kong and Taiwan. On her return, she told me, "Maria, you have to go to work with the Chinese people. They are really open to learning." One year later, three people from Hong Kong came to our Process Community and to Module Two. They invited us to Hong Kong to do a workshop there. That trip would be the first of many, many workshops and a catalyst for Satir Centres to develop all across Asia. I proceeded to do workshops in Taiwan, Bangkok, Thailand, Singapore and later in mainland China.

My triad co-founded the Hong Kong Satir Institute, the first Satir Centre in Asia, which was inaugurated in 1986. Virginia's foresight, and her wish to expand her work into Asia was becoming a reality. John Banmen and I, along with others, continue Virginia's work in Asia to this day. In the last few years, our students who graduated in Taiwan and Hong Kong have continued to be my assistants in mainland China. We now have second and third generations teaching the Satir Model in Asia.

In 2004, as a continuation of my work in Hong Kong and Taiwan, I received many invitations to teach the Satir Model, relationships, communication, family reconstruction, and family therapy in mainland China, including Nanjing, Shanghai and Beijing. I have continued to teach regularly in China ever since.

The Satir Model fits very well with Chinese culture because of its emphasis on family, particularly family of origin. I admire how Chinese people treat their elders, how they clean the graves of their ancestors, how they respect their parents and grandparents, regardless of what may have happened in their lives. Chinese culture is rooted in family. There isn't a preoccupation with being happy or being loved. Preserving family ties is simply inherent in the culture, and people make it a priority. There is an unconditional love for family, and an unconditional acceptance that family is the foundation of life. This is one of the reasons that, in my opinion, there is a wider demand for learning about families in Asia than in the Western world. Family is important, regardless of levels of happiness or unhappiness, finances or other issues. For this and other reasons, it is a privilege, as well as a personal challenge, to work with Chinese families and Chinese students.

Chinese students are hardworking, serious and curious. For me, they are a joy to teach. Because of China's extended family system, children grow up in a community. Caring for others, and a sense of belonging, are deeply rooted values. I believe that my contribution has been to teach my students to maintain a balance between service to family and personal congruence.

Looking back, I realize how much I have learned about myself through every family and every group I have been in contact with. Working in different countries has helped me to grow and move beyond the issues that separate people. I know and believe that on the level of humanness, we are all connected, regardless of race, colour or creed. Virginia knew this and taught this. I have come to realize there is a profound difference between hearing it from her and experiencing it first hand. This is why I am so grateful to have worked with many people of different backgrounds and cultures. My experience has proved to me the truth and applicability of her theories.

# PART TWO

## *The Family Therapy Teaching Project*

## Chapter Three
BACKGROUND, STRUCTURE, AND GUIDELINES

The cases presented in this book are drawn from a family therapy teaching project which took place in Shanghai and Nanjing in 2011 and 2012. In this chapter I want to give some background to the project and explain its structure and goals. This information should be useful to you as you read and reflect on the transcripts that follow.

Family therapy is relatively new in mainland China, just as it was in the West in the pioneering days of Virginia Satir, Murray Bowen and others in the 1950s and 60s. In China I was first invited to teach family therapy to the students of the Normal University of Beijing in 2004. Later, the Universities of Nanjing and Shanghai extended similar invitations. I was genuinely moved to share what I knew could help nurture the growth of individuals and families, and happily accepted.

Then, in 2010, one of the participants in my family reconstruction workshop asked me if I had a dream related to my work. I told her it was to teach practicing family therapists and to have the opportunity to work with Chinese families and learn from them. She provided the support, funding and resources to make my dream come true.

First, I needed to find between 50 and 60 therapists. They would provide me with families I could work with in order to demonstrate my therapeutic processes. Therapists and university professors in China make very little money, so the program needed to be subsidized. I already knew professional people who could locate and invite participants from Nanjing, Shanghai and Beijing universities. A branch of the Shanghai University Counselling Service offered to organize and administer this group.

Participants committed to three workshops of six days each between 2011 and 2012. They came from all over China and were invited to present families they were working with who were willing to be interviewed by me and videotaped. The families would then follow up with their own therapist. Nine families participated in the program. In the 18-month period of the project, we were in fact able to follow up with some families more than once.

By 2011, I was fortunate to know people who had graduated from Satir Model training in Hong Kong and Taiwan. Some of them were invited to join the program as small group leaders. They helped me with their feedback and hard work, every evening discussing the process and asking questions. It was wonderful to see my students growing up, continuing my and Virginia's work. In addition, I was happy to see the growth and positive changes in the individuals and families that we worked with.

Around the same time I was also invited to teach a Family Therapy program in Beijing. The program had the same structure, this time over 15 days, and was designed for the doctors and staff of a hospital for mental health patients, a teaching hospital of the University of Beijing. They generously agreed to have one of these family interviews published in this book ("Anorexia: A Cry to be Loved and Valued").

## Structure of the experience

The 18-day training program comprised three sessions of six days each. It involved 60-plus people, who were divided into small groups of 8 to 10. Each small group had a leader who led discussions and reported on what the group was learning. The participants and the group leaders had very specific guidelines on what to look for (details follow later). They were to observe and assess how the process reflected the goals, objectives and basic elements of the Satir Model. Most importantly, participants had to observe me as a therapist.

They were expected to observe and integrate such therapeutic elements as how to create safety, how to connect with the family and how to use oneself to enhance the process. My intention was to demonstrate all the basic ingredients of the model through my own work. I expected the participants to notice what I was doing and also what I might miss. In the evening, the small group leaders would gather with me to discuss what the participants were learning from the live family interview. They also had the opportunity to raise questions about the process.

The teaching process consisted of five events:

1. The therapist's presentation about the family
2. The actual interview with the family
3. Group participants sharing with the family their own feelings and experiences related to the interview
4. Discussion and questions with small group participants
5. Small group leaders' summary and questions

The therapists, who had invited their client family, had guidelines on how to present their family previous to the interview. They were asked to present:

1. The family maps of each person
2. The iceberg of each person
3. What each person wanted to change and
4. Their experience so far with the family – including a description or a sculpt of each session, any change, and their process so far with the family

On a personal basis, each therapist was asked to explain:

1. What they wanted to learn by presenting this family
2. What they hoped would change through my intervention
3. The desired outcome for this family from this session

I made it clear that I saw myself in the role of a consultant. I emphasized that my seeing a family was not going to make a big, magical difference. The primary focus was on learning for the participants, not on solving all the family's problems. Of course, some change for the family was expected, since a new change agent – me – had entered the process. The therapists were encouraged to identify the family's coping strategies, to look at the family as a system, and to identify how the family system related to the "identified problem." This reflects a basic principle in the Satir Model, that "the problem is not the problem. Coping is the problem."

My goals for the students and families during these 18 days included:

1. Participants would learn and understand that we, *as persons*, are the most important tools in the whole process.
2. They would realize that we, *as therapists*, are not the change agents of the family. We are there to challenge the family to access their resources and educate them to help themselves. Therapy is basically education. If we can teach people to become congruent, to stand on their own feet, to say what they want, to share their feelings, to be responsible choice makers and, most importantly, to accept and respect themselves, then the whole family system can grow.
3. They would understand that the presenting issue is not the one to focus on. It is the underlying processes in the family system that

we are looking for – the unspoken feelings, the fears and anxieties, and the unmet expectations. This is a very different view from the traditional "helping" process that I, and most of my colleagues, learned in the school of social work and many other learning settings.

My own university training had taught me that my role as a therapist was to make an assessment, set a goal and then decide what is best for a person, family or a couple. But in the Satir Model, the first questions are: "What do you want to change? What would make your life better?" In other words, it is the client or the family who gives me a direction to follow. I then assess and intervene at the same time.

When I meet with a family the first time, I may not know anything about them. However, what I do know is that we all have our internal processes, expectations, values, beliefs and resources. I know what is universal about human beings. I know that the family members have their life force and their resources. We connect on the level of our shared humanness. As therapists, our most important tool is our own self, and we must connect on the level of our authentic energy connecting to their authentic energy. I often use the metaphor of a river. I, the therapist, am on one side of the river and the family is on the other side. I cross the river to meet the family, maintaining my authenticity and integrity while respecting their authenticity and integrity. I bring my authentic self to meet each person where they are. I leave my baggage and my ego behind.

I knew that I was teaching an approach that was almost opposite to what my students were learning in their university programs. I wanted them to understand that we cannot change anybody. We can only demonstrate and facilitate. The change is up to the family. Virginia developed many exquisite processes to build a bridge between therapists and families. The intention of these processes is for people to accept themselves, to get in touch with their resources, and feel free and safe to connect with each other. It's essential that they first and foremost accept themselves.

I reminded the students of the basic elements of Virginia's model, along with the goals of Satir-based family therapy and the guidelines for the entire process for achieving them. The therapist needs to consistently look at all of these. The small-group instructions, which are outlined in the following pages, were intended to help guide the students in their observations. For the reader's benefits, I will refer back to these basic elements and the therapeutic goals after each case study.

It is important to realize that all the therapists participating in this project already had considerable experience in using the Satir approach. What follows is therefore brief and assumes previous knowledge of the subject. Therapists who are interested in learning Satir's family therapy must be knowledgeable and competent in the theories and foundational processes of the Satir Model. In addition, they must be experienced and have integrated the Model personally, as well as in the role of therapist. They must demonstrate that they have internalized the beliefs and processes of the Model. It is essential for a family therapist to have experienced their own family reconstruction, to minimize the possibility of being triggered or impacted by the family in front of them.

For more details, readers are referred to *Personal Alchemy: The Art of Satir Family Reconstruction* (Gomori and Adaskin, 2008) and *The Satir Model: Family Therapy and Beyond* (Satir, Gomori, and Gerber, 2006).

## Characteristics of the Satir Model
The Satir Model is (1) experiential, (2) systemic, (3) positively directional, (4) focuses on change, and (5) utilizes the therapist's self.

1. *Experiential.* Therapy must be experiential in order to provide as much of an awareness of positive life energy as possible. Often, body memory is accessed as one of the ways to experience the impact of early life events. When we experience both the past and the present life energy, an energetic shift can take place.

   We learn from experience. The communication stances are metaphors for what and how the body feels when we are placating, blaming, super-reasonable, irrelevant or congruent. Using the stances, or any kind of body position, helps a person become grounded in the here-and-now and connected to his or her internal processes. For example, if someone comes to my office and says, "I am depressed," I might ask the person to get into a body position to represent what that feels like in the present moment. I would then ask to see a body position reflecting how he or she would like to feel. The change in the body position can create new awarenesses on many levels, providing insight in questions such as: What baggage do I carry? What do I need to let go of? How does my desired outcome (my yearning) look, feel and sound?

2. *Systemic.* Therapy must work within the intra-psychic and *interactive* systems of an individual's life. Transformational change is an energetic shift in the intra-psychic system, which then impacts the change process in the interactive system.

    The intra-psychic system includes emotions, perceptions, expectations, yearnings and the authentic essence, "I Am" – all of which interact with each other as parts of a system.

    The interactive system includes the relationships that an individual has experienced throughout his or her life, both past and present.

    The two systems, intra-psychic and interactive, impact each other. Some therapeutic approaches focus only on the interactive or interpersonal, what is happening between people. Others deal mostly with the intra-psychic, focusing on a person's internal experiences. In the Satir Model, however, we aim for change within each person *and* change between people. A profound transformation will affect every level of the experience. As a result, our perceptions, expectations, feelings and coping will change and we can meet our yearnings.

3. *Positively directional.* The focus is on health, possibilities, growth, and accessing resources rather than on pathology and problem solving. It's about connecting with the person's positive life energy rather than any negativity in their life. When a symptom is expressed as physical pain, the focus is on finding where the energy is stuck in the body.

    Positive intention means that we don't focus on illness or symptoms or on the "identified patient." Often, one person in the family is identified as the problem. For example, let's say there is a boy who refuses to go to school. If we look at this as a symptom to deal with, we label the child as the problem. Sometimes parents will take such a child from doctor to doctor to find out what is wrong with him or her. The Satir Model, on the other hand, looks at the whole family system. In this case, we suggest the priority is to look for and access the child's and the family's resources and strengths to unblock the energy that is blocked within the system. In this model, the very act of asking people what they want to change indicates that change is possible. There is always hope.

In the traditional model the therapist would attempt to be empathetic and supportive. "Poor you. What happened to you? You must feel awful. I support you." This is the traditional way of helping someone, and it's how I learned to provide support, reassurance and sympathy. But it ultimately does not help at all because the person ends up feeling even smaller and more dependent and we end up reinforcing weakness instead of nurturing strength.

Using the Satir Model, with a different tone of voice, I would say: "How did you get out of that alive? What resources did you use? You have lots of strength." I know that if the person is sitting in front of me and is alive, she had the resources to cope. I use the same approach within the family system. If there was abuse in the family, we don't focus on the abuse but rather the resources the person used to cope and to survive. This is the meaning of positively directional. No matter how sad, depressed or deprived, as soon as the family is in front of you, they are here now and they have coped. They have their survival energy and their resources, and the question is how can we help them to use their own energy to make the next step. We can only support their own energy; this is a different approach from the medical model, where the doctor does it for the patients. We would say that even though the doctor performs the intervention, the patient's participation is very important. The patient participates in and promotes his or her own recovery.

The underlying idea is that we are all energy and that symptoms merely indicate that the energy is stuck somewhere within the system. We all are part of a universal energy, and therefore we are all connected. This is why we can so effectively role play each other's family members. I believe that when a group like this gets together, a kind of synchronicity occurs. There is always a reason why we are brought together. We can learn from each other, both individually and collectively.

4. *Focuses on change.* All Satir therapy is focused on transformation and change. The first thing we ask when working with people is "What do you want to change?" rather than "What is the problem?" This is not a problem/solution oriented approach. Rather, we ask everyone in the family what they want. This question reflects the idea that change can happen and the therapist's faith in the change process.

We believe in energy transformation, so we ask people to consider, "What do I want to change?" Change requires me to access my resources positively. If I have been using my energy in a certain way for a long time, that pattern becomes ingrained. For example, as an adolescent, I rebelled against everything. A great deal of my energy was spent on acts of rebellion. Being rebellious likely saved my life a few times, but later, when there was nothing useful to rebel against, I had to learn to transform that part of my energy into something more adaptive to my current life situation. Many people continue to use resources acquired in childhood long after they have stopped being helpful or relevant. For example, children often develop the ability to become silent because there was a family rule that children should be seen and not heard, or that youngsters shouldn't talk back to their elders. That repressed energy can be released and transformed into an ability to be open.

5. *Utilizes the therapist's self.* The congruence of the therapist is essential to create an atmosphere of trust, safety, caring, acceptance, hope, genuine interest and authenticity. The use of self is the main tool for change and building trust is an integral part of the therapeutic process. The therapist is a companion and a partner in the change process. The therapist-client relationship is a partnership, the purpose of which is to access resources for making new choices, where the focus is on health rather than symptoms. It is this authentic human connection that sets the stage for the therapeutic process. The emphasis is on empowerment and the context is the learning and growth that occurs between the therapist and the client/patient. The therapist is expected to model congruent behaviour and needs to be fully present and in touch with his or herself, feelings, and thoughts.

Satir used the metaphor of a musical instrument for the therapist's use of self. It is the experience and creativity of the player that determines how the music sounds. The instrument is the self of the therapist. In other words, the therapist needs to tune in to his or herself. The therapeutic process is the meeting of the therapist's self with the self of the person, patient, client, or family. When this occurs, it creates the context for vulnerability and an opening for change. People have all the resources they need to grow. The task is to help to access and utilize those resources.

The therapist's beliefs are also of utmost importance. A therapist who believes that all human beings are sacred will help clients live up to that belief, while one who believes that people are victims will try to rescue them. Therapists who believe that people are to be manipulated will themselves find ways to manipulate clients. The Satir Model places high value on humanity and the life force inside every human being. It is grounded in the belief that all people are equal in value, and can change, evolve and grow.

In summary, to use the self of the therapist as an effective tool in the change process, a therapist must first know him or herself. That means dealing with one's own family issues and being clear and aware of personal vulnerabilities and potential pitfalls.

## *Goals of the Satir Model*

Traditionally, goals in therapy were the specific objectives set out by a therapist based on their assessment of the patient. In the Satir Model, goals and objectives are not content-oriented in this way. The overall objective is for people to grow, to value themselves, to stand up for themselves and to be congruent. If I have high self-esteem, I stand on my own two feet, am responsible and make my own choices. That is the definition of a mature grown-up.

The goals are the same whether we work with an individual, family or group. A family is a system, and in a healthy system everybody stands on their own feet and is connected to every other member. A healthy family is made up of healthy, integrated individuals. Achieving this level of systemic health is a process. First, we find out what everyone wants and what is standing in the way of their getting it. Generally speaking, what people in every family want is to feel loved, validated and connected, and to live in harmony. I have worked with countless families who, when asked to sculpt what they want, stand together in a circle, wanting to be connected and to experience their own individual dignity. If clients do not leave with at least some hope, we have not done good work, and they may not return. Even a small amount of hope makes a difference; people need to believe that change is possible.

In the Satir Model there are four therapeutic meta-goals:

1. *Raise self-esteem.* Self-esteem is one's own experience with one's interpretation about one's own value – not just how one feels. It is a state of being which includes self, other and context.

2. *Foster responsible choice making.* Encourage people to become their own choice makers. We always have choices, and with greater awareness and self-awareness, we can make better ones for self, other and context.

3. *Encourage self-responsibility.* Self-responsibility is part of maturity. It includes actions, feelings, thoughts, and experiences involved in trying to meet our yearnings.

4. *Facilitate congruence.* Congruence is a state of awareness, acceptance and openness manifested as one's genuine, authentic self. It represents internal harmony.

## Assessment and intervention

When I see a family for therapy, there are six general areas that I look at: communication, self-esteem, family rules, system, attitude towards change, and productivity.

1. *Communication.* You can be sure that when an individual or a family has problems, their communication is incongruent. If the system were congruent, they would not need help. Our aim is to help family members move from incongruent to congruent communication.

2. *Self-esteem*. A family that comes for help usually has low self-esteem. It's important to remember that having high self-esteem isn't about being happy. It's a level of awareness, an experience of validating self and others. Imagine you wake up feeling depressed. Your mood is low and you feel miserable. You can still have high self-esteem and value yourself while feeling low. If you can accept your current state, you may even share your feelings with a friend. The core objective of this model is to help people get to a different level of self-validation.

3. *Family rules*. In an unhealthy family system, the rules are rigid and inhuman and offer no choices. We try to help families change rigid rules into guidelines and boundaries with consequences instead of punishment.

4. *System*. Incongruent communication, low self-esteem and rigid rules create a closed and rigid system. In the process of learning congruent communication and self-validation, the system will hopefully become more open and flexible. In a family system, members interact with each other all the time. If we can get one person to learn to validate him - herself, that can have a ripple effect and change the whole system step by step. I look for the person who is most ready to grow. Sometimes it is the person, often a child, who needs help who is most ready to engage in the change process.

5. *Attitude towards change*. Unhealthy, closed and rigid family systems fear and reject change. We hope that as the system moves towards congruence and health, it will become open and more welcoming toward change.

6. *Productivity*. In unhealthy families, members feel insecure, unsafe and chaotic. As members shift their communication, they gain more self-validation, change their rigid rules and become open to change. Their productivity or performance – at school, work, or around the house –will become more grounded and secure as a result.

The overall intention is to help people transform unhealthy into healthier family systems, as follows:

| | | |
|---|---|---|
| Incongruent, destructive communication | → | Congruent, constructive communication |
| Low and self-destructive self-esteem | → | High and self-validating self-esteem |
| Rigid, inhuman family rules | → | Guidelines and boundaries |
| Rejection and fear of change | → | Open to/welcoming change |
| Closed and rigid system | → | Open and flexible system |
| Chaotic and insecure productivity | → | Stable, grounded productivity |

## Some guidelines to remember

In every therapy session there are fluid and moving parts that I weave together with the elements and goals of the Satir Model. They are not linear, but used interdependently to create a safe environment and process for hope and change. These parts include:

1. Establishing a relationship
2. Establishing trust
3. Asking each person what they want (not what their problem is)
4. Observing and listening
5. Introducing emotional aspects
6. Considering family-of-origin and cultural aspects
7. Discussing issues
8. Utilizing Satir Model processes as they fit the context
9. Encouraging the sharing of vulnerabilities
10. Concluding each session with an anchor for hope, reflecting positive progress and commitment
11. Homework related to practice and integration of their learning

1. *Establishing a relationship.* It is important to make equal contact with all the family members, establishing a relationship with every

member of the family and promoting interaction between members. Notice everything and comment appropriately. It is important to instill a sense of hope for change.

2. *Establishing trust.* I pay a lot of attention to establish a level of trust. Sometimes I ask the question, "What do you want to know about me?" I do whatever I can to create rapport and a sense of safety. (In regards to the cases presented in this book, the context was a workshop environment where families were being observed by a large group. Their home life was being exposed to more than 60 strangers. This was an unusually difficult situation in which to establish trust and safety.) Therefore, it is essential for the therapist to always be aware of the context. Establishing trust and safety in a public session is more challenging than in a private session.

3. *Asking each person what they want (not what their problem is).* Give equal time to each individual and direct family members to talk with each other as soon as possible, rather than to the therapist. Regardless of the number of people in the family, we need to make equal contact with each person. It's easy to spend more time with one person, especially when you move from individual therapy to family therapy. It's tempting to talk to the person who wants to talk to you. When I first began working with families, I was happy when one person kept talking with me and I inadvertently neglected the other members. If you focus on only one or two people and don't give equal time or interest to everyone, some will feel excluded or neglected and the family may not come back. Nobody wants to be left out, not even a child who does not want to communicate with you. In that situation, you can simply comment, "I notice you don't want to talk to me." Making contact with everybody is very important. Everyone needs to be noticed and heard.

   Create a sense of hope for change. The question, "What do you want to change?" already implies there is hope. The therapist needs to really believe that change can happen. You can't pretend. If you don't believe it, don't say it.

4. *Observing and listening.* The following are useful questions to consider:

- How do the family members interact with each other?
- What is their communication pattern (verbal and non-verbal)?
- Who does most of the talking? Who does the least?
- Who seems to have most of the power?
- How do people relate to each other?
- What bridges or walls exist between people?

After asking everybody what they want, I will direct my questions so that members can talk to each other. For example, if there are four people (parents and two children), everybody will initially talk to me and then I will direct them to talk to each other. If the wife says, "I want him (husband) to spend more time at home," I would turn to the husband and ask, "Do you know she wants you to be at home more?" Maybe the husband then says: "I'm too busy." I will then ask the wife to talk to him directly about this. I will position them so they're communicating face to face, looking at each other, and I might say to the wife: "Would you tell him you want him to be at home more?" I will encourage husband and wife to talk to each other about this issue.

Next, I would ask the daughter what she wants. It might be something very different. I would ask her parents whether they know what she wants. Again, they can talk about it with each other. Step-by-step, each person's hopes and wishes come out into the open and communication is directed to be between family members as much as possible.

Generally, people tend to avoid talking about certain things, especially their own fears, wants and needs. Often it is children who don't want to talk. In that case, I will ask the mother whether this is the child's pattern at home. I can quickly find out who the identified patient is. There is usually one scapegoat in a family system, and by this time, they have already decided who it is. Even if that person does not talk, we can have indirect communication and offer support and acceptance.

The focus is never on the problem or the symptoms. The symptom indicates that there is an energy block in the system and how people cope with their pain. It won't take long to find out how family members cope with the identified patient or scapegoat. Father may be blaming, mother might be frustrated and sister may be supportive. In one family we saw, the mother had her way of coping with her daughter while the husband had another way of coping with her. He didn't worry about the symptom. The mother worried and amplified the daughter's symptom.

Sculpting helps the family members to find out about each other's perceptions. For example, if it's a family of four people, you can say, "I have a picture of what is going on in your family. Can I show you?" I show them my picture so they can learn about the coping stances. Then I ask each person to show me his or her perception about themselves in connection to every other family member.. A sculpt is a powerful way to help people to discover each other's perceptions. The daughter, for example, will sculpt the family based on how she perceives her parent's relationship with each other and with their children. Step by step, I ask that everybody, including the scapegoat, sculpt their perception. This allows them to express themselves without words. It's especially helpful with children who don't want to talk as it gives them a chance to demonstrate, non-verbally, how they feel and how they think power is distributed in the family. Children will show us their picture about power and control and distance and closeness, as well as their wishes and their desired outcome. It is very important that you always ask each person to show how he or she would like the family to be. The desired picture demonstrates the individual and mutual yearnings within the family. An important point is never to end a session with the stress picture. It is the desired outcome that creates hope and positive direction. This means asking each person to sculpt how they wish every member to connect with themselves and with each other.

5. *Introducing emotional aspects*
   - Explore each person's internal experience (iceberg) as they express feelings of hurt, anger and indifference, as well as love, caring and acceptance
   - Assess their level of self-esteem, self-protection when express ing feelings, closeness and distance, and how they share their feelings and affection
   - Find out their rules, beliefs and judgement about self and each other
   - Assess each person's energy, strength and openness to change.

6. *Family-of-origin and cultural issues.* It is helpful to become familiar with certain details related to family of origin and some history of the parents. For example:

   - What are the parents' families of origin?
   - How do the parents' patterns repeat those of their family of origin?
   - How are these patterns reflected in their current roles, as a sibling, parent or spouse?
   - How did the parents meet?
   - What did they hope for?
   - What expectations did they have of each other?
   - Are there religious and cultural issues and differences?
   - What is the impact of in-laws and extended family?
   - What are their child-rearing practices and issues?
   - What are their resources and supports?

7. *Discussing issues.* Specific issues will become evident as dialogue progresses. As a therapist it may be appropriate to use a topic as a "teachable moment" or to gain more insight into the individuals' perceptions. Some universal issues that arise in family therapy are:

   - Child rearing
   - Relationship with in laws
   - Health issues
   - Finances
   - Stressors at work
   - Demands on time
   - Decision-making
   - Task-sharing

8. *Utilizing Satir Model processes as they fit the context.* These may include:
   - Teaching congruent communication
   - Encouraging members to communicate with each other
   - Directing family members to listen to each other
   - Checking out what was heard
   - Using communication exercises
   - Demonstrating and encouraging high self esteem

- Sculpting and processing the sculpt (see below for more on sculpting)
- Revealing family members' perceptions of each other
- Encouraging "I" instead of "You" messages
- Checking out each person's meaning and mind-reading assumptions
- Reminding people to look at each other when they are talking
- Accessing resources and utilizing them
- Encourage expression and acceptance of vulnerabilities such as fear, anxiety and shame
- Reinforce and recognize positive feelings and characteristics
- Use re-negotiation
- Use the "As If" technique to help re-establish trust
- Use a "paradoxical suggestion" to amplify the symptom and shake up behaviour patterns

9. *Encouraging the sharing of vulnerabilities.* This is a basic ingredient of congruent communication. Enhancing the freedom and safety to establish congruent communication is essential in the building of connections within the family system.

10. *Concluding a Session.* When concluding a session it is important to emphasize and reinforce the strengths and resources of the family. Make sure they have learned something new in the session and have had an experience that gives them hope, no matter how small. Ask for commitment. Therapists must remember that therapy is a learning process. It's not about fixing, solving or eliminating problems, but rather adding awareness and resources.

11. *Homework.* Give homework only for what people have already practiced in the session. Include a commitment between members to work toward desired change. Make a contract for no more than four sessions.

## *Sculpting*

Virginia utilized many therapy models and tools. Sculpting is a process in Satir-based therapy designed to help externalize an internal experience. People are guided to "make a picture" by placing themselves and others in positions that they experience within the family dynamics. As early in the process as possible, we like to provide families with an experience, and sculpting provides an enriching opportunity for assessment and intervention. A sculpt reveals what words cannot express and provides a family with new information. Sitting in a circle, it is hard to talk about feelings, perceptions and expectations. It can be everybody's perception, for example, that mother blames father. That may be a difficult subject to discuss openly, but in a sculpt, it becomes explicit through making a picture using the coping stances. It is important to note that we can only introduce sculpting after we have formed a relationship with the family and achieved a certain level of trust. Joining with the client is the art of therapy. The therapist is the most important tool in the process. Who you are as a person, how you present yourself, how you demonstrate congruence, the extent to which you have dealt with your own family issues and how much of yourself you can share in a professional manner will determine the quality of your relationship with a family or a star. Making contact is a priority.

## Conclusion

This chapter is based on the guidelines I gave to participants in the training project and that are the basis of the feedback and discusssion that are included in the transcripts that follow. Bear them in mind as you read on.

## Chapter Four
### CASE SUMMARIES

The following are brief synopses of the five interviews that are transcribed in the rest of this book.

### CHAPTER FIVE *Anorexia: A cry to be loved and valued*

In this family, anorexia was a symptom used by the identified patient, a 17-year-old girl, as a weapon. She yearned for validation and connection and, at the same time, autonomy.

In this family system, the mother was in control. There was an unexpressed rule to never disagree with her. This applied to the father as well as the daughter and her 28-year-old brother.

Both parents raised their children based on what they had learned in their family of origin. Mother never expressed nor demonstrated affection. She had never hugged her children. Father had disciplined them by beating them. The couple's relationship lacked communication and affection. The primary role models were mother's control and father's placating. With good intentions but without discussing it with the girl, the parents decided to have her hospitalized. As a result, the daughter felt betrayed by them. They lost her trust.

Before this interview the hospital staff had been working with the girl as a patient, along with the family. They were now ready for change and eager to learn. The family connected in a new way on many levels. Sculpting helped them to become more aware of their feelings and perceptions. Enhancing direct and one-to-one communication encouraged them to listen to one another. Sculpting the daughter's resources raised her self-esteem and self-acceptance.

This also revealed her adult capabilities to the family and contributed to the overall positive change in the family system. A lot happened in this two-hour session. Building trust, validation and connection between the family members was the purpose of the interview. This is a good example of how change is possible once we are ready and open.

CHAPTER SIX
## *The taxi drivers' family: Change is always possible*

In this family, the identified symptom was the alarming behaviour of an adolescent boy. The parents were hard working and had good intentions but no understanding of child rearing and family life. The family, as a system, was disconnected and appeared hopeless. The parents were very distant from one another. In the past, mother would discipline by beating the boy, while the father's attention was focused solely on the boy's academic achievement. Everybody in this family felt neglected, unloved and disrespected. The boy yearned for love, encouragement, attention and trust. It was his acting out and behaviour at school that brought the family to therapy.

The parents needed step-by-step education about parenting. Through sculpting and role play, they got concrete information and examples of what their son's basic needs were. In addition, the boy learned to say what he wanted. The parents' relationship changed when they became aware that they were following the ways of coping that they had learned as children. Sculpting their family-of-origin patterns created a significant new awareness in the whole family system.

This family made remarkable changes following the three therapy sessions in the group and numerous therapy sessions in between. They were open to learn, they kept their commitments for change, and with consistent hard work they found harmony and peace.

The dormant energy that was always in the family came forward. They made significant connections with their life energy. There is no hopeless family. Change is always possible.

## CHAPTER SEVEN *Letting go: From child to man*

In this family, a boy's anger was seen as the symptom. Actually there were many issues in this family system that contributed to his anger and his violent behaviour. The mother's enmeshed love smothered the boy. The parents were distant. Mother had no personal interests and was lonely, while the father was not present and spent a great deal of time at work. These factors all created barriers for growth in the family system.

The mother's entire life and existence focused on her son. She consistently called this 17-old-boy her "child." Although not the mother's intention, this relationship was impeding the boy's emotional growth. He lived away from home with his grandmother and had no friends. He felt mistrusted, devalued, hopeless and angry.

He expressed the family's pain through anger directed toward the school, carrying a knife in his pocket and threatening to kill his teacher.

The interview focused on creating an opportunity for the whole family to connect in a new way. The parents needed to hear each other and to hear the boy's wish for more freedom and self-responsibility. The mother needed to accept that her son was no longer a child and that it was necessary for her to create some of her own interests in life. The father needed to pay more attention to his wife and their marriage.

When the channels for communication opened up through the sculpt, every member learned to express themselves congruently and made new commitments in their individual life and family relationships. In this climate the boy became more hopeful and opened to learning how to express his anger in a new way.

He seemed to recognize the opportunity to live his life with self responsibility and freedom to express himself. My opinion is that it would have been useless to focus on the anger as a main issue unless the mother let go and the whole family learned to connect in a new way. Even during the interview the anger seemed to dissipate as we progressed with the underlying issues that contributed to the famiy's dysfunction.

## CHAPTER EIGHT
### Parenting in the shadow of family-of-origin experiences

This family was supported by an external multi-system team, including an adopted grandfather. In this family the boy was identified as the symptom, by the mother. However, the real issue was that the parents had no constructive role models in their families of origin for dealing with anger or how to be warm, loving and supportive parents. The boy experienced more warmth and acceptance from people in the community and school system than he did at home. He was lonely and yearned for warmth, hugs, and connection.

The mother did not know how to deal with her anger and beat her son, repeating the abusive pattern of her family of origin. The father never attended high school. Consequently, his parenting was focused on his son's homework and higher education.

The couple's relationship was violent. They needed to learn how to parent and express their feelings in ways that were different from what they learned in their family of origin. Those old patterns included anger and violence.

The main focus of the process was to encourage the boy to express himself and to be heard. Involving the adopted grandfather, teacher and counsellor in this process was significant, as they provided and set examples for support that the boy needed. Based on their modelling, the parents were enlightened with an entirely new understanding of their son. They learned how to listen, support their son and make positive changes.

The family learned that feelings can be shared and commitments can be made and kept. In this family hugs were unknown, and became a necessary new experience for them. Their homework included giving each other daily hugs.

## CHAPTER NINE
### *Three sisters and an attempted suicide: Breaking the silence*

In this family, a suicide attempt opened up an opportunity for the family to voice their suppressed feelings, expectations and assumptions. It was a wake-up call in a family system in which there was love without expression and relationships based on obligation. There were rigid rules to never disagree and never express feelings. The family members protected each other by avoidance and this naturally led to distance between them. The outcome was a lack of self-validation to the extent of despair and suicidal ideation and acting-out.

The three interviews focused on communication. It was a very slow process because the family was stuck in a cycle of dysfunctional communication. Each person protected the others at the expense of expressing themselves. The family looked perfect from the outside but because they were hiding their real feelings the real outcome was resentment, guilt and self-destruction. Two of the sisters had considered suicide as a solution.

There was genuine love and protection, which was never verbalized.

Consequently the relationships were dishonest and self-destructive. Everybody's authentic yearnings for giving and receiving love were well hidden, so the three sisters were involved in a web of unspoken, desperate, attempts to connect. Each one felt alone, unloved and guilty.

This family needed to learn that loving has to be expressed with words, and breaking the silence is necessary if the members in the family system are to grow. They still have a long way to go. This is an example how difficult it is to change the intention of being "a nice family" when it is based on the old learned patterns of communication and rules.

This family system is universal. It reflects how learned rules influence communication in family systems through generations in most cultures. The rules that we should be nice, humble, and never angry, that we should take care of others and not hurt people's feelings, and so on, lead to incongruence and devaluing of the self and others. An extreme result of this is often suicide.

## Chapter Five
### ANOREXIA: A CRY TO BE LOVED AND VALUED

During my work in China, I facilitated an 18-day family therapy training program for the Beijing University Mental Health Program. Participants were mainly hospital staff, including doctors, psychiatrists and nurses. The family and medical staff kindly gave us permission to publish this case; I appreciate their cooperation with the Shanghai Family Therapy program. This hospital has a special ward for children and for patients who have been diagnosed with anorexia.

According to her therapist's report, the 17-year-old girl in this interview developed anorexia nervosa when she was 14. At one point, her weight dropped to 26 kg (just under 60 lbs). Her parents had duped her into going for what she thought was an outpatient check-up when, in fact, they had already made arrangements to have her hospitalized. She felt cheated. Since her hospitalization, she had continuously criticized her parents and would not forgive them for their perceived betrayal. At the time of this interview, she was living at home and visiting the clinic as an outpatient.

The girl did not trust her parents, but wanted to learn how to relate to them. She believed she needed to be cautious in her relationship with them. She also expected herself to be perfect, and had doubts about her future.

Her older brother, 28, was a quiet person with high expectations of his sister. When she was depressed, he had moved out of the house in order to avoid conflict, although he maintained a pleasant relationship with her. The girl and her mother, father and brother all agreed to come to the interview, which the girl's doctor also attended.

## Interview

COMMENTARY *I began to create safety by greeting the family at the door. When they sat down, I asked the group to introduce themselves. As the girl looked around, she noticed an additional doctor and nurse were present, and asked them to participate. I invited them to sit with us in order to support the girl.*

MARIA Hello, my name is Maria. This is Marie, who will translate. I am very happy to meet you. Your therapist already told us about your background. I can imagine it was hard to come to a big group like this. I want to tell you that everybody here is learning about family therapy. Many people are working with families. We learn from every family we see. We also learn about ourselves. We are privileged to have you here. I will invite people to say their names and where they are from so that you can feel more comfortable. Is that OK? [The family agrees and participants give their names, one by one.]

COMMENTARY *In the part of the interview that follows, I start by asking every family member what they want to change, and what they hope for in change, by coming to this session. This is the usual practice in the Satir Model. It is important to include everybody equally in this part of the process.*

*I start with the mother, asking her what she wants to change. She immediately stands up, indicating to me that she holds the power in the family. Before responding to my question, the mother insists on introducing her family. As she introduces them, she asks them to stand up, one by one.*

*When the mother describes her family, she uses a metaphor: "The four of us are a family, and we love each other, but in the last two years, it has been just like four fishes in a pool and the four fishes don't enjoy swimming on their own." Three of the family members remain standing; only the girl sits down.*

*Mother is aware that her family is disconnected, and she realizes they need to learn how to communicate better. She sees them as enemies. She fears she has done something wrong and is taking on that responsibility. I encourage her to turn her yearning into action. I ask her to talk directly to her daughter, son and husband, in an attempt to begin teaching them to communicate. The goal is to help them create an actual connection. I will do this throughout the interview.*

MARIA Mama, when you came here today, what did you hope for? What would you like to change so that everybody would be happier in this family? What is your wish?

MAMA The four of us are a family, and we love each other. But in the last two years, it was just like four fishes in a swimming pool, and the fishes don't enjoy swimming on their own. As a couple, we really suffer. We are privileged to have a therapy session in front of so many specialists and I hope that Maria can help our family become happier and live in harmony.

MARIA What do you think you need to change so that in this swimming pool those fishes can all be happier and get along well? I want that too.

MAMA We have not been able to communicate, especially in the last year.

MARIA It is important. I agree with you. Who would you like to communicate with first, in a new way? I think I can help you to communicate differently.

COMMENTARY *This is turning yearning into action.*

MAMA To be honest, so far I have felt that I have lots of enemies around me. I could not communicate with any of them.

MARIA Everybody is an enemy? Your husband, your son, your daughter? They see you as an enemy?

MAMA No, sometimes I think I don't play a good role myself. When I am facing my husband, I am not playing a good wife role. When I am with my children, sometimes I think somebody else should be the mother instead of me. Because I don't know how to do mothering any more. They are all my biological children. He was born in the 80s and she was born in the 90s, so I am the mother of children born in two different decades. It brings special challenges.

MARIA They both grew up, so you did something good.

MAMA But at this moment, I feel confused. I don't know how to be.

MARIA She is almost grown up. He is grown up, so that usually changes the relationship. How would you like to be with your two children? Can you tell your son what you want with him?

COMMENTARY *I encourage her to communicate directly with her children to create an actual connection.*

MAMA [to Maria] Me?

MARIA [points at son] Tell him. What would you like to happen?

MAMA [still looking at Maria] Seems like he is not accepting whatever I say.

MARIA Tell him directly, you want to learn communication. Communication first of all means that you look at the person and you tell them directly. So tell your son what you want and then give him a chance. Everybody in the family will have a chance too. What do you want from him? Do you want to communicate more, do you want to be listened to, or do you want him to talk to you? You want to be respected? I don't know what you want.

MAMA I want my son to be independent when he is 30.

MARIA [asks son] Is that your wish too?

SON I ... I ... I wish my mother to be healthy ... and peaceful.

COMMENTARY *I encourage the son to stand up to his parents rather than placate them. He begins to express his feelings as I encourage him to talk directly to his mother. He asks for clarity in her meaning and acknowledges that her expectation for him is normal for parents.*

MARIA Would you tell your mother when you are 30, you will be on your own? You are grown up. You will do what fits you. Is that true?

SON [nods] Yes.

MARIA My son got married when he wanted to, not because I wanted him to marry. But it is true that it is your mother's wish. It is important that she can tell you.

SON I can accept the wishes of my parents.

MARIA You can also decide when you will do it because you are 28 years old.

SON If there is an appropriate person, I might marry.

MARIA Wonderful. [To Mama] Is that OK with you?

MAMA Yes.

MARIA Your son is a grown-up person and as his mother you want him to find the right wife, one who is right for him.

MAMA Yes.

MARIA OK. So you have now started to communicate.

COMMENTARY *I encourage the son to look directly at his mother as he shares his wish that she allow her children to move on independently and experience the challenges of adult life. He also expresses his most important wish, that his parents be healthy, live in harmony, and be safe.*

*It is important to encourage communication between all family members. I ask mother to talk to her husband. She speaks in generalities and placates. I encourage her to be more clear and she reflects on how she has influenced the family dynamics, particularly her relationship with her daughter. Since mother resists talking about the relationship with her husband, I move the process along as she shares an insight gained from a note where her daughter described her as the decision maker who everybody had to listen to.*

MARIA Mama, what do you want to say to your husband? What do you hope for from him? What do you want to change in your relationship with your husband?

MAMA We have been married for 30 years. We are loyal to each other, so we keep our commitment. That is what I feel most happy about.

MARIA Do you communicate with him?

MAMA That's my difficulty. We have difficulty with communication. We often have different ideas. But most of the time, he follows me.

MARIA In every couple's relationship, the two people may have different ideas, because each person comes from a different family. The question is how to deal with it when we have different backgrounds. So when you have different ideas, who gives in? Do you win or does he?

MAMA In the first 30 years, I have always been the winner.

MARIA Do you mean you are very powerful?

MAMA That's with my daughter.

MARIA What does it mean between you and your husband?

MAMA My daughter wrote me a note about her impression of me. She said that I always have been the decision maker and everybody had to listen to me.

MARIA You agree with that?

MAMA I got this message one month ago. I have reflected on this for one month. I can accept this feedback. I am doing everything for this family.

MARIA So, you want to change. So in that pool, you are the big fish and you want to be a smaller fish so that everybody can have more water and space. True?

MAMA Yes.

COMMENTARY *I use her metaphor to make a point and challenge her on her commitment to change. I continue to take the opportunity to encourage her by offering appreciation for her and her ability to self-reflect. I affirm what she wants when I say, "You want the other people to have equal water and space." Again, I use the metaphor to make meaning of the mother's wish.*

MARIA OK. That is what we are going to talk about. Is this what you want? I have a real appreciation for you. You can reflect on yourself. From what you are saying, you have a lot of power in this family. Your good intention was that you wanted every fish to swim your way and now you are saying the fishes started to swim another way.

MAMA Yes, I am the only one swimming.

MARIA Yes, and then you are alone. You are very smart. So, now you are giving a message to everybody, that you want the other people to have equal water and space.

COMMENTARY *When mother expresses her new wish about what she wants in the relationship with her daughter, I hear her placating and I challenge her. At the same time, to build safety and trust, I refer to her willingness to be a good support for the family. I encourage her to value herself and stop blaming herself as a bad mother. I teach her that we learn from our experiences and gain resources in the process. I encourage her to talk directly to her daughter. This becomes a pivotal part of the process.*

MARIA What do you want to say specifically to your daughter? How would you like to change your relationship?

MAMA My daughter is going to be 18 next year. The reason that we are seeking help is so that in the future, we can be equal. I would like to discuss with her everything about the family. I want to listen to her ideas. I hope that she could be my guide in the future because from what I see and what I hear, I think she can see things better than me.

MARIA She doesn't have to be the guide. You can each guide yourselves. When she is 18, she can guide herself and you continue to guide yourself. I really appreciate what you have gone through to understand this now. So, you can be a big help to these people. And I know that you want to help.

MAMA Am I able to?

MARIA Yes. But first I would like you to make your own change to no longer blame yourself. You did everything you could with your good intention. You know we all learn from our experiences. You know now that you did not know how to deal with some situations. That doesn't make you a bad mother. That just means that you didn't know. We all make mistakes and I am very happy that you are standing on your feet and you are telling every member of your family what you want.

[Points to daughter] What do you want from her? [Mama has been standing from the very beginning and now the daughter stands up.]

MAMA I just want my daughter to be happy and healthy.

MARIA Tell her, "I want you …" You have started to communicate.

MAMA I just want you to be healthy and happy, to do things you like to do and that you are capable of doing.

MARIA So, you want to give her freedom, to be herself?

MAMA Yes.

DAUGHTER What I want to tell my mother is that I don't want her to be the bigger fish in the pool. We are almost similar size and we can swim in the direction we want to, but we don't need to deny it when the other person is wrong.

MAMA I am sure that I can do it because I feel tired of swimming alone now. I really want to swim, following you three fishes.

DAUGHTER Do you mean that my father, my brother and I made you worry too much, so that right now you are so exhausted, you are not willing to?

MAMA No.

MARIA She did not say that.

DAUGHTER But I feel when I am communicating with my family members, I am always negative.

MARIA You are. So, you want to change, too?

DAUGHTER I want to change.

MARIA Tell your mother, you want to change.

DAUGHTER Mama, I guarantee that in the future, I will keep myself positive. I will make myself believe that my family members are the people who care for me most and love me most in the world. They will not cheat me anymore. I am sure you have good intention, whether you were right or wrong.

MAMA I believe you.

MARIA You are doing very beautifully. Thank you. Well, I will get back to you two. [Maria now turns to father. Mama and daughter sit down.]

COMMENTARY *This is the first time mother has sat down since the beginning of the interview, signalling to me that she is feeling safe and experiencing a connection.*

*I now include father and ask what he hopes for. It is important to encourage father to be more specific about his wish. Usually, people will first offer a general idea. As therapists, we need to help them express their wish with clarity.*

MARIA I would like to ask Papa. Papa, what do you hope for?

PAPA [standing up] My wish from this group is to help us to get out from being stuck and to help resolve the issue, which is a blind spot for us.

MARIA So, what is it? What do you specifically want that could resolve the issue? Mama said she will change. What else do you think needs to happen?

PAPA I think we still have communication problems in our family.

MARIA I can see that. Number one in communication is that you look at each other and talk directly. Number two is that you really say what is in your heart and that you are not afraid to say what you want.

PAPA I want everybody in the family to treat each other from the heart and to feel solid. Also, I want everybody to trust each other that whatever we say is from our hearts.

MARIA That's beautiful. So, what would you like to tell your wife directly when you have a disagreement?

[Mama stands up.]

PAPA I want to tell you, she has been married to me for so many years.

MARIA "You." [Maria encourages Papa to speak directly to his wife.]

PAPA You have been married to me for so many years. You have suffered a lot for this family, and have been working very hard, I appreciate that. The children are grown up now. We should let them go. You worry too much for them. You always are thinking for them. You care about them, but it could be that they don't understand your ideas. The children are already grown up, so they can have their own ideas. They can take off and fly. They can have their freedom. Whatever you think is right, they might not agree with you. So, if it is time to let go, just let go. That's what I am thinking.

MARIA That is very important. Very beautiful. So, you will help your wife to let go. You know, this is the most difficult thing to do for all parents. It is difficult. But it can be very helpful when you both are closer to each other because then you have each other. The more you have each other, the more easily you can let go of the children. Thank you.

COMMENTARY *I turn to the girl as Papa and Mama sit down. At the beginning, the girl was the "identified patient." Throughout the interview I have identified the challenge as the communication between the family members. It is clear that the lack of communication between everybody, especially between husband and wife, is the real issue. The parents have not been good role models for a healthy relationship. As Virginia taught, the "presenting problem" is not the problem. It is now time for me to connect with the girl and create a connection by helping her communicate directly with her family.*

MARIA [to the daughter] What do you want to change in this family so that everybody's lives and your life are better?

DAUGHTER I wish my parents could be closer and that they would love and respect each other. I wish they wouldn't focus so much on my brother and me. I wish my brother would be more open and more generous so that I can feel more secure.

MARIA I hope you heard what your father said. Your father is ready to let the children go.

DAUGHTER My wish is not only that they let me go, or us go, but also that they can love each other and live for themselves.

MARIA Yes, they lived with each other for over 30 years, so that tells me that there is a relationship. How they deal with each other is their business. I know your wish.

DAUGHTER But I don't think they really have affection for each other. They get together just for my brother and me, for our development.

MARIA What do you think would be best for them?

DAUGHTER I wish they would be considerate of each other and live happily. If they can do that, then my brother and I won't worry about them. Then we can move on with our own lives.

MARIA I think you love them very much. Can you tell them how much you love them rather than tell them how they should be? [Daughter suddenly stands up and faces her parents.]

DAUGHTER I wish that you could live for yourselves more because I am afraid of your distance. I feel this family is not in harmony. Then I feel powerless and I am afraid to move on. [Sitting down] That's all.

MARIA You didn't tell them that this wish has to do with you loving them. Is that true?

DAUGHTER How can I express it?

MARIA Do you love them? Is that why you have this wish?

DAUGHTER Yes, I love them.

MARIA Can you simply tell them? In this family, people don't tell each other that they love each other?

DAUGHTER Never.

MARIA You never heard your Mama say that she loves you?

DAUGHTER No.

MARIA Papa, neither?

DAUGHTER Even worse!

MARIA Do you have the feeling that they love you, care for you?

DAUGHTER I can feel it, but I don't know how much.

MARIA I don't know whether a scale can measure love but I know that loving is a feeling, and sometimes in families, the problem is they don't know how to let each other know. Each person expresses it in different ways. I think Mama's best way to express her love is to take care of you. She loves you by telling you what to do. That's one way to love somebody. I would like her to change that.

COMMENTARY *I encourage the girl and all the family members to express their feelings. As we move on, the daughter begins to express a universal issue: that we are all defined by our parents because, as we grow up, they are the only criteria and reference points we have for self-validation.*

DAUGHTER I don't like my mother always warning me that I should do this or do that. I want more validation from her for what I do and for her to appreciate me for who I am. I don't want her to always blame me and tell me what I missed.

MARIA So, you would really know she loves you if she expressed her appreciation and validation. That is important for you.

DAUGHTER Only when they validate me do I know that I am a good daughter.

MARIA You don't value yourself.

DAUGHTER I don't know what is right. Only my parents … I only know my value based on how my parents define me.

COMMENTARY *It is a universal yearning to be validated by our parents.*

MARIA I would like to show you today how you can value yourself as well, because you are already almost 18 years old. You know, when we are children, we only know our value from what our parents say. To be grown up means that we value ourselves, and I am sure from what I heard from your therapist that you already have lots of reasons to value yourself. It is very good to have the parents' validation. I wish that you learn to value yourself. You understand what I am saying?

DAUGHTER I think how my parents value me is more important than how I value myself.

MARIA It's very important. When you are 25 years old, or even 19, I think it is very important how you value yourself. That's very important to learn.

DAUGHTER I want to learn, but I don't know how.

MARIA I will show you, but first I would like to ask your brother. [Turns to brother.]

COMMENTARY *I establish the goal and contract for the Third Birth – acknowledging our parents as individual people and accepting responsibility for ourselves. I now involve the son by asking his wish.*

MARIA [to son] What do you want? What do you think can make this family happier?

SON I think we need smoother communication. Even though in daily life we don't do everything well, I wish everybody reflected on his or herself. Starting from the self, we should try our best to play our role in the family, as a father, mother, brother and sister. Whatever we learn here we can practice and implement in our lives. At least, we can move step by step to the future in a positive way. We cannot totally change just by one session. But at least we need take action and move to a better level, and then move on. That's what I want so far.

MARIA What do you think about what your sister was saying?

son What she talked about is the same reality that I am also currently facing.

MARIA So, you agreed what she said?

son Yes, I agreed.

MARIA And you also agreed when she said that in this family people don't know whether they love each other?

son We have love in our hearts but we never express it with words. We manifest some action to represent our love, but never from our mouths. We have very little verbal expression.

MARIA Would you like to? Would you like to know whether your parents or you sister love you?

son I am sure that we love each other.

MARIA I believe you. How do you know they value you, because your sister was not sure?

son This is a fact. I know all the family members love me and care about me, but we don't know how to express it in words. This could be related to our personalities.

COMMENTARY *I remind the family that communication and rules are learned in our family of origin. We repeat our childhood learning and we repeat the familiar. This normalizes their current family experience.*

MARIA No, it's related to your rules. I think there were unwritten rules in this family, to not say how you feel.

son I agree.

MARIA People do that in many families. Your parents maybe learned it in their families.

MARIA Mama, in your family, did people talk about feelings?

MAMA [shakes her head] No, my background affected how I am now, just like my son. He is now 28 years old, and I have never hugged him. In my memory, I never hugged him ever since he was young. If my daughter did not get sick, I would not hug her either.

MARIA Did your Mama and Papa hug you?

MAMA No.

MARIA So, you didn't learn it. You know, we learn in our family as we grow up how to express feelings. So, if you never experienced love through hugging, how would you know how to hug your children? But you can change that if you want. Certainly you can.

MARIA How was it in your family, Papa? Did people talk about feelings?

PAPA My family was the same, in not expressing feelings and not saying "I love you" or hugging. I was also beaten when I was young.

MARIA Did you beat your children?

PAPA Um ... I did. I did.

MARIA You did what you learned in your family. We continue to do the same thing that we learned. We can change. Your children can raise their children differently. It is important to know what they want.

MARIA I know Mama wanted a warm pool where everybody can swim freely. On the feeling level, that means everybody understands and loves each other. As a matter of fact, your family tells me that you have a lot of good feelings. Yet, as children, you didn't learn how to express feelings and did not feel validated.

[Looks at Mama] Now, how would she know you value her if you don't tell her? I hope that you will learn to express your feelings more, and that your therapist will help you.

[Turns to daughter] I would like to pay more attention to you because you have some very important wishes here. You want to know that they value you and how you can value yourself.

COMMENTARY *At this point I feel the timing is right and the trust level high enough for a sculpt. I explain that we will look at everybody's communication and perceptions about each other, including their desired changes, through positioning themselves into a "picture." I begin by demonstrating my sculpt in order to provide a model for the family to see what I am talking about. I explain that when a person is perceived as powerful, I will ask them to stand on a chair. We demonstrate closeness and distance through spatial proximity. I then ask the daughter to be my co-producer and show me her perception of the parents' communication when they don't see eye to eye.*

MARIA When a person is perceived as powerful, I ask them to stand on a chair. Could Mama stand on a chair? Mama said that when there was trouble in the family she used her power. Mama, are you willing?

MAMA Yes, I can. [Moves to stand on chair.]

MARIA Papa will support you. I will show you my picture and then we will look at everybody's picture. Papa, can you help Mama so she doesn't fall?

So, Mama you are very powerful. Now where was Papa, how close to Mama? On the stage. [Papa is about a metre away from Mama.]

DAUGHTER He is a little bit shorter than Mama.

MARIA Does he agree with Mama? Does he say "Yes" to Mama? Does he support her or does he blame her?.

DAUGHTER He agrees 80 to 90 per cent of the time.

COMMENTARY *I show Papa the placating position and then ask the girl to place her brother in the picture at a time when he was in junior high and the family was in a stressful situation. She places him outside the family with his back turned, blaming both parents. Mother was blaming father and father was placating mother. I then asked the girl where she was in this sculpt. She moves to the furthest corner of the room and curls up to make herself as small as possible.*

MARIA [to daughter] Mama is blaming father, not you.

DAUGHTER What do you mean?

MARIA Mama blames Papa, she is not blaming you. Nobody is blaming you, so why are you so far away? What are you afraid of?

DAUGHTER They are on a battlefield, but the reason was because of me, so I feel helpless.

MARIA You felt helpless. That was some time ago.

DAUGHTER That's what I experienced in the past year.

MARIA I just want you to know this is the past year. You are no longer that small.

MAMA How do you feel in this picture?

MAMA I feel that I am the only one standing here. I don't have much power and no help. I wish somebody would help me come down from the chair. That was what happened in 2010 when my daughter was choosing to go to senior high. That was the structure when we decided which school she would go to.

MARIA You know how she feels? How far away she feels from you? You see when people don't talk in the family they don't know how the other one feels?

MAMA I know I have to choose for her. She is not able to choose by herself about which school she is going to.

MARIA That's one thing. Another thing is that you make an assumption that she is unable. I don't think you give her the opportunity to make a choice.

MARIA [to daughter] Did you have the opportunity to say what you want?

DAUGHTER I had the opportunity, but they always rejected me.

MAMA Yes, yes.

MARIA Papa how do you feel in this picture? Does that make sense to you?

PAPA Even though she was above me, I had my own idea. I just didn't tell her.

MARIA You didn't communicate with her?

PAPA Sometimes I communicated with her.

MARIA Tell her now what your idea was then, so that your daughter hears it.

PAPA If you think you are right, I won't argue with you. So, whatever you say, I say yes, so there is no anger here.

MARIA [turns to son] How do you feel, being out here and seeing this picture, with your sister there?

SON I think everybody is selfish and not considerate of the others. Actually, we are all coming from good intentions.

MARIA I know. In this picture, I can see that it is very difficult to have communication. This picture illustrates what Mama said in the very beginning about the swimming pool.

COMMENTARY *I am starting to teach congruent communication between the girl and each family member. I will ask each person to show me their desired picture through a sculpt. I see that the girl has stood up in the corner of the room.*

MARIA Now, Papa would you have a different picture? What will be your picture? This was your daughter's picture. Give us another picture. I will ask everyone's picture.

[To daughter, who has stood up in her corner] I am happy you stood up. Come here. You were there long enough.

[To Papa] How do you feel in this picture?

PAPA She completed the entrance examination and was admitted to a school she had chosen, but her mother did not let her go. Mother decided she'd go to another senior high school and paid the tuition fee.

MARIA Did you know what she wanted?

PAPA I knew, but my wife said, "This is my idea and that's where she is supposed to go."

MARIA So, you did not help her to get what she wanted. But even so, you agreed with her.

PAPA At that time, I think my wife had her own reason. I did not know that she had already paid the tuition fee. But she did not respect my daughter.

MARIA [to daughter] Do you believe that your father understood what you wanted? But in a way, he was helpless.

DAUGHTER It seems to me my mother made a decision and my father didn't care about it.

MARIA He says he did care. Ask him now, today, if he cared.

DAUGHTER I felt you didn't care about making a decision. What consequences are you are willing to accept because you didn't make a decision?

MARIA What do you mean, consequences? What can he do now about what he didn't do then? What do you think he can do? We cannot change what belongs to the past, but we can change the present.

DAUGHTER He can tell us about his idea. He can talk with my mother on behalf of my brother and me.

MARIA That's a very good idea. Can you tell him? You say, "Papa, I expect you to be equal with Mama and discuss with Mama." You stand up for yourself.

COMMENTARY *Encouraging congruent communication, I hold the girl's hand and lead her to stand in front of her father.*

DAUGHTER Papa, I think a man is very important in a family. I wish you would be responsible and be equal with my mother, and fight for my brother and me regarding our opportunities.

MARIA Are you willing to do that? That's a change you could make.

PAPA Yes, I am willing to. I already let go. You and your brother can do whatever you want to do.

DAUGHTER This is your attitude, not my mother's attitude. My father said he let us go, but my mother disagreed.

MARIA OK. We will get to your mother. This is between you and your father. Do you believe he can stand up like a man? If your mother got down from the chair, then could he stand up? I know that your Mama wanted to get down from the chair.

DAUGHTER I don't think my father is capable of standing on the chair.

MARIA I don't think anybody needs to be on the chair, not even you.

DAUGHTER We need to have leadership in the family.

MARIA The leadership in the family is not about standing on the chair.

It is about standing on your own feet and respecting yourself and the other. We will make that picture, too.

DAUGHTER It is very difficult to do.

MARIA I agree. Change is difficult, but everybody said an hour ago they want to change. Today we only can decide what you want to change. Change is a difficult process because we go from an old way to a new way. If there is a commitment, then the family can go in that direction. I believe as I look at your Papa, he is a strong man. When your Mama steps down from the chair, which in her mind she already did, Papa doesn't need to be on the chair either. Nobody needs to be more powerful than the other. Everybody can be of equal value and strength in this family. What you want is Papa to stand up to Mama.

[Turns to son] How do you feel here? You are very far from her. How did you feel at that time?

SON I feel that even though we are a family, we are so separate. We are all individuals.

MARIA This is in your head. I am asking what you felt when your sister was out there, about a year ago? [Points to the corner where his sister was curled up earlier.] I can see that you wanted to exclude yourself and you did not want to be in the mess here. But you felt for her, didn't you?

SON I felt anxious and sad.

MARIA Did you ever tell her?

SON I only told her in my head, not from my heart.

MARIA You just said it now. I really appreciate what you just said. [To daughter] Did you know that he felt anxious and sad for you?

DAUGHTER I knew, but he only gave me a speech.

MARIA Yes, I noticed. That's how he protected his feelings. How did you protect your feelings?

DAUGHTER I don't accept his idea.

MARIA Tell him. This is communication.

DAUGHTER You just impose your dream onto me and you want me to fulfill it for you. But that is not something I want, so I wouldn't accept your idea.

MARIA Tell him what you want.

DAUGHTER I don't know. I wish that you wouldn't criticize or deny what I am doing.

MARIA He criticized you from his head.

DAUGHTER He thinks that what I did was not good.

SON I just tell her my ideas and how I see things. That doesn't mean I decide for her.

DAUGHTER You measure what I do in my life based on your ideas, and are judgmental about it.

MARIA What would you like your relationship to be with your brother, now that you are both grown up?

DAUGHTER If I want to do something and I am not able to achieve it, I wish you would help me.

SON I wish we were a team, that we could work together. I am willing to help you.

MARIA Do you believe him that he could be a team member with you?

DAUGHTER I believe he wants to, but right now he doesn't have the ability. He needs to raise his ability.

MARIA What kind of resources do you think he is missing?

DAUGHTER Other than learning a theory, I wish he could be more practical, not only saying it and then not doing it. He needs to do whatever he talks about.

MARIA You are a big judge! You decide how he should be, but you resent it when he decides how you should be.

DAUGHTER He said he wanted me to do something, but even he cannot do it. How can he ask me to do it?

MARIA Well, I really wish you wouldn't tell each other what the other should be doing. I wish you could just hear and support each other. Both of you could become what you want. Can you see that as a possibility? In this family, everybody has to tell everyone else what to do, but nobody supports anyone to be who they want to be.

DAUGHTER Now I don't want to think so much. I just do whatever I want to do.

MARIA You are doing the same thing with your brother that you resent your mother for. You want to tell him how to live and he wants to tell you how to live. Neither of you like what Mama was doing. But in a way, you both learned from Mama to tell others what to do. I wish that everybody could be free in this family and yet be connected. That's a possibility if you give up that pressure on each other.

Can you accept him, that he will live in the way he wants to, even if you don't like it?

DAUGHTER As long as he doesn't interfere with what I am doing. Then, he can do whatever he wants to do.

MARIA OK, you will not interfere with him and you can ask him not to interfere with you. That doesn't mean that he cannot tell you his thoughts. There is a difference when someone says, "I am telling you all I see and I leave it to you to decide."

Personally, I don't think I have any power over anybody. Neither do you. I hope that everybody will let go of controlling each other. I heard from your doctor that you were very much controlled at that time, and it was very painful for you. Nobody needs to control. Everybody is grown up here.

How do you feel about what I am saying? I wish for everyone to be free in this family. We are getting there. But as long as you want to control him, you won't have a relationship as brother and sister.

DAUGHTER What I am doing now is accepting the reality; accepting my family for who they are.

MARIA Good, can you accept your brother?

DAUGHTER It takes time.

COMMENTARY *Next I ask the girl to identify resources she can appreciate in her brother to help her to connect with him.*

MARIA OK. Is there anything nice about him that you can tell him? Anything you appreciate and can learn from him?

DAUGHTER He is kind.

MARIA "You" are kind.

DAUGHTER You are kind and considerate and you are doing OK.

MARIA That's very beautiful. I am really impressed that you can see his strengths.

MARIA [to brother] What kinds of resources do you see in your sister?

SON My sister is more competent in summarizing, much better than I am.

MARIA Can you say, "You are."

SON I think you are outstanding. You are still young. In the future, you can be healthier mentally. As a brother, I will try very hard to improve myself. If I improve myself, I think my family members will be very happy for me. I think I made some mistakes in the past.

DAUGHTER Right now, I feel so happy because I have a brother. I feel so secure.

MARIA Can you come closer to him and really appreciate you have a brother who can support you? *(Girl moves closer to her brother)* Can you make a commitment that this is how you will look at each other? You are being grown ups, you can tell each other everything, but always see and each respect the other's strengths.

DAUGHTER I wish we could be friends and siblings. You are not a substitute for my father.

SON Yes.

DAUGHTER OK.

MARIA Do you know what she means?

SON Yes.

MARIA She does not want you to be a substitute father. She wants you to be a brother and a friend.

SON I know what she means.

MARIA Is that what you want?

SON Yes. I wish we can have more communication rather than tell each other what to do. Sometimes we can give each other our suggestions, but it's only a reference. We don't really need to put them into action.

MARIA Yes, you learn very fast. No more control. You can make suggestions, but she will make her own decisions.

MARIA [to daughter] Feels good?

DAUGHTER Very good.

MARIA You have a big support here.

MARIA OK, let's look at Mama. What do you want to tell Mama? What kind of relationship do you want to have in the future? Is there anything from the past that you did not share with her?

DAUGHTER I wish that you treated me just like your jacket, so you would feel really warm to me.

MARIA What do you mean by that?

DAUGHTER I want my mother to know I really trust her and love her.

MARIA Tell her.

DAUGHTER I really trust you and love you. I wish you would support my ideas and validate me. If I cannot make it, you can help me rather than stop me doing something because you think I cannot do it.

MARIA Tell her what you want to do in the future. I suggest you no longer talk about the past. You are standing here on your own feet. Tell her your ideas, about yourself, about what you want to do, about your school. I believe that you really know what you want.

DAUGHTER After graduation, I want to go to university then begin my own business. You can help me.

MAMA Can I say something now? Two years ago, my daughter already told me, "After I graduate from high school and university, I want to develop my own career and I am not going to stay in Beijing. I want to have my career in another country." I said, "Don't have such an unrealistic dreams, because many children go crazy when they go abroad to start their own business. You are lucky if you can find a job in Beijing. You should be satisfied."

MARIA You said that. Are you saying that now?

MAMA I think that was my mistake, how I said that two years ago.

MARIA So, what do you think, feel and say now?

MAMA Now, I am telling you from my heart. No matter where you go, I, your Mother, will do my best to support you.

MARIA Do you believe it?

DAUGHTER Yes.

MARIA I believe that you can do anything you want. I am on your side. I know from my own experience. If we believe in ourselves, we can get what we want. I know from your history that you have a lot of strengths. You can use your strengths for your dream. Do you believe now that Mama will support you, whoever you want to be, and whatever you want to do with your life?

DAUGHTER I believe.

MARIA Are you sure? I want to make sure. How can you convince me?

DAUGHTER I want my mother to get down from the chair.

MARIA I think that is a good idea. Forever?

DAUGHTER Yes.

MARIA [to Mama] Are you willing?

[Daughter walks to mother and helps her come down from the chair.]

MAMA I wanted to come down long ago.

MARIA I think that's great. So, now you are on an equal level. You no longer have to be small, feel small, and you no longer have to be out there in that corner. Now tell your mother again. Get as close as you possibly can and tell her anything else that you never told her, because there is a lot between you.

DAUGHTER I did not express myself to you, so you were not able to help me. From now on, I will tell you everything I want so you can help me to fulfill those possibilities.

MARIA I would like you to ask her to support you rather than help you. You don't need help. It is different. You are not helpless.

DAUGHTER I wish you could support me to do the things that are possible for me, not to deny me before I even start.

MARIA This is difficult for your mother. She is not used to that. I'd like you to be at a distance so that you can see each other. When you are too close, you don't see each other. You are two separate people. I love the idea that you want to hug your mother, but you are also two separate people. Mama, what do you want to say?

MAMA I think my daughter really has grown up.

MARIA Talk to her.

MAMA You really are grown up. I don't want to mention the past anymore. In the future, you can have more validation. We can be equal and be a team.

DAUGHTER Let's forget the past and let's have a new beginning.

MAMA I believe it and it can happen. [Girl hugs Mama.]

COMMENTARY *Next I use the metaphor of the museum as a place to put unmet expectations from the past. I know that the family, especially Mama, can relate well to metaphors. I continue to use Mama's metaphor to express my wish that they will all swim in the pool as equal grown-ups.*

*Having laid the groundwork for congruent communication, I turn my attention to resources. My intention is to assist her to value herself and be validated in her family. I ask the girl to tell me some of the resources and qualities she really appreciates in herself. She describes herself as enduring, considerate and practical. I ask her to find people in the group who will represent and role play these qualities. I remind her that she must be smart, since she can be the top student. She then proceeds to choose the doctor to role play the quality of Studying Well. Additional resources she chooses include Understanding and Being Outstanding. I then ask if she had any resources she wanted to hide or that got in the way, for example anger, or anything else she'd like to repress.*

DAUGHTER Sometimes I don't like Understanding.

MARIA When you don't like Understanding, what is it, what makes you not like Understanding?

DAUGHTER I am too considerate of others. I make others a priority.

MARIA Oh, I think what you miss is Self-validation or Self-acceptance. Accepting yourself or self-care. What do you call it?

DAUGHTER Self-acceptance.

MARIA OK, so choose somebody to be Self-acceptance. Is there any other resource you would like to hide?

DAUGHTER No more.

MARIA So, if you could have Self–acceptance I think you would value yourself.

DAUGHTER I don't know how to value myself.

MARIA You don't know how to value yourself, yet you want other people to value you?

DAUGHTER Yes.

MARIA That feels very sad for me. I think this is very important. If I met you and looked at you, what would be the first thing I could notice about you? Would it be that you study well?

Let's make a sculpt of your resources.

DAUGHTER I don't know what you mean by sculpt.

COMMENTARY *I explain how she can represent her perceptions about herself and her resources by making a sculpt. This is done by her placing role players in positions based on how she presents herself to the world. Some of the resources will be in the foreground, some in the background, and some will be hidden. We can arrange these resources based on how we feel we are using them. We can also rearrange resources and use them as we want. We are in charge.*

*She places Endurance, Studying Well, and Outstanding in the front, close to each other. They represent the first resources people will see. Outstanding is standing on the chair next to Studying Well.*

MARIA These are all parts of you, within you. You have lots of energy. So does Mama. I do, too. We use our energies in different ways, and this energy is expressed through our resources. Sometimes we are not willing to show all of them, so we select only what we want the world to see. Do you understand?

COMMENTARY *The girl continues to arrange her resources by placing Practical beside Understanding, in close proximity to Studying Well and Endurance. Self-acceptance becomes very small and is pushed away into the distance, far away from the other resources and from the girl herself.*

MARIA I want to suggest something that I believe in strongly. As long as Self-acceptance is small, all your parts will become smaller and almost invisible. You really can't value all your other resources unless you accept and value yourself first. My wish for you is that Self-acceptance will stand up, so all of your resources can shine. As long as you don't accept yourself, you cannot use your other resources.

[Maria asks all the resources to become small and invisible.]

COMMENTARY *At this point, the girl puts Self-acceptance in the front. I want to make a strong point that she cannot simply ask Self-acceptance to move until she has a dialogue to connect, accept and value Self-acceptance.*

MARIA First of all, you have to talk to her, for her to stand up.

DAUGHTER [walks toward Self-acceptance] If you were sitting here for many years, how would you feel to not be accepted?

ROLE PLAYER (SELF-ACCEPTANCE) I did not know that I was so influential for those parts. I am afraid and I worry.

MARIA She represents your own internal energy, your life force, your self-validation.

DAUGHTER I don't understand.

MARIA You said earlier you don't value yourself. You only accept yourself when Mama acknowledges you. I know that you have this resource of self-validation because you are a human being. You have had to hide her, did not accept her, because you saw yourself in the corner and nobody nurtured that resource in you. You need to connect with Self-acceptance and all your resources in a new way.

[Girl invites Self-acceptance to stand up and walks with her to join her other parts. All parts are standing up.]

MARIA This is a metaphor. Do you understand? I hope that you begin to value yourself. All your beautiful resources and many more that you have can now stand. You can be whoever you want to be. I would like to ask you to make a big decision now to validate yourself for everything you did, including in the past. You protected yourself the best way you knew how. When you stood up to your Mama, you did not know how to do it differently. Sometimes you acted against yourself because you made yourself sick. But you had the endurance to get better. You were able to get better with the help of your doctor and your resources. All these resources inside you helped you to survive. I want you to really appreciate all your parts and yourself. In this family, it is very easy for you to stay small. But right now, all your resources are standing, and I want you to make a commitment to yourself that you value yourself. When you value yourself, everybody else in your family and other people will know how to value you, too, I believe this and I know it from my own life. I had to learn to value myself first. Then other people valued me. Do you believe me?

DAUGHTER Yes.

MARIA Can you make a commitment that you will never put yourself down again? When you do, stand up right away. Sometimes fear puts us down. I hope that you remember this moment and this experience of valuing yourself. Deep inside, I am sure, you survived because you valued yourself. That's important not only for you, but for everybody. All of us human beings have our life force, our life energy. When we are not aware of this energy and we put ourselves down, other people put us down. Your family had the best intentions when they told you what to do. This is universal in many families. You did not learn how to be, to value yourself and to love and accept yourself. Do you understand what I am telling you?

DAUGHTER I need to have my own principles and have the courage to do the things I want to do, because I am great.

MARIA Can you tell the Self-acceptance role player that you value yourself and you are great?

DAUGHTER Should I say, "I am great" or "You are great?"

MARIA Say, "I" am great.

DAUGHTER Actually, I am great and I am outstanding. Other people see me as great even though I don't see myself that way.

MARIA And will you love yourself, along with all the many other parts?

DAUGHTER I do.

COMMENTARY *By integrating the resources, I am asking her to have a dialogue with each resource, accepting, valuing, connecting and making a commitment to each resource.*

MARIA OK, would you tell each of them what you like about them, talk to them. This is your Understanding. You understand things really well. They are your resources but you are in charge of them.

DAUGHTER Because I am so understanding and considerate, I often show my caring to others. Because I am so practical, my parents don't need to worry about me. Because I am so outstanding, my parents, family members and friends are proud of me. Because I can study well, I can have a good foundation and in the future I can have a good career. Because I have endurance, I can be persistent and I can fulfill my dreams. Because I often look into details, I can discover a lot of problems and I can resolve those problems. Because of my self-acceptance, I can own all these wonderful qualities. I can grow and I can develop more.

MARIA And you believe all that?

DAUGHTER Yes.

MARIA I am really happy and I want you to know you have many more qualities. I have another suggestion for you. In order to use all that, you need to take care of your body. Our body wants food. Our body wants to move. We could not do this here right now without our bodies. Your body is also part of you.

COMMENTARY *The girl is invited to give appreciation to each family member. This creates an additional awareness of where her resources have come from. It also creates a stronger connection and appreciation for her parents and brother.*

MARIA Knowing now that you value yourself, look at your family. Can you tell your Papa and Mama what you appreciate in them? Even if they didn't always do the best, they have the best intentions. You learned every resource from someone in the family. You can now use them differently, it's up to you. Every part of you was learned from them. What did you learn from Mama?

DAUGHTER I learned from my mother to Study Well and to be Outstanding. I learned from my father Endurance. I learned to look into details, and to be Practical and Considerate from my brother.

MARIA So, you learned from every one of them. You can always appreciate these and know they learned from you too.

COMMENTARY *I invite each family member to sculpt their desired picture of the family system. I want them to leave with a clear picture of all the possibilities of congruent communication, which is what each sculpt will represent.*
*The girl's picture includes Papa and Mama in the middle with brother standing next to Papa. The girl stood next to Mama holding her hand; Mama takes the initiative to hold Papa's hand and the son follows.*
*Mama's picture has the family standing in one line, from left to right*

*– the girl, Mama, Papa and the son. Mama puts her arm on Papa's and her daughter's shoulders. The son puts his hand on his father's shoulder and then the father puts his hand on the son's shoulder.*

*Papa comments that he doesn't like this picture and proceeds to create his own. He wants more distance because he believes that with more distance they can understand each other better. Otherwise, they are enmeshed. Papa's picture has the family of four still standing in one line, but with each person having some distance from the other.*

*The son has two different pictures. The first one is the whole family in a circle holding hands with one another. In the second picture, each family member raises one of their hands and holds the others' hands together in the middle of the circle. It represents being related and listening to each other's heart. We are facing the future together, supporting each other.*

*At the close of this interview, I suggest that the next step will be to work on the couple's relationship. I also suggest to Mama that since her children are grown up, there is no need to treat them like children.*

*I ask the girl if she wants feedback from her role players before we de-role them. The role players share their experience, feelings and feedback with the girl.*

*To end the session, I ask each of them what they learned in order to anchor the learning and to make a commitment to the changes they agreed to.*

MARIA I would like to ask you, Mama, what you learned here today and what you will commit yourself to. Papa, brother, I will ask you the same later.

MAMA This is our honour. Even if we sometimes lose our way in the future, I do believe I will have lots of help from the doctors here. I can even be greedy, in the future. Maria gave us some instruction how to live so that we can get onto a normal track. So, all the specialists here can feel relieved for us.

MARIA I hope that you will see the doctor regularly with the whole family.

DOCTOR. Sure.

MARIA OK. Thank you. Papa, what did you learn?

PAPA Through this interview, I saw things I was not aware of in the past. I discovered lots of issues in our family. In the future, we should improve, especially my relationship with my son and daughter. I learned I should give them the freedom to take risks and not limit them. Just let them fly as free as birds.

MARIA Yes. And you can even improve your relationship with your wife. [Turns to girl] That is their business, not yours. [Turns to Mama] There is always the possibility that we can change.

MAMA I will try.

MARIA Brother, I know that you would give us a good lecture about what you learned. I am curious.

SON Sometimes it is very difficult to express verbally. Sometimes we have to experience in our heart rather than express with words. I was complaining that my parents only asked us to study, but did not teach us how to be human beings. Today I learned that there were lots of things we couldn't express in words. Just like the quality of kindness, I learned this from my parents, day by day.

MARIA Yes, you can express it in words if you make an effort. From now on, I want you to study in your computer all the words which have to do with feelings so that you can find the word for every feeling you have, then teach everybody how to use it.

SON I am thankful now. I appreciate all of you and appreciate dear Maria. [Stands up and bows to Maria.]

MARIA Thank you.

MARIA [to girl] How about you? What kind of learning and commitment you can make?

DAUGHTER I discovered everybody is unique. No quality is good or bad. Everybody is a miracle. So, I want to accept everybody, especially myself.

MARIA Good. That's a commitment. Now I would like to give you homework. Mama, could you write it down? We will practice here, right now. Every day when you meet, you give one appreciation to everybody. It doesn't have to be a big thing. You can make a phone call for each other, cook something, or any small thing, and you [the girl] can be in charge of it. At first, it has to be structured, and later you will learn to do it automatically. In every family, especially in yours, people notice what goes wrong but they do not notice what people do for each other.

Let's practice now. [To girl] You give one appreciation to each of your family members. Start with Mama.

DAUGHTER I really appreciate you taking everything seriously and taking care of things for so many years.

MARIA Now an appreciation for Papa.

DAUGHTER I like how you say things straight. You never pretend, and from you I can learn to treat others with my heart, and allow people to be genuine to me too.

Brother, you are a curious person. You want to learn everything. I learned from you that I like to keep learning. You are a wonderful role model.

MARIA Do you have an appreciation for your doctor?

DAUGHTER You are very patient and you know how to work for us. I admire you. I hope I can become better under your leadership.

MARIA Mama, you have appreciation for everyone.

MAMA I appreciate my husband.

MARIA Say to him "You."

MAMA I appreciate you being so honest. Sometimes when you say things, you are gentler than me. I got married before falling in love, because we got married through a matchmaker. So, out of aware-ness, I became the mother of my husband. I did not prepare myself to become the mother of my daughter. I didn't play a good role as a wife, and as a mother. Let's learn from each other in the future. I tried to be a good wife and tried to be a mother. I couldn't be a woman because I did not know how. When I saw my daughter, sometimes she reminded me of myself. When I was young, 17 and 18, I had a dream but I did not go for it. I got married, but made a mess of this family. I am really proud of my daughter and son.

MARIA Can you tell your son what you appreciate about him?

MAMA I appreciate that you don't have any bad habits or addictions. You did not make me worry about you for 28 years. Not even a little. I felt quite comfortable to have a son like you. I felt quite solid to have a marriage for 30 years with my husband.

MARIA Good. What do you appreciate about your daughter?

MAMA I gave birth to you when I was 36 and you are my best gift. I am very lucky. Even though I am not good at mothering, I think I have a kind of competence. I can do better in the future.

[The group claps for her and she stands up and bows.]

MARIA You can be proud of the family, Mama. Papa, can you say your appreciation to everybody?

PAPA First, I want to talk to you, Mother. Don't worry in the future. Don't be so controlling.

MARIA Remember, it's an appreciation.

PAPA I appreciate your contribution to this family. I am so happy you gave me a son and a daughter.

MARIA What do you appreciate about your daughter?

PAPA You are so outstanding. You always want to win. My wish for you in the future is for you to be more relaxed, not to exhaust yourself.

MARIA How about your son?

PAPA In the past two years, you didn't cause any trouble for this family. You are very honest. You are filial to your parents. In the future, you can think for yourself. [Mama reminds Papa that we are doing appreciations.]

COMMENTARY *Filial is an important concept in Chinese culture, requiring that a person is 100 per cent devoted to their parents and ancestors. This includes a very deep, traditional value to respect, cherish, value and take care of parents and ancestors. It is a matter of honour. If you are filial, you are considered to be a good person. Being filial is a normal expectation.*

MARIA Brother.

SON I appreciate my sister. You have the competence to become out-standing. I will always support you. No matter whether you succeed or fail, you are always my only sister. You are one of the best. Whether you succeed or fail, you are always one of the family members. Always come back.

Mother, you are very kind. I can receive the love of my mother, which is unconditional and the best kind of love.

Father, you like to do housework and you have a good sense of humour.

MARIA OK, so, you know what I mean. Appreciation every day for every little thing. You can try.

COMMENTARY *I conclude with a hugging exercise for the family.*

MARIA Thank you. I have one more wish for you, which is learning to hug each other. [To girl] You give one hug to Mama. [The girl immediately stands up to hug her mother, her father and her brother, one by one.] You can do that every day. Papa and Mama didn't learn that. You can always learn hugging.

[Girl hugs Maria. Maria reminds Papa and Mama to hug each other. Mama hugs Papa and then Mama goes to hug her son.]

MARIA You learn fast!

MAMA This is something we need to learn in our family.

MARIA That is very easy to learn. You need to practice every day.

MAMA My son is already 28 years old, yet he never holds a girl's hand. Never. Now that I hug him, maybe he will dare to hold a girl's hand.

MARIA He needs to learn at home. So, every day you hug him so that he learns it.

MARIA This is your homework. And you [girl] remind them.

MARIA OK. Thank you very much.

[The session ends. Mama hugs Maria. Maria hugs the brother and Papa bows to Maria.]

## Group feedback

COMMENTARY *I asked the family if they would like to receive feedback from the large group of participants who had observed the process. They agreed. The following is feedback shared by those professionals who were involved in helping the family, followed by feedback from other participants.*

MARIA Doctor, would you like to say anything?

DOCTOR. It is an honour that I can have this kind of interview with the whole family. It was such a deep experience. Now I know where the daughter learned not to accept herself. I wish I also had the opportunity to help mother to look into her own resources, to help her value herself, too. I think Maria made a very important step today. In the future, you [the girl] need to help your family to do this every day.

I have strong emotions because of what the brother said to his sister. I also feel very touched by the way he talked to his father. It is just like a copy of my own family. So, I not only learned a lot, I also feel a lot. I am sure I will continue to work with you and the family. Thank you, Maria, for giving us such a wonderful interview.

MARIA Thank you, Doctor.

OTHER DOCTOR I was always here. I was very touched by the many pieces here. I was also touched by the mother. I can also see the strengths from the father. And I can sense the brother is always supporting the younger sister. I see lots of hope in this family. I would like to see you become better every day.

NURSE You were in my ward when you came to this hospital for the first time. You look much better now than at that time. I met your parents before. Mother, you look much better emotionally. At that time, when I met you, you were very anxious and always tearful. I think there is a big change in this family today. It is so real. You showed yourself and disclosed yourself so honestly. I think you will become better every day. My best wishes to you, that you can go back to school and be healthy.

PARTICIPANT My learning is about self-acceptance. When Maria did the sculpt, Self-acceptance was so far away, and all the other resources sat on the floor. I was so impressed with this picture. Later, the role player of Self-acceptance said, "The more I looked into my resources, the more I wanted to approach them." I think this is a good method of increasing self-acceptance. When the girl was standing in the centre surrounded by her resources, she asked them to help her any time she asked, and she said she was always there for them. She was surprised she was so distant from them, because she was sure she was together with the resources. She felt loving and powerful when she was standing with the resources. I enjoyed this.

PARTICIPANT When Maria asked what the star wanted in the very beginning, she was not sure. I could understand her at that moment because I have had a similar experience. When I saw her quickly take Self-acceptance to the center, I felt very relieved because we only can say what we want if we can accept ourselves. This is how we grow. That's the reason I chose to be here. Thank you. I saw my journey in yours.

PARTICIPANT I was quite shocked by this case because I have experience not accepting myself. I tried to hold on to this until August last year, when I had a car accident. I broke my lower back and then I had to stop to really reflect on myself. Then I became aware that I have not paid attention to myself for a long time. Sometimes I felt what happened this morning was a movie of my own process. I did not validate myself. I did not accept everything that was happening to me. From the star, I learned about power. I was tearful when I observed the star's process, so I am really thankful to you. [To son] I am really proud of you, too. You are so great. You remind me of my son. He is also quite sensitive. It's difficult for him to live in a super-reasonable family. So, I can feel your feelings. My son lives in this kind of family himself. He has overcome it. So, I learned lots from you, and now I know how I can be with my son when I go home. Thank you very much.

PARTICIPANT I felt touched today, especially when you hugged your mother. My parents never hugged me when I was young. I only touched my father's hand when I received an award, and I suffered from that. I always wanted my parents to validate me. One time, I asked my father why he never appreciated me. He said, not blaming you is already appreciation. I was able to understand. I just made myself live better. I am thankful for your process today.

## Evaluation notes

The following is my own assessment of whether this interview conformed to the goals, basic elements, and directives of the Satir Family Therapy Model as outlined earlier in this book.

### EXPERIENTIAL

The first sculpt was the girl's perception of her younger years when she felt ignored in the family. This set up the opportunity for the girl to eventually have a dialogue with everyone in the family.

During most of the interview, the mother was on the chair, demonstrating her power and control in the family.

The second sculpt externalized the girl's resources in order to raise her self-esteem and to connect her on an adult level with her family members. The acknowledgement that she learned these resources from her family provided another level of connection.

### SYSTEMIC

Everyone in the family was involved throughout the entire interview. The interview also included the larger system – the hospital and the two doctors and the nurse who cared for the girl. The nurse came at the girl's request.

### POSITIVELY DIRECTIONAL

In this interview I helped the family focus on goals that would create a positive change in their individual choices, the dynamics within the family, and their connection to each other. Mother coming down from the chair and the girl increasing her level of self-esteem moved them towards congruence within self and with each other.

### FOCUS ON CHANGE

The priority for change was for the girl to reconnect with her family members in a positive way. Since mother indicated at the beginning that she wanted to step down from the chair, her relationship with her husband was already changing.

There was more focus on changing the relationship between the girl and the family members than the relationships between husband, wife and son. These need to be included in the follow-up interviews.

### THE THERAPIST'S USE OF SELF

I made sure to create safety, encourage communication, and maintain a balance between providing feedback to mother and supporting her. I was congruent about sharing feelings when it was appropriate to do so.

### ENCOURAGE SELF-ESTEEM

Externalizing the girl's resources and encouraging her to stand up to her parents were done to raise her self-esteem. I had to keep a delicate balance between this goal and encouraging the mother to step down from her position of control and develop a new sense of strength in the family. The father and the son were encouraged to speak up for themselves. I also consistently validated their thoughts and feelings.

### FOSTERING SELF-RESPONSIBILITY AND CHOICE-MAKING

The priority in this process was to help the parents recognize and accept that both their children can make their own decisions and be responsible for their own lives. The process that creates a new connection between the parents and children is demonstrated by the picture the family sculpts at the end of the interview. They each take responsibility for self through their posture.

### FAMILY OF ORIGIN

Both parents revealed that they had been raising their son and daughter based on how they had been parented. Mother had not experienced any affection in her family, and father had been beaten. Neither knew how to express their feelings. I assured them that they had been parenting the only way they knew how, based on what they had learned from their parents. Now they could change. I also emphasized to the son and daughter that they could make choices about how they would parent differently once they had their own children.

### FACILITATING CONGRUENCE

Mother's opening statement, wanting the family to be four fishes swimming together, set the tone for promoting congruent communication among family members. My questions and comments were all geared toward teaching family members to be congruent. The son felt safe to talk about his vulnerabilities and express his wants. The exchange between the girl and her brother was congruent for the first time. I supported both the girl and her brother to express yearnings and wants congruently. The parents were then willing to hear and accept the yearnings and, as a result, the whole system was opened up for congruent communication.

COMMENTARY *At the celebration of the Chinese launch of this book, in Shanghai in March 2014, I met the girl's doctors. The doctors reported that the girl was doing very well; she had been discharged, and as far as they knew the family was OK.*

## Chapter Six
### THE TAXI DRIVERS' FAMILY: CHANGE IS ALWAYS POSSIBLE

Two therapists had previously worked with this family, which comprises a mother and father and their son. They had more than 20 sessions with the first therapist, starting in December of 2009. They were referred to the second therapist in February 2011, not long before seeing me for the three sessions recorded in this book, at which time the boy was 15. The boy had been displaying extreme anger and violence – hitting his mother and threatening her with a knife, overturning furniture, chopping at doors, and cutting himself and writing curse messages about his family in blood on the wall. When his parents had tried to punish him, his behaviour only escalated. He was performing poorly in school and his attendance was sporadic.

The parents were taxi drivers and took turns staying at home. They tried to convince their son to go to school, but his anger continued to increase. Feeling this was not a good environment for their son, they arranged for him to live with friends and attend school in another city. His school attendance and performance improved briefly, but he soon reverted to his previous behaviours. The following incident occurred. The mother needed to travel to her hometown because her father was dying. She asked her husband if their son was going to accompany them, but because the boy had hit his mother the previous night, his father intended to leave him alone at home. The couple left without providing their son with money or food.

For the next 11 days, the boy had to ask his friends for food. They earned their money, he said, by collecting so-called "protection fees," meaning they asked people for money and threatened to cause trouble if they weren't paid. When his parents returned from their trip, the boy became very angry and set fire to the house. His parents called the police, but did not lay charges. His anger continued to escalate. The boy's mother was scared to leave the house because her son would lock the door as soon as she stepped outside and would only unlock it if she gave him money. He went to school only when he felt like it and slept on the sofa in front of the TV.

It was around this time that the first therapist decided to refer the family to the second therapist. The latter saw the parents at the beginning of March and the boy attended the second session. The boy was annoyed that he had not been informed about the new therapist. The therapist guided the mother to talk to her son, suggesting that she tell him, "No matter what you do, I still love you." The boy was touched, but did not believe his mother. He suggested everybody mind their own business; that his parents drive their taxis and he go to school. He did admit that he regretted hitting his mother.

At the time of the first session with me, the family has had two interviews with the second therapist. The therapist reports a lack of communication in the family. The boy is angry, hurt, frustrated and confused and appears to have deep sorrow. He yearns to be loved and connected. Even though the relationships are so distant, there is motivation for change in the family. According to the therapist, although the family has a long way to go, there is hope.

## Family background

The couple met through mutual friends and married when he was 34 and she was 26. He was attracted to her submissive nature. He was born in Nanjing and graduated from university, while she was born in a small village in Canton Province. His family did not like her, so he cut ties with them. She doesn't have much contact with her family either, but in her case mostly due to physical distance. The husband looks down on his wife. The couple aborted their first pregnancy because of financial hardship. They were better off by the time their son arrived, but the mother later had another abortion due to China's one-child policy.

In terms of communication styles, the therapist reported that the father was mainly super-reasonable and sometimes irrelevant. His wife was placating and sometimes blaming. Their son was often controlling. The father loves his son conditionally – only when he succeeds academically. When the boy did well in elementary school, his father gave him twenty dollars even though he had only asked for five dollars. When the boy failed to do well in junior high, he only received three dollars. The mother said her son started hitting her with a comb when he was six years old. Her husband seemed unable to support her in this matter.

The therapist presented the following sculpt. The boy placed his parents in two distant corners. Father blamed mother. Mother blamed both father and son. The boy blamed both parents. The mother cried and the boy said, "You always want me to take your side when you have an argument with father." The mother disagreed and said she was only telling him what was happening. The father said he never blames. The boy was looking at his parents while they were looking away from him. As soon as they made eye contact, arguments ensued.

In the session, the boy had said, "I would feel happy if my parents would give me money and leave me alone for the rest of my life. I know it is not realistic. Sometimes, friends are more reliable than family members." The mother's ideal picture featured the three of them standing next to each other with father in the middle. She wants support from her husband. The father agreed with the picture. The boy wants the same picture, but with more distance.

The therapist suggested a picture with three of them standing in a circle and reaching out to each other. They all agreed, although the boy expressed some doubt.

## First interview

COMMENTARY *I create safety by greeting the family at the door and asking the participants to introduce themselves by stating their names and where they were from. I then set the context by explaining that the observers are learning about family therapy.*

MARIA I heard from your therapist that everybody in this family is working toward better relationships. I am impressed that you have already made lot of changes. You have a really good therapist who is a good teacher for you.

[To boy] I was told that you have learned a lot and are very good at school.

[To father] I also know, Papa, how important it is to you that your son does well.

[To mother] Mama, you sometimes have difficulty being a mother. I have lots of appreciation for you, and [to therapist] for you. When you came here, Mama, what did you hope for? What do you want to change?

MOTHER I wish my child would go to school, and that he would be willing to go from his heart rather than have us push him every day.

MARIA That is what you would like for him? That would make you feel good. What about for you?

MOTHER That there is warmth in our family.

MARIA Do you want more warmth for yourself?

MOTHER For this family.

MARIA Do you want more warmth with your husband?

MOTHER Yes.

MARIA Could you look at your husband and tell him that you want to feel more warmth?

COMMENTARY *I want the couple to learn to look at one another and to be direct with each other.*

MOTHER I want him to understand me, and that we need warmth in this family. [Weeping] I want him to be more accepting of us as a couple and more accepting of our child.

MARIA Turn toward him and ask him whether he would like that.

MOTHER [to father] Are you willing to stop saying that you want to move out and rent an apartment for yourself? I don't want to live like this.

MARIA Would you [father] like to respond to this? Look at her.

FATHER I think this is the only way because I'm seeking a way out. I'm doing this for our child. I made a lot of effort. I tried different ways. I only want our child to be better. I'm willing to pay any price. That's OK for me.

MARIA Are saying that you are only in this family for your son?

FATHER I will move out because of him.

MARIA Have you moved out already?

FATHER Not yet, but I plan to.

MARIA Why?

FATHER Because I did everything for this child to help him go to school. I bought everything for him. Everything he wanted, I would do for him. I made so much effort, yet this child did not go school.

MARIA I understand he is going to school now. [To boy] Are you going to school?

FATHER He did not go to school on Monday.

THERAPIST [to boy] Is it because they didn't drive the taxi, so that's why you didn't go school on Monday?

SON Before Monday, it was Sunday night and I was not able to fall to sleep that evening. I watched TV until 2 or 3 in the morning. They said they tried to wake me up, but I don't remember that. I was not able to get up.

MARIA You're saying that you don't feel responsible to go to school. You knew if you watched TV so late, you wouldn't get up. Is it not your responsibility?

SON But I think even if I made myself lie on the bed, I might not be able to fall asleep.

COMMENTARY *I want to make a point that it is the boy's responsibility to go to school. Self-responsibility and choice making are goals of the therapeutic process.*

MARIA Do you feel responsible for getting to school or don't you care?

SON Actually, at 10 o'clock on Monday morning, my uncle and aunt came. He is my father's brother. They got me off the sofa and blamed me a lot. They kept nagging and I was so annoyed. By that time, whether or not I went to school that day was not important.

MARIA You felt bad? They blamed you?

SON Yes.

MARIA [to boy] I asked everybody what they want to change. Mama is concerned about you. She also worries about your father. Papa wants to move out if you don't go to school. And all you [father] want for yourself is for your son to go to school. You don't want any relationship with your wife?

FATHER This relationship is very important.

MARIA With your wife?

FATHER Yes.

MARIA Tell her.

FATHER You are very important to me. Did you know that?

COMMENTARY *I connect the couple through direct dialogue. They begin to share what they want and hear how each other is feeling.*

MARIA She wants to know. You both turn your chairs to face each other and tell her more.

FATHER I want to tell you something else. Sunday evening, I was driving a taxi. The boy went to an internet café. His mother went to the shop to look for him. He didn't listen and then he also kicked his mother. I came back home at 4 o'clock in the morning. I asked him to go home. I love my wife very much. How can I protect her? Should I beat him for this? I was not able to protect my wife, so I want to take her away from the house. That way my son can experience the pressure of living. That's the method I want to use.

MARIA So how do you show your wife that you want to protect her and care for her? She said she wanted some warmth from you. Ask her what she needs. I don't know what she wants from you. I know that you care for her.

FATHER What do you want from me? What can I do to for you to feel warm?

MOTHER Because he feels the family is hopeless, he suggested that I move out. He said if I don't move out, he will move out for two years.

FATHER I did not say that.

MARIA Tell her. Let's clarify that.

FATHER Whether I move out totally depends on his [the son's] performance.

MARIA You are husband and wife. You need to stay together. That doesn't depend upon your son's behaviour. If he doesn't behave well and you move out, that doesn't help your wife. Can you decide that nobody moves out? We have to work on the premise that everybody stays in the house. Moving out is not a solution.

FATHER You are right for us to stay at home. The therapist told us we all need to give in a little bit to make some adjustments.

MARIA Yes, we will talk about that. First we need to settle her worry. Mother, are you always worried that he may move out?

MOTHER Yes.

MARIA OK. Father, you are threatening that you'll move out if your son doesn't behave. You are giving him too much power. Your relationship does not depend on him. I want you to understand that this is about your relationship with your wife. If you threaten to move out, she gets very scared. You give your son a lot of power. Mama and Papa staying together does not depend on your son. Do you understand what I am trying to say?

FATHER I understand.

MARIA Tell me how you feel about my suggestion?

FATHER As a husband, as a father, I feel that I am helpless when mother and son have conflict. I feel really frustrated.

MARIA Yes, I understand. When they argue or there's violence, you feel helpless, so you say you will leave.

FATHER No, I want to take her with me.

MARIA [to mother] You heard that?

MOTHER I heard that.

MARIA Do you appreciate that? He also wanted to protect you. Tell him how you feel about that.

MOTHER I'm feeling better.

MARIA Tell him what else you want, because he says he is not going to leave you.

MOTHER We should raise this child together.

MARIA You have been doing that. Right?

MOTHER We've been doing this, but he said my son always beats me and he kicks me. That is why he said we'd better move out.

MARIA [to son] Is that true? You kicked your mother and you hit her? What's going on with you when you do that?

SON I have no feeling.

MARIA Why do you hit her? You must be very angry. Anger is a feeling. Usually we're angry because we want something and we don't get what we want. So I would like to ask you to do something. Maybe you didn't do it before. Would you turn to your mother and tell her what you want from her? You can turn your chair and your therapist will support you here. Tell her what you want, which may be something you never told her before. Mama, I feel angry when I don't get what I want. I am not talking about the internet or another car, or bicycle. What would you want in your heart from your mother? Tell her what fuels your anger.

COMMENTARY *I help the son learn more about his internal experience by giving a name to his feeling and explaining why people may sometimes feel angry. This helps the son to develop awareness about what he wants. It then opens up an opportunity for me to create a new connection between mother and son.*

SON I want to have freedom.

MARIA What kind of freedom? Can you explain?

SON I want to have freedom to stay out late or even not come home. I don't want them to keep calling me or sending me messages with threatening words.

MARIA How do they threaten you?

SON Once it happened. I went to a distant place to have fun with my peers. My father sent me a message and called me a few times. He said if you don't come back home on time, then don't come back at all. I felt powerless, because it was rather late and there was no vehicle for me to go back home. I had to spend the night there. After then, they became stricter with me. Because of that, I did not live with them for half of the last year.

MARIA You want freedom. They can only give you freedom if they can trust you and if you'll be responsible and think for yourself. Is that true, Mama? Can you trust him?

MOTHER No, I cannot trust him when he is like this.

MARIA If you could trust him to be responsible, could you give him more freedom?

MOTHER He hasn't shown me any reason to trust him.

MARIA In what way don't you trust him? That he can't take care of himself, or that he can't be responsible?

MOTHER I don't trust him. For example, we told him that we would come here today. But last night, he went out and we searched for him until 5 o'clock this morning to take him home.

MARIA You go away and they don't know where you are.

SON They knew where I was.

MARIA If they hadn't searched for you, would you be here right now?

SON No.

MARIA Do you want to be here?

SON Yes.

MARIA How do they know that you will be responsible?

SON They don't trust me.

MARIA I don't think they can because sometimes you don't go home. Would you like them to trust you?

SON I don't care.

MARIA I don't believe that. I think you care. Are you sure you don't care? You don't want any relationship with these two people who care for you so much?

SON Actually, I don't see the evidence that they care about me.

MARIA How do you know? Tell Papa how you would know he cares for you? It's very important. [To son] What do you really want from Papa so that you know he cares? [To Papa] Do you want to hear?

FATHER I do.

SON Actually, I don't even know what caring is because I have not experienced loving from my parents for a long time. If you asked me whether there has been anyone to support me and help me to survive until now, I would say it has been my peers, my friends.

MARIA That is how you feel. From what I hear, they show their caring by trying to find you when you don't come home and by wanting you to go to school. That is how they think they care. How would you like them to show that they care? I think I have a guess but I want to hear from you.

SON Maybe sometimes they did care about me but they used the wrong method.

MARIA What would be a good method, one that you really yearn for?

SON I don't know, but definitely not pushing or pulling me when I am having fun.

MARIA They worry about you and that's their way of caring. They want you to do your school work and that's their way of caring. Can you see that? [To father] How did you know that your Papa cared?

FATHER When I was my son's age, we were very poor. As long as my father bought something small for us, we felt really content.

MARIA That's how your father cared? Did he sometimes talk to you, play with you?

FATHER [weeping] Very little.

MARIA What do the tears mean?

FATHER I want to use the loving and caring from my parents to raise him. I think what I am doing is much more than what my parents did.

MARIA Tell him how you care for him. I think he needs to hear it.

FATHER I care about you. We have an agreement that you will go to school. I quit work very early in the morning. I bring some breakfast for you. Generally, we have similarities, but we also have some differences. As long as he's willing to go school, I don't look at other mistakes. If I buy something and he says he doesn't like it, that's OK.

MARIA How would you show him that you love him? I know you do.

FATHER Maybe when we have too much sugar, we don't feel sweet. That means if you offer too much, they take it for granted.

MARIA Do you feel you offer too much?

FATHER He wanted to get on the internet. He wanted to learn. Compared to other children, he spends less time studying. My own family is poor. When I first married my wife, our family was in poverty, yet he was in grammar school. The way our financial system works, we had to find social welfare. But even then, I spent more money on him. The teacher thought he came from quite a wealthy family. I support his studies so that he can attend different competitions. Even the school principal said if we couldn't afford it financially, don't go. But I said, "That's OK. Even though I am poor, I don't want my son to suffer. I want him to get an education even if we miss out a lot at home." His school principal was very touched.

MARIA That is how you show you care. Did you hear that?

SON I heard.

MARIA What would you like to tell your father? What else do you want from him? What else do you need in order to know that he cares? Tell him.

SON At this point, I don't think I want anything from him.

MARIA Tell him what you wanted but didn't get.

SON Encouragement. For example, if I won some awards from those competitions, or if I got good grades in the school, he would just glance at the report and did not really appreciate me. He thought it was simple and that I got it easily. He did not see the effort I made. So I don't want to make an effort anymore.

COMMENTARY *The son has begun to share his unmet expectations, which creates a turning point in the session. I now think about externalizing his wants to make the discussion more concrete.*

MARIA You really want appreciation.

SON Yes, I did.

MARIA And encouragement for your efforts. That's what you want from your father. [To father] Do you understand that?

FATHER I understand, and I offer something. Last November, he was fifth in the class.

MARIA Talk to him and say "You."

FATHER You were staying with the couple and I took you there. On the way there, I asked you what you wanted and what kind of food you'd like to eat before we arrived at the couple's house. At that time you said you didn't want anything. Do you remember that?

SON No, I don't remember.

MARIA OK. Do you mind if I try to find out what he wants from both of you, so that you can connect more? I understand that you both give him everything you can. There is something inside him where he doesn't feel appreciated. Maybe you didn't know that. If you had known, you would connect with him more. [To boy] You want encouragement and appreciation.

SON Yes, I agree.

MARIA And trust? Do you agree?

SON I wanted that in the past, but not anymore.

MARIA I hope you never give up your desires.

SON I'm sorry, I don't trust them anymore. If they cannot offer, then forget it.

COMMENTARY *I move into sculpting to externalize the boy's yearning and support him in making his yearnings clear to his parents.*

MARIA I'm trying to find out what they can offer and what you can offer so that we can make some changes. I would like you to stand up and look around. Find somebody to represent your father's encouragement and his appreciation. That is what you really want and didn't get. This will help both you and Papa learn something. Everybody in this room knows about all these things. I want you to come with me and look around and find people who you think know about encouragement.

First of all, a father's encouragement. Who should represent the encouragement you want? You could show Papa what you want. I know he knows what encouragement is. Papa, you also know what trust is. Sometimes we know something but don't know how to show it to the other person, because we are so anxious. We can all learn something. Find somebody to role play encouragement. It's going to be fun. You like to play. This is my game.

COMMENTARY *The therapist wanted to help the boy choose his role players and I disagreed with this idea. I explained that he needed to do this himself. Finding role players involves a certain energetic component, specific to each individual. The boy chose a male group member and everyone clapped.*

MARIA Good choice. Who will role play appreciation, showing Papa how you would like to be appreciated?

[The boy chooses a female group member.]

MARIA Do you think trust is the third thing?

SON Yes. [He chooses another female group member.]

MARIA Good choices. OK, let's show what you expect from Mama. What do you like to receive from Mama when you do well in school? How could she show you that she really loves you?

SON Similar to father.

MARIA So you want encouragement.

SON Yes, more or less the same.

MARIA What else from Mama?

SON I can't remember. I cannot recall anything now.

MARIA Let's think and you look at Mama now. I want to trust you. I want you to trust me, to encourage me, to appreciate me and what else? You want her to love you? How would you know that Mama loves you?

SON I don't know how she's loving me.

MARIA Ask her.

SON Mother, how are you loving me?

MOTHER I care about the food you're eating and the clothes you're putting on and your learning at school.

SON But you did not do those things.

MARIA You didn't experience that? She didn't care for your food, your clothes?

SON For example about the food. Most of the time when I go home, there's no food on the table. So I have to buy instant noodles myself. Talking about clothing, she did not buy those clothes for me or with me. I don't even remember when did she buy clothes with me. Talking about studying, she did not help me study at all. So I don't sense what she said.

MARIA [to mother] You want to respond to him.

MOTHER Son, don't lie. You asked me not to buy for you. You only wanted money.

SON When did you ever take me to buy clothes?

MOTHER Even last week, I wanted to take you to buy clothes for the spring but you said you don't want to.

SON I don't remember. I don't remember anything.

COMMENTARY *I move the dialogue to future expectations so the family can let go of the past.*

MARIA We don't want to spend time on the past. What do you want Mama to do to be helpful for you? Sometimes to buy clothes for you and what else?

SON I don't need any more.

MARIA So you don't want anything?

SON I don't believe them. I don't trust them anymore.

MARIA What can we do? You don't believe.

SON I want to see the evidence if they make any change.

COMMENTARY *I suggest a commitment for something concrete that Mama can do.*

MARIA Your parents can learn. We can talk about it and then your therapist can help you. Let's negotiate. If Mama agrees to cook for you, in the next two months, would you be there to eat?

SON I would.

MARIA Mama?

MOTHER I will cook.

MARIA And sometimes go and buy clothes for him?

SON I don't need any more clothes.

MARIA OK, so Mama can cook. What else, one more thing Mama can do? How can she show you she loves you?

SON I don't have anything particular I want her to do. Let me think.

THERAPIST I heard you say last time that you want them to respect you. You want to be respected?

MARIA Do you want both of them to respect you?

SON But I don't think they can do it.

MARIA You have to give them a chance. This is why we are here now. We give everybody a chance, including you. Your therapist will help you. Choose somebody to role play both parents' respect. Who will be the person that represents your parents' respect?

SON My therapist.

THERAPIST Thank you.

MARIA Do you feel she respects you?

SON I think so.

MARIA Good. That's very good and I am happy because then she can teach your parents. Do you believe she is a good teacher?

SON I believe so.

MARIA OK, she can teach your parents how to show respect.

SON I hope so.

MARIA Now we have a very few important pieces here. You wish for a change that your parents can give you. Now ask your parents: What would be one important thing their son could commit to change?

COMMENTARY *I ask the parents to communicate what they want from their son so he can learn to grow in self-responsibility.*

MOTHER If I cook the meals, you'll come and eat, and come home on time. Come home right after school. You make me feel safe at home.

MARIA Can you commit to that? She will have a meal for you and you need to come home.

SON Yes.

MARIA He commits to that.

MOTHER I want to feel safe at home.

MARIA I know you want to go to school. True? School is a weapon for you. You know that this is the best weapon you can use against your father. We are now talking about your weapons. We will talk about a way that you no longer have to use your weapon. There is another weapon for you, which is not coming home.

Come and choose your weapons. Which one is the school weapon – "I don't go to school?" That really, really frightens your father. Which is your school weapon? [The boy picks up stuffed toys to represent his weapons.]

COMMENTARY *I plan to extend the sculpt to identify the boy's negative behaviour as weapons, then externalize them as stuffed animals so he can hold them as his own. This is how I help him acknowledge what he is doing. My intention is to reframe his negative behaviour into resources.*

MARIA Which is the one you can use to hurt your father the most and to worry your parents? [He picks a yellow bear.] OK, which one is this, school or staying out at night?

SON Staying out at night.

MARIA This is Staying Out at Night. Now choose one for School.

[He chooses a green ant for School.]

MARIA OK. Now what other weapon do you have? You have a third one, I'm sure you have.

SON The third one is Ignore Them.

MARIA Oh, yes, that is a good one! Choose one. [He picks a turtle.] Good, let's go back. You have more weapons than they have. So Mama said she would cook. You said you would go home after school. Now Papa. What do you want from Papa?

SON That's all.

MARIA It's all?

FATHER I feel it's enough if he can manage those.

MARIA He can manage. Role players, would you like to come closer? Let's look at them. You want encouragement from Papa when you are doing well in school. There was a time you really missed it.

[To Encouragement role player] Tell him what the event was so that he can help Papa say what he could have said to encourage you. Tell him when the event happened. Don't lose it.

[The boy drops the toy ant onto the floor.] You don't lose your weapon.

SON Long ago there was a boy who studied very well.

MARIA Who's the boy?

SON Of course, it's me.

MARIA OK. Good. That's very good. [Everyone applauds.] How long ago was that?

SON I used to always place first or second in examinations, until Grade 6. At that time, many junior high schools wanted to accept me as one of the students, but my father favoured one of the very famous schools. I was not accepted, and at the same time, I lost my opportunity to attend other high schools. I ended up in this school. When I first enrolled in the school, I was not willing to participate. For one examination, I was an hour late. I tried my best and I was accepted to the best class in the school. I was disappointed in this school. For the first final examination, there were more than 500 students and I was numbered in the 400s. Even though I am talented, many teachers and my peers thought I was a bad student. At that time, I made a decision. I wanted to study really well so they would see me differently. I went through lots of difficulties and finally I got fifth in the examination last November. Both my teachers and my peers looked at me with different eyes. But my parents stayed the same.

MARIA What did they say?

SON I don't remember what they said. I only remember they did not encourage me.

MARIA [to Encouragement role player] Maybe you can say what he would have liked to hear from Papa and Mama.

COMMENTARY *I ask the role players to demonstrate to the parents how to express encouragement, appreciation and trust. They role play how the parents could have been, and can aspire to be. This is a very distinctive kind of sculpt, using the role players as teachers.*

ENCOURAGEMENT ROLE PLAYER Actually, we like you very much. We are also proud of you. But I don't know how to encourage you and how to appreciate you. We believe that you can make it. You are so smart. You are so great.

MARIA Is that what you would like to have heard?

SON Yes.

MARIA Papa, did you feel this? Maybe you felt it, but you couldn't say it. Do you feel what encouragement is?

FATHER I thought I said that to you. I said those things to his mother. I wanted to invite the couple that he was living with to celebrate together.

MARIA Did he tell you that?

MOTHER He did.

MARIA But I think he [the boy] didn't hear it.

FATHER We even discussed with them that we wanted to celebrate together for you. Did you know that?

SON Aunt didn't tell me.

MARIA Now that you know, do you believe your father? [To father] Would you tell him more about that?

FATHER I mentioned earlier the time when I gave you a ride to the couple's place. I said to you then that you are great. It's not only us who need to tell you. You need to tell yourself. This is a mutual understanding.

MARIA Your father needs to hear from you.

SON You just took it for granted that I did things well, so you deleted those encouragements.

THERAPIST I remember in the counselling room, you told me that your son is beautiful and smart, and you are proud of him. Why don't you tell him now? Just tell your son what you told me. Telling me is useless unless you also tell him.

FATHER You are very right. I told you to walk together with us and we can face any difficulty when you need the help. Do you remember this?

SON Then what did you say when I solved the difficulty all by myself? "How come your answer is different from mine? Is something wrong with you?" That's what you told me, and then you left me.

MARIA That's what he said?

SON He said those things to me and then he left.

MARIA Do you remember?

FATHER I don't think so. I don't remember this part, because my personality stops me from doing this.

MARIA You're learning. You are a fast learner. You are doing beautifully. Tell him more.

FATHER You want me to tell you verbally.

MARIA Yes!

FATHER We express ourselves more on the behaviour level. I'm not sure if I put it into words that you will believe it. [To son] You are great!

MARIA Do you believe it now?

FATHER Very good. As long as we work hard, we will always be successful.

MARIA Do you hear him? Your father has to learn to put words to what he thinks.

[Turning to Mama] Mama, what did you learn from Encouragement? How do you encourage him more? What is it that you didn't tell him then?

MOTHER I will tell him, and I will encourage him when he does well in the school.

MARIA Right now, what can you tell him for encouragement?

MOTHER Son, we like you. We love you.

MARIA Can you say I?

MOTHER Once I see you have improvement, we will encourage you.

MARIA [to boy] Do you believe what you hear? What they are saying here is on video, so they cannot take it back. You can have that video.

SON I wish they would say those words from the heart and not after being pushed.

MARIA Am I pushing them?

SON I feel that my father was kind of reluctant to say that.

MARIA I don't feel I pushed him. Your father needs to learn to put words to how he feels. I encourage him to do. In this family, people don't say how they feel. You don't say it either, because you have been using weapons to say what you feel, not words. So let's see about Appreciation.

[To Appreciation role player] What would you like to say?

APPRECIATION ROLE PLAYER I really appreciate you because I see there are many things about you that deserve to be appreciated. I think you are a very smart boy. I appreciated you very much when you told your story. I notice you have high awareness about yourself and you reflect a lot about yourself. I notice you are really willing to be responsible for yourself because you helped yourself get to the top from the bottom in your grades. You discipline yourself and you have a strong will. I think it is not easy for the kind of boy you are.

MOTHER He's smart and he's cute.

MARIA And you appreciate him.

MOTHER I appreciate him. I appreciate you.

MARIA Mama, I would like you to learn to give him one appreciation every day. We are all learning that. It's helpful. Could you do that?

MOTHER I'm willing to.

MARIA You know, we appreciate our children just for being our children. They don't have to do anything. Do you appreciate him in your heart?

MOTHER I do.

MARIA I believe that. He needs to hear it. We need to let others know it. Papa, can you tell him that you appreciate him?

FATHER Recently your performance is really good. You are even better with Maria's guidance.

MARIA Do you appreciate him for himself?

FATHER I appreciate him.

MARIA You can be proud of having a son like that.

FATHER I appreciate you because you are good quality.

MARIA This is a good time to tell him what qualities you see in him and what he learned from you, because your son learns from you. What did he learn from you?

FATHER The way of learning things. That we don't need to work hard, yet we can learn. We are good at thinking and can see things through. You will be highly appreciated if you become better.

MARIA He has abilities just like you. Can you be proud of him?

FATHER Very competent, yes. I often say you have both sides and you are not in the middle.

MARIA You really appreciate him. [To the boy] Don't drop your weapons. [Some fell on the floor.]

MARIA You believe what Papa says?

SON Yes.

MARIA How do you feel? Did you know that before?

SON No.

MARIA Now you do. OK, now about trust. You want your parents to trust you.

TRUST ROLE PLAYER I believe as long as you decide to learn something, you will learn it well. I really trust you that you are willing to go to school. That's how I felt.

MARIA Mama, do you trust him? How would you express that?

MOTHER Son, I trust you.

MARIA Do you believe it?

SON I don't believe that she trusts me.

MARIA Tell her what you want from her so that you can trust her.

SON If she could really trust me, she would offer me enough freedom and not lock me up at home.

MARIA If you give him freedom, what would it be? Papa and Mama, you two discuss how much freedom you can give him.

[To son] You cannot have the freedom to not go home at all. I don't agree with that.

[To parents] If he goes out to play, what time does he have to be home? You discuss this together. If you trust him, how much freedom would you give him?

COMMENTARY *I suggest that they both need to participate in parenting, including making clear decisions about shared expectations of their son. I encourage concrete commitments in how much money he gets, what time he has to be at home, and what time he has to go to bed. I ask the parents to state these expectations for their son.*

FATHER The big problem is not that he goes out to play but that he stays in the internet café. He is addicted. I trust him when he goes out with his peers from the school. I don't even care how late he comes back.

MARIA Yes, I think you should care. You have to have a time limit. Unless you set a time, he won't come home.

FATHER But if he goes out with his friends from school, that's OK.

THERAPIST No, he still needs to come home.

FATHER I'm sure he needs to come home.

MARIA Papa, he has to go to sleep at a certain time so that he can get up and go to school in the morning. Parents have to set a time.

COMMENTARY *I stress the parents' responsibility to set guidelines and to be consistent in following through.*

FATHER I want you to have enough sleep. I want you to sleep in your own bed. [He asks mother if son goes out with his classmates is it OK for him to be home at 8 p.m.]

MOTHER How can you be at home at 8 p.m. when school ends at 6?

MARIA You know, he's 16. I suggest he has to go to sleep at a reasonable time. [To the boy] You have to go to sleep every day at 11 o'clock so that you can get up. It is every parent's job to have guidelines for their child. [To parents] Tell him: I want you to have enough sleep. Therefore, you need to sleep in your own bed.

FATHER Yes, yes, yes. You are right.

MARIA Is it OK with you? Mother said he needs to get up at 6:30. You two decide. He needs some freedom but he also needs some boundaries. You give him the freedom to play on the internet but he has to follow the guidelines for when he has to be in bed, among other things. This lady [the therapist] will keep track of it. You parents will keep track of what you promise and he will do the same for what he promises.

FATHER I guarantee I will keep that promise.

MARIA Good. Papa, I want you to promise you will learn about encouragement. You tell him when you are proud of him. You give him appreciation. You can let him play on the internet because you can trust him.

[To the boy] Now, very important, this lady [the role player] represents Respect. You tell Papa and Mama how you want respect. What does it mean for you?

SON I feel they never respect me.

MARIA How would you know Papa respects you?

SON For example, if I play, I go out and play and I'm home late. When I have too much fun, I lose the concept of time. I don't want him to call me and blame me over the phone. Talk to me gently and ask me to come home.

COMMENTARY *I decide to teach them, through role playing, how to communicate with respect.*

MARIA OK. Tell your father and show him. Let's imagine a father and son are talking to each about the son coming home late.

[To the son] You be the father.

[To the father] You be the son.

[To the son] How would you talk to him? How would you want him to talk to you? How would you say, "You are late" with respect? Show him.

SON [as the father] How come you are home late today?

FATHER [as the son] It's none of your business.

MARIA That's what you say? OK.

SON He did not respect me, why should I respect him? Forget it, forget it.

MARIA Are you saying that you want to be respected? Same with Mama. How is Mama not respecting you?

SON I want to try it again.

MARIA OK. Try again.

SON [as the father] Didn't you say you would be home at 9:30? How come you are still out until now?

FATHER [as the son] It's too much fun. So I stayed until now. I forgot.

SON [as the father] Is it OK for you to stop playing?

FATHER [as the son] It's so much fun. I like it.

SON [as the father] So that means I cannot give you money next time. What do you think? Can you spend your money appropriately when you get money?

FATHER [as the son] At the moment, as a son, that's OK. Don't give me money.

[Father steps out of the role] But then afterwards, he will be nagging us, asking his mother, "Please give me five dollars."

MARIA That is the past. You understand now. Do it again. Practice that you are late and Papa phoned. You wait. Papa phoned.

COMMENTARY *I suggest they role play so they can understand each other's feelings. In the following role play, they act out a typical scenario that happens between them.*

FATHER Where are you?

SON A long way away.

FATHER Where did you go?

SON I'm playing with my friends. I stayed here because there's no more transportation.

FATHER Just come back tomorrow morning.

SON I have no more money now. Will you give me a ride?

FATHER Yes.

SON So would you come immediately?

FATHER I will.

SON I'm drunk. I'll wait for you at the door.

FATHER It'll take me an hour to get to your place.

SON Would you come sooner?

MARIA At this point, I would get angry if I was your father. I do not think that is very respectful. You want respect. Father worked all night and you want him to pick you up. If you want respect, you have to give respect.

COMMENTARY *I share my perception to teach the boy and the parents that they have to impose consequences if their son doesn't keep his commitment.*

SON Because it is late, I have spent all my money.

MARIA Yes, but that's not good planning. If you want to get things from your parents, you also need to respect them and be responsible. It's not only one way. You don't stay out without money until the morning. You see Papa, I'm suggesting all these things are important. But you both also need to have consequences. If he's not at home at 11 p.m., there are consequences. Do you know what consequences are?

FATHER I heard the word, but I'm not sure if it is right or wrong.

MARIA If he is not at home at a certain agreed-upon time, then next time he wants to do something, he cannot do it. I don't want to use the word "punishment." If he doesn't follow through on what he promised, then you are not obligated to keep your side of the agreement. You both need to be responsible.

FATHER That's what I'm thinking. Sometimes he would say, "I have spent all the money." So if I don't give him any, he can find different ways to get money and that really bothers me. Because the consequence doesn't help.

MARIA We are talking about the future. You have to learn new ways as well.

FATHER You are right. He said, "I don't get the respect but I want to get the money."

MARIA [to the therapist] OK. I am suggesting that in the next sessions, you negotiate the guidelines, because in this family there are no guidelines. In one way, there are lots of expectations, so he can do whatever he wants. He doesn't know what the limits or consequences are. I am suggesting that you discuss boundaries in the next sessions. He wants freedom and he needs it, but there are boundaries attached. In a way, he has too much freedom and he has no reason to come home.

Sometime I would like you to discuss with Papa and Mama how they can a have better relationship. They can model for him how to have more warmth in the family. Something very important for them to learn is how to show respect.

I'm suggesting there is much more work to be done for the boy to get what he wants from his parents, and for his parents to communicate what they need.

[To the boy] I hope you will get the love, respect, encouragement and support you need from your parents. I think it's all there; they just didn't express it. Then you would no longer need to use those weapons. What are you going to do with those weapons if you get respect, encouragement and trust? Tell your parents.

SON If they are able to do this, I will gradually put down my weapons.

COMMENTARY *I move into commitment and a contract by asking the boy which weapons he is willing to let go of.*

MARIA: What commitment do you make to Papa and Mama? Put it in words.

SON I make this commitment not only for you, but also for my future. I definitely will go to school.

MARIA I believe you.

SON I believe, too.

MARIA Thank you. I'm very happy. Now which one is next and when? This one. This one is heavy – Staying Out at Night. What about this one? Are you willing to negotiate with the help of this beautiful lady [role player] about Staying Out at Night?

SON If they can be like other parents and encourage me, appreciate me, trust me, respect me and love me, then I would go back home because in that way, it will be a home and not a house.

MARIA That's really well said. Did you hear that, Papa?

FATHER Yes.

MARIA What meaning do you make of that?

FATHER [to son] If you will go to school, I definitely welcome it.

MARIA What about this weapon, "Not Coming Home?" What do you think? [To the father] He made a commitment and I ask you how you feel about it, because it is a negotiation. He wants something from his parents. He doesn't need to stay out. Do you understand that?

FATHER I know. We will try our best, but you are comparing us with others. What I worry about most is that he couldn't see what we have done for him, or he disagreed with what I did. It's about trust. I said he could play with his classmates and that he can play for two hours. This means I trust him. I think I love him more than the parents of his classmates. I don't think those parents can make it. Maria said what we are looking for is consequences.

MARIA What about this one – "Ignoring Them?" Can you throw that away?

SON Not now.

MARIA Not yet? When your trust is growing, then you can slowly throw that weapon away. This is still a weapon he is going to use. If he doesn't feel encouragement, appreciation, trust and respect, this is the weapon he will use. You understand that. From now, everybody has a commitment here.

FATHER Yes.

MARIA Papa, what is your commitment? What can you tell your son? What did you learn here today?

FATHER What I will definitely do for the family is earn the bread. I will take care of my wife and my son. I can definitely do this.

MARIA Do you commit as well to what your son needs?

FATHER I've been appreciating that he has quality. That's no problem. It's not a big issue of trust. I didn't go for encouragement because I could not encourage you at this stage.

SON When I'm successful, I need more encouragement than when I fail.

FATHER OK, I am encouraging you at this stage.

THERAPIST Father, do you appreciate him already?

FATHER It's very good that you are willing to let go of not going to school. If you can manage it, I'm sure you can be successful. As long as you work hard, you can be anything you want. That is something I really feel. It's totally true.

MARIA Do you feel encouraged? [Son nods his head.]

COMMENTARY *I am anchoring all the learnings for each family member.*

MARIA: Papa, you are learning. Mama, what did you learn here today? What's your commitment?

MOTHER I learned to show my caring to him. I'm very happy that he is willing to go to school.

MARIA What about all these things – encouragement, appreciation, trust and respect? Can you do that?

MOTHER I will, and I will also be cooking.

MARIA Papa, can you assure your wife that you will no longer think about leaving, because she worries about that. In your own words, tell her about that.

FATHER We will try our best, so that we can get the result we really want.

THERAPIST I'm happy to hear that. Did you see how, if you let go, your son lets go as well?

FATHER I am not giving up. I wish he would co-operate.

MARIA He is co-operating. We are not talking about the past; we are talking now and in the future.

FATHER From now on, I'm definitely staying.

MARIA You commit to your wife that you will stay in this home. Tell her.

FATHER I won't leave if he goes to school.

MARIA No. This is not your son's business. From today on, this is between you and your wife.

FATHER Both of us can be together all the time. We are together forever.

MARIA Good. Your son is not responsible for your relationship.

SON Do you mean you're going to move out if I don't do any studies and you will take mother away?

FATHER I will try my best to stay.

MARIA That's not good enough for me. He made many new commitments. She did, too. This is the most important commitment: that Papa is going to stay no matter what.

FATHER No matter what, I will stay home.

MARIA Good. We will end here right now. You will continue to work with your therapist. I have a lot of faith that everything will move ahead. I want everyone to de-role themselves and share how you felt in your role. Is there any wisdom you can offer?

COMMENTARY *I ask the role players to give feedback. Each role player shares his or her feelings in their role. They also appreciate and support the boy in letting go of his weapons.*

THERAPIST I'm happy that you let go of your weapons.

MARIA From now on, he is going to get more and more diamonds and fewer weapons. Thank you. So we'll have a few minutes of feedback if you want to hear from anybody in the group who wants to say something. Who would like to share feedback?

COMMENTARY *The participants give feedback to the family sharing their own experiences and learnings. Some of them identified with the boy, providing support and commenting on his intelligence. Some teachers in the group encouraged the boy in his pursuit of education. One participant admired the fact that the boy accepted his parents' limitations and respected their commitment to change.*

MARIA I want to thank you for being here to share your life. I would like to have a commitment. Especially from you [the boy]. Can you commit to no violence ever? No matter how much anger, nobody may beat anybody in this family. Can you make a commitment?

SON Yes.

MARIA If you feel angry, you can say so. I want to shake your hand. Are we friends? No beating Mama. You can say, "I feel angry now." Mama, can you commit? No violence, no beating. I know it is hard when we're angry. But you are learning so much. This is very important because all that learning cannot take place if you hurt each other. Can you, Mama, say to your son, "I feel really angry now"? But do not beat him.

[To son] Can you do the same? And Papa? What do you want to say to Papa?

SON I am thankful for all the teachers here. And I'm very thankful to you.

MARIA I believe you will keep all your commitments. I also know you will go to school. I will hear from you and from her [the therapist] how well you are doing. Mama, do you want to say something?

MOTHER I received lot of help here. Our family was helped to become warmer.

MARIA That's what you want? To feel more warmth?

MOTHER I received lot of help from everybody here and the help from the teacher. So I believe I have.

MARIA Papa?

FATHER Thank you all. Once we put things on the table and we work hard from that, I am sure we will be successful. Thank you all.

MARIA Thank you, Tina [the therapist], you did good work.

## Group feedback and discussion

I divided the large group into smaller groups to discuss the process. One person in each group then reported back to me, as outlined below. The group's feedback consistently touched on the importance of:

- Creating safety
- Therapist's use of self
- Including all family members
- Sculpting to move the process forward
- Focusing on change
- Commitment for change
- Teaching congruence

GROUP LEADER 1
We learned to take risks and to reflect on our process.

GROUP LEADER 2
Our learning was not just about personal growth but also about Maria's use of herself. Our discussion on how to use oneself raised more self awareness. Maria also demonstrated the different levels of the Satir Model so that we understood congruent counseling through real demonstration. She followed the family's process in the interview. We learned how to build safety in the room for the family members.

GROUP LEADER 3
Maria demonstrated how to connect with the client's process in the interview. We discovered that a therapist's personal growth and professional growth are important. To be an effective therapist requires

a long journey of learning. In fact, we realized that therapy is an art. We learned how to use family sculpting. Maria connected the family members and used herself to connect with persons in a human way, whch she demonstrated to help the family. She was totally present.

## GROUP LEADER 4

The seven points for discussion were good guidelines and helped us to uncover the process of the family interview. We saw Maria not just practice the Satir Model in an interview, but connecting with human beings. She used a few questions to review the needs and yearnings of the family members and let them open up for their journey, let the family members understand and accept each other. Our group wished to express our appreciation to the role players for their congruent communication to the family members.

## GROUP LEADER 5

Our learning in the whole process was about how to create safety, giving support for the client to open up himself. The use of sculpting in the interview reflected the whole picture of the family's process. Moreover, Maria used her life force to connect the life force of the family. She also followed the family's process closely and patiently. We learned to be more focused on the family by supporting them. We also wanted to learn how to set the sequence for the family interview and set priorities for choice points in the future.

My learning as a group leader was to become less influenced by the feedback from others. In the past when I said something which did not receive positive feedback, I thought I had done something wrong and would feel anxious.

## GROUP LEADER 6

Our group learned how to live in the present and accept the family members where they are. As therapists sometimes we cannot be in charge of the process. When we are stuck over the family argument, making use of the resources is a great learning.

We felt the family's flow of energy. After Maria's contact with the family, the dynamics of the family became fluid and flowing. They could listen to each other. The use of Satir's beliefs is powerful and important in the therapy. We also saw that we could use different types of skills within the Satir Model.

GROUP LEADER 7

We saw the soul of Satir behind Maria in the past six days. She demonstrated her great curiosity about the family. She considered the individual problem as a family problem, and she let all the family members see the family problem as a whole. This was very powerful and helped the family members to accept each other. Maria was very patient with the clients, which we had not been in our normal interviews with the family. She gave enough space for the members to grow at their own pace. Also, we saw the impact of family sculpting, which we intend to use more in future. Maria put the beliefs of Satir into practice. We were amazed that she still remembered to remind the family not to use violence at the end of the interview.

## Questions and answers

QUESTION *The mother beat her son and he did not want to talk about his feelings. How do we deal with the client who does not want to talk about his painful experiences?*

MARIA: Good question! The Satir Model focuses on the positive parts and not on pathology or negativity. If the client does not want to share, he is his own choicemaker. I was not curious to find out about his trauma. I concluded that he has shown he has the energy and resources to survive.

QUESTION *You had father and son switch roles during the interview. What was the purpose of this role play?*

MARIA: It was meant to be a learning experience for them. I could see the father had difficulty understanding his son, and the boy did not trust his father. It is a good learning experience when one has to identify with another person. Through the role play, the father could acknowledge the needs of his son and show more understanding. Using the toys to represent the son's weapons helped the family see it in a fun light rather than something that is "bad." I also wanted to expand their vision so they weren't only focusing on studying. School work was the boy's only way to get his parents' attention.

QUESTION *We learned that therapy is not only in the therapy room and that homework can be used as an extension and to anchor the learnings. We also saw that homework can be used to prepare for the next session. Were there any other purposes for homework?*

MARIA: To let the family practise and to help them connect with each other. I also tested their readiness for change. If I gave them too much, they would not do it. It is important for them to know that they are responsible for their work and for whatever changes they want to make. It is important to remember to practise the homework during the session.

I ask myself how I can get the message across to the parents that the boy needs help. The symptom was related to schooling, but all the family members have been neglected. It is easy to get carried away with the symptom. Whenever the boy came home, he needed love, but he felt lonely at home. What he needed was attention and love. I needed to do something so the parents could learn this instead of focusing on the problem. The key was to treat the whole family as a system. In this family, everybody was neglected. I needed to focus and bring the most important message to the family.

## Evaluation notes

### EXPERIENTIAL
1. To externalize the boy's unmet expectations and teach the parents how to respond to his needs, I used role players. Their feedback helped the parents to become more aware of the boy's needs.
2. To externalize the boy's resistance, I used stuffed animals, which I called his "weapons," and actually transformed his negative behaviour into strengths. For example, not going to school was first perceived as a negative behaviour, yet in the sculpt it emerged as a positive resource to express his anger and yearning to belong.

### SYSTEMIC
The interview included every member of the family, as well as their therapist. She had an active role in the process in order to establish continuity going into follow-up sessions. My intention was to build trust between the therapist and the family in order to extend the work into the larger system.

## FOCUS ON CHANGE

The priority for change was to build connection between each member of the family. The parents needed to learn to connect and to learn about parenting. There were no relationships between anyone in this family, so the focus needed to be on building awareness of expectations and responsibilities. The parents had no awareness of their responsibility toward themselves and their son. They also lacked awareness of the impact their reactions were having on their son's behaviour. They simply lacked parenting skills, although they had good intentions. They needed to learn how to recognize and respond to their son's needs. The boy needed to learn how to express his expectations in such a way that he would be heard.

There was a great deal of teaching required in this session. At the end, the commitments to change needed to be anchored. There is hope for change in this family because they were so willing to commit to the new learning.

## THERAPIST'S USE OF SELF

I focused on creating safety, teaching and demonstrating in a way that was free of judgment and an opportunity for learning. The feedback from participants indicated that my use of self helped them to become more self-aware.

## RAISING SELF-ESTEEM

In this family, I was aware that I needed to raise self-esteem gently, one step at a time. I tried to show that I value them so that they can value themselves. The parents had been so busy with their basic survival that they had no concept of valuing themselves or their son. They are good people, focusing only on the basics of earning a living. The main issue was that they didn't value the boy, because they didn't value themselves either.

## FOSTERING SELF-RESPONSIBILITY AND CHOICE-MAKING

This was accomplished through the sculpt, and in the commitment they made. An example is when I had the father and son switch roles and "walk in each other's shoes."

## FAMILY OF ORIGIN

In this family, it was very important to be aware that the parents' background did not prepare them for their parental responsibilities.

Based on the limited information I had about how they were raised themselves, I suspected that what they learned in their respective families was basic survival, and that feelings were neglected. Both had had experience of being physically abused, which they understood and accepted as "normal." In turn, they repeated these patterns with their own child.

FACILITATING CONGRUENCE
Throughout the interview, I tried to support everyone to express their needs congruently and to hear each other and be heard. The couple, for instance, actually had to learn to share information with each other directly.

I was willing to challenge each of them, by sharing my perceptions, my expectations, and my feelings for them. For example, when the boy expressed that he wanted to be trusted, I shared my perception that his behaviour of not coming home was not responsible and therefore would not help him to earn trust. He agreed and became more aware that he has a role to play in ensuring his expectations are met.

\*\*\*

## Second interview

THERAPIST'S PRESENTATION
When the therapist met the family for the first session after Maria's interview, the father looked very happy and the mother seemed very calm, but the boy did not come. The parents explained that their son had not come home the evening before. He had been at the internet café, hadn't gone to school, and was now at home sleeping.

What had happened after Maria's session? After the interview, the boy had started attending school and had requested money from his parents as a reward. The mother gave him the money and he went to the internet café, frequently returning home early in the morning. The boy said he was too sleepy to go to school. The mother continued giving money to the boy. The father had packed his bags and left, as he had previously planned to do.

The therapist reminded the parents of their commitments. She said that unless the father moved back home, she would not see them. Consequently, he moved back home.

In the second session with the therapist, all three came. The boy had returned to school. The therapist asked him what made him put down the "Not Attending School" weapon. The boy said he needed to think about his future. He said he now realized his parents loved him and he had decided to go to school. The therapist asked the boy to verbalize how he knew that his parents loved him.

In the previous week the boy had set fire to the house. It had to be put out by two fire engines. In the past, when the mother reported that she was being beaten by her son, the police had ignored it. This time, the police wanted to arrest the boy. The parents did not want the police to take the boy away, so they protected him. The boy was touched by this gesture.

## DISCUSSION WITH THE THERAPIST

COMMENTARY *In the following section, I am talking only to the therapist in order to get an update before the family arrives.*

*I asked her if she knew why the boy had started the fire. She said that the mother has beaten the boy since he was young and had found nothing good in him. They had had many altercations and the boy had a lot anger. After the fire incident, however, the boy was moved that his parents protected him and he was willing to see the therapist. He talked with his parents about his expectations.*

MARIA I remember everybody made a commitment. The boy will go to school, the father will live at home and the mother will cook.

THERAPIST The biggest issue is that they made commitments but did not follow them. Mother has to be reminded to cook. During the holidays, the boy had only two meals a day, but he was satisfied with this.

MARIA When did you see them last?

THERAPIST Two weeks ago. There is a big improvement in their relationship. Up until now, the parents never cooperated, they just did their own thing. Now they have discussions and they know that they need to agree on issues involving their son.

MARIA Is the father living at home now?

THERAPIST Yes, he's living at home.

MARIA Did the mother cook?

THERAPIST Actually, she didn't cook much.

MARIA What about all the other commitments, such as trust? Did they acknowledge the boy?

THERAPIST I don't think they trust the boy. After the boy started high school, and he went to school every day, the father did not talk to him for more than two months. Even when the boy was at home, the father still ignored him.

MARIA Why do you say their relationship is better?

THERAPIST Recently the father responded to the boy.

COMMENTARY *The therapist had given them homework to appreciate each other. The boy was designated "chairperson" for this homework. The therapist also reports that the mother was physically abused in her family of origin.*

*The whole family agreed to another session because the husband wants a more harmonious relationship with his wife. The therapist wonders how she can help the wife let go of the past and be present to her husband. The boy is now in boarding school and returns home on weekends.*

*I asked the therapist to sculpt the family relationship as she saw it. The couple was facing each other. When the husband reached out to touch his wife, she refused his approach. The husband said every time he touches his wife, she reacts as if he were harassing her.*

*The therapist also showed another picture of how things were at home. It portrayed the parents blaming each other with the boy in the distance, helplessly watching them. The boy reported to the therapist that his parents argue a lot, but that he has less anger.*

MARIA It seems to me from what you are saying, that the mother does not want a relationship with the father. Is that true?

THERAPIST She said she did, but her behaviour said no.

MARIA OK, I will ask her. I wanted to see them again because I believed that they would keep their commitment. It seems to me that the commitment was not realistic. The only one who kept his commitment is the boy. He goes to school. The father kept his commitment and stays home now. Mother didn't keep hers.

[To the therapist] Thanks for your work.

From what I remember, the boy's wish is not that his parents love each other. His wish is to be understood, respected and loved, and not neglected. He did not say that he worries about his parents' relationship. Why should we worry?

THERAPIST The boy wants harmony in the house. He doesn't want his parents to argue.

MARIA OK. That's what we can talk about. It seems to me that you want them to love each other, but this is not what they want. We can't expect people to have a relationship that they don't want.

THERAPIST Maria, I'm also thinking about myself; I usually don't work with people over such a long period of time.

MARIA Now you are talking in a different voice. I can hear you. [Therapist laughs.]

THERAPIST I have reflected on why I continue seeing them. Out of 17 visits, I have only been able to see the boy seven times. I asked myself, "Would Maria be disappointed if I stopped seeing this family?" I didn't think you'd feel disappointed in me, but you might feel regret because the boy's life is precious. I don't think that's the real reason. The most important thing is, I treasure his life. I really love him.

MARIA So my question is, what would be the best thing for him?

THERAPIST I think the main objective is to work with this boy. He has two faces – one face is a beautiful angel; the other face is someone who gives up easily. He's just like his father. He only accepts the positive parts of himself and not the negative parts. I wonder how we can integrate his resources so that he can see all his parts and accept and appreciate himself. He has his own goal for his life, but he cannot discipline himself.

MARIA What do you think are the negative parts?

THERAPIST He often follows his own wishes and has no discipline.

He's afraid to suffer or face difficulties. He gives up easily.

MARIA How about the positive parts?

THERAPIST He's very smart, sensitive and caring. He is very good at connecting with and understanding other people.

MARIA I agree with you. I saw all these parts but I think that what he is missing, as he said in the last interview, is appreciation, respect, trust and encouragement. Encouragement is the most important. Do you think he is getting them now?

THERAPIST I discovered it's very difficult for the parents to encourage the boy. When I was working with them, I asked them to appreciate each other. In the session, they did not know how to show appreciation. I asked the boy to demonstrate for his parents. He appreciated his parents first and then they were able to say a little in return.

MARIA How old is he now?

THERAPIST He's now 15.

MARIA How many more years does he have to save his parents? How many years before he graduates? Three? I'm thinking about helping this boy. He needs to be saved from his parents.

THERAPIST I want him to save himself. When I saw him last time, I gave him homework to save himself. I want him to appreciate himself every day and write it down.

MARIA Good. Is he doing it?

THERAPIST That's the homework I gave him two weeks ago. We can check with him this time.

MARIA I appreciate that you continue to see them. I think you are the only positive person in the boy's life. Now we are out of time. I just want to know how it happened that they came back. Who wanted to come back? You? The parents or the boy?

THERAPIST They all wanted to come. I didn't know why they wanted to come, but I know why I came. [Laughs] Maria, you are right. I'm angry with them.

MARIA I'm not angry with the parents. They really did not know how to handle a child. I see that many parents know how to make a child but many of them really don't know how to deal with a child. I hope you'll continue to work with them.

THERAPIST I want you to work with them, and then I don't need to work with them anymore.

MARIA [waves hand] No interview if you don't follow up. This is a basic issue.

THERAPIST I will follow up.

MARIA [shakes hands with therapist] A commitment.

COMMENTATRY: *When I work as a consultant, I will only work with a family when I am sure their therapist will commit to follow-up sessions.*

MARIA You are doing a good job. It's a very difficult family because we don't have the parents' cooperation. When we have parents who don't want to be parents, there's nothing we can do. There are many children in that situation. I think this boy deserves our attention. I think you are the only person in his life who cares, even when your voice is angry. OK, thank you.

## *The interview*

COMMENTARY *I greet them at the door. The boy is the first to walk in. As the family enters, the entire group applauds and welcomes them back. I tell them they are the only family that I have seen so far for a second time.*

*I turn to mother and ask her what she hopes for in coming back.*

MAMA To fix this family.

MARIA I cannot fix it. You can only fix yourself. [Leans toward Mama] Do you know that?

MOTHER [nods] Yes.

MARIA So, how would you like to fix your family and yourself?

MOTHER I learned a lot from the last interview.

MARIA Did you keep your commitment? I will write down things. [Family members look to a large flip chart where commitments were written down during last interview.]

I know that you made some commitments, including cooking meat for your son and trusting him more.

MOTHER I did all that.

MARIA You did?

MOTHER Partially.

MARIA Partially. So, what was difficult?

MOTHER [hesitates] A few things. Maybe it's a matter of time.

MARIA So you need more time. [Mother nods her head.] Has there been any change?

MOTHER My son.

MARIA [points to son] Tell him what has changed.

MOTHER [looks at son and he looks back] His attitude, and he went back to school.

[Maria points to the son and reminds Mama to talk to him directly and say "You" when addressing him.]

MOTHER [turns to look at the son, who looks at his mother] I like your attitude and I like that you went back to school.

MARIA That's nice.

MOTHER [looks at son] And you respect your parents.

MARIA It's good to hear. Was your experience with your husband good?

MOTHER Um … Yes.

MARIA Did he stay at home?

MOTHER Yes. He stays home and he's helping me to do the housework, too.

MARIA [points to father] Tell him.

MOTHER [looks at husband] Husband, I would like you to continue to be like this and to help this family.

MARIA [pointing to husband] So, one wish is for him to continue what he is doing. What else would you like to change today?

MOTHER Um … That we can trust and help each other.

MARIA So you would like your husband to trust you more and help you more?

MOTHER Yes.

MARIA [points to the son] Your son, too?

MOTHER Yes, my son as well [nods].

MARIA So that would make your life better?

MOTHER [nods] Yes.

MARIA So we'll talk about trust and help.
[Turns to father] How about you, Papa? What was good? What happened for you in the past few months?

COMMENTARY *I encourage father to speak directly to his wife and son.*

FATHER [to Maria] At first, after the education from all of you, my son changed a lot.

MARIA [points to the son] Tell him directly.

FATHER [turns to look at son] Son, since last time 'til now, you have made a big change. You improved very quickly in school, as well as how you treat family members, how you deal with life, and many other aspects. [Looking at Maria] I don't know how other people think. As a father, I'm quite satisfied.

MARIA Do you often tell him that?

FATHER [looks at son] I did. We are having good communication now and we have good interaction. If anything happens, we can discuss it. We have mutual understanding on many issues.

MARIA I'm very happy to hear that. So what is your wish?

FATHER I'm very happy, too. [Laughs and then turns to look at the group.]

MARIA What you would like to discuss today that could make your life and the family's life even better?

FATHER I didn't think much about this. I became so emotional when Tina [the therapist] told me you were coming. So I already decided I just want to meet you. I want to meet you and everybody here [looks round the group and laughs]. I feel excited.

MARIA Very nice. I want this meeting to be useful for you, so we'll go one step further. What could make your life and your family's life even better? Your wife said she would like to have more trust and more support and help.

FATHER The respect and trust is a mutual thing. [Looks at his wife] I want to tell you that I trust you and believe in you. And something you need, other people need too.

MARIA [to the wife] Look at him, he's talking to you.

FATHER How you want your son to treat you, I think your son also wants that same thing from you. Sometimes when there is a conflict, we don't really need to deal with it face-to-face. We sometimes go around to deal with it, and that would be like a spiral, going up and up. That's what I want to tell you.

MARIA Give me an example. I find it very interesting because if I want to say something to Marie [translator], I'll say it. I don't go around in circles.

COMMENTARY *Father proceeds to report on an event that happened on the way to this interview. Mama wanted to take a picture of her son but he didn't want to do this. Papa got annoyed because she insisted rather than respecting the boy. Mama took the picture anyway, because it was the first time they'd been in Shanghai together and she wanted the picture as a memory.*

MARIA [to son] Is that true? [Son nods his head.] So Papa protected you from Mama. Can you say, "Mama, I don't want the picture taken"? Do you need Papa to tell her?

FATHER [interrupts] No, no. He had told her.

SON [turns to speak directly to Mama] Actually, I told you but you didn't hear. I find it's difficult when I talk to my mother. Sometimes I'm reluctant but she pushes me to do things. I become helpless. That's why I need help from my father. Sometimes it is difficult for my father too, and so he just avoids it.

MARIA The two of you [father and son] are together when you don't agree with your mother. How do you [mother] feel when they are together saying "No" to you?

MOTHER Since our son grew up, we've never taken a trip to Shanghai with him. I would have regretted it if we didn't take that picture.

MARIA So you had good intentions.

MOTHER Yes.

MARIA Did your son know that you would like to keep a good memory?

MOTHER He won't treasure this. [Turns toward son] This is a rare opportunity.

MARIA I hear you. [To son] So I would like to ask you: How was it for you in the last two months? Did your parents keep their promises? I wrote them down last time. You wanted respect, encouragement, trust and appreciation. Remember?

SON Um … [looks at the paper].

MARIA [to son] You must remember. You don't have to read them.

SON Mother did less.

MARIA So, what's your experience with your father?

SON My father did more.

MARIA Father promised to stay home if you go to school. You went to school and father stayed home? [Son nods] I'm very happy to hear that. You kept your promise. I hear from your therapist, that you did not go back to school right away, but eventually. [Son nods] And I'm very happy to hear that you met the therapist many times. Right now, what would you want to change so that this family has a better way to live?

SON That my parents can live in harmony. [Parents look down at the floor, expressionless.]

MARIA That's your wish for yourself? [Papa looks at son for a while and then looks down again.]

SON Yes. And that my mother will consider my feelings more.

MARIA Can you give an example, other than the picture? Tell your mother how you want her to consider your feelings.

SON [turns to Mama] Sometimes I need to go shopping with my friends. Sometimes I like certain clothing, but you always have comments. You say I should buy something else. So, in the end you feel unhappy and I feel unhappy, too.

COMMENTARY *I use this example to encourage direct communication and continue to remind them to use "you" when addressing each other. The dialogue reveals continuous contradiction between mother and son, which develops into misunderstanding and confusion.*

MARIA Mama, do you want to respond? Can you turn to face each other? What do you, Mama, have to say in response?

MOTHER When he said to buy some clothes ...

MARIA [interrupts] "You."

MOTHER [to son] In talking about buying clothes, I only recommended. I had good intentions. You only spend money on buying clothes that don't fit.

[Son looks away from mother. Mother looks at Maria and then turns her chair more to face the son and looks at him.]

SON [looking at Mama] Everything you said was negative, at least from my understanding. From what I remember, you always push me to do this and that. I don't hear any recommendations from you. Maybe this is our generation gap.

MOTHER You don't trust me.

SON You don't understand me.

MOTHER Just take a simple example, your trousers. [Points at son's pants] You spent eighty dollars to buy these pants, and I think they're too tight and you should change to a bigger size, but you didn't change it. You kept this size.

SON Yes, I like these. Why do you comment on these pants and push me to change to a bigger size? As long as I think these are good, they're good enough.

MOTHER Son, to be honest, you bought these pants, you told me you wanted to change them. [Raises voice, points blaming finger at son.] You said you wanted to change them, but you didn't.

SON [raises voice] I never said I wanted to change. I only said I can change.

MARIA [turns to father] Papa, what's your opinion about this?

FATHER [takes microphone from son, who sits with arms crossed looking helpless. Father lectures mother in a serious tone and points a blaming finger at her. Mother sometimes looks at the floor and sometimes looks at her husband.] I think you need to respect him. He likes these pants. If they're too small for him, it's up to him to change or not. My feeling is these are his pants. What I have said is just say "Yes," approve this. If they don't fit, he will face the challenge. That's something he needs to learn from the challenge. That's my feeling.

MARIA [to son] This is one example. Can you give me another example, when you feel your mother doesn't understand you?

SON You still compare me with my peers and say they are better than me. You don't want to acknowledge that I'm the best, but I think I've already tried my best. So in your eyes, I'm always a little less than the best. I don't think you really appreciate me.

MOTHER Son, how can you say these things? Your teacher sent me a message. When you came home, I told you, "Son you did very well this term." I got the message from your teacher you placed fifth in your class. I said, "Pretty good, pretty good. You did very well in school." How come you said I was not satisfied?

SON You had a "but" after you appreciated me. You said "but." [Group starts laughing, then mother and son join in.] The key point is what came after "but." What you really want to express was what you said after "but."

MARIA What is the "but"? Tell him now. Do you want him to be Number One?

MOTHER [still laughing] According to the message from the teacher, five courses he did very well, but the other three, which are the major courses, he did not do so well.

MARIA And he has to be perfect? He has to be the best?

MOTHER As long as he tried his best.

MARIA He says he does.

MOTHER I would be happy if he doesn't violate the school rules.

MARIA Are you happy?

MOTHER Yes, I am.

MARIA I see a big change. He has been going to school. Last time, we had an issue of whether he goes to school. A lot has happened. This question is already resolved. I remember what he wanted – encouragement, trust, loving. What else was there on the big paper? Appreciation. I don't think, Mama, that it is encouraging to tell him that fifth is not good enough. "Fifth is very good" would sound like encouragement. Trust is, "I trust you." How do you show "love"? How does he know that you love him? [To son] Do you know she loves you?

SON Yes.

MARIA How do you know? How does she let you know?

SON [Mama turns to look at son] Sometimes, when I'm doing homework at home, she will cook some snacks for me or offer me some fruit. Then I know, at least, this is the way she's showing her love to me. She cares about me.

MARIA Are there any other ways you want her to show that she loves you?

SON I wish she could show it verbally.

MARIA Then she would tell you?

SON Yes. Seems like she never says that.

MARIA [to Mama] You never told him that you love him?

MOTHER When you came back on Friday night, I asked you what you would like me to cook.

MARIA Is that how you tell him? [Mama nods] That's one way. How else do you tell him?

MOTHER I take him along to buy new clothes for him when it's getting cold.

MARIA In your family, Mama, when you were about his age, did you know that your parents loved you? [Mama nods] How did you know?

MOTHER When they didn't beat me or scold me, and when they bought the food I liked to eat and clothes I liked. [Smiles.]

MARIA So, that's how you knew?

MOTHER Yes.

MARIA You could wear the clothes you wanted?

MOTHER Um … I didn't choose. I was just happy that they bought clothes for me.

MARIA So you are trying to do with him what you learned from your family. You give him food. You want to buy him clothes.

MOTHER I also show concern about his studies. Right now he is in boarding school.

MARIA Mama, nobody ever told you "I love you" in your family, with words? Not your Mama or Papa? I'm curious.

MOTHER They didn't tell me with words.

MARIA Can you tell your son that you never learned that yourself, therefore you don't know how to say I love you? We repeat what we learn from our parents. But our children still want to hear the words. Maybe you can tell him it is difficult for you. If you feel in your heart that you love him, maybe you can learn to put words to it, because that's what he needs.

MOTHER [turns to son] Mama really loves you inside. If I didn't express it well, I apologize.

MARIA Do you really feel that? Or do you only say it because I asked you to?

MOTHER It's from my heart.

MARIA OK. Look in his eyes and tell him a little more slowly.

MOTHER You should know, son, I'm speaking from my heart to tell you I love you. I told you before, you are the only one I feel intimate with. I told you many times, I will love you forever. I'm always loving you. You are my good son.

MARIA [to son] Do you believe what you hear?

MOTHER [interrupts before son can answer] Believe me. I didn't say much. I'm sorry.

MARIA Do you believe your mother?

SON I believe her.

MARIA OK. Would you tell your mother that you love her?

SON I love you, too.

MOTHER Thank you.

MARIA I'm very touched that you can say "I love you" to each other. I would like you to do that more often. We need that. I believe that maybe you would have liked it for yourself when you were a little girl. But your parents didn't know that you would like to hear that. We don't have to repeat the past. We can do more when we are parents ourselves. Do you understand?

MOTHER I understand.

MARIA I would like you to tell your son often that you love him.

MOTHER I will do this in the future.

MARIA How often can you tell him? He wants to hear it.

MOTHER When he comes back home. When I see him, I will.

MARIA [points at son] Tell him.

MOTHER Son, when you come back from school, I will tell you I love you. I'll cook for you, but don't tell me you don't like this and you don't like that. [Group, including Mama, laughs.]

MARIA Can you cook what he likes sometimes? He's only at home on the weekends.

MOTHER I did go to his room to ask him what kind of food he likes. He always says, "Go away. Leave me alone."

MARIA This will be different from now on because he knows you love him. [To son] True?

SON Yes.

MARIA So your mother said she doesn't like you to push her away. What can you do about that?

SON Um … I can change.

MARIA Mama, would you tell him what you would like? Now it's your turn. He told you what he wants, and you said yes.

MOTHER [to son] When you come back home, when I ask you, don't reject me, and communicate with me about what you want. [Mama laughs and son smiles].

MARIA That's not a big request. How do you want to respond?

SON When I come back home, I will tell her what I want.

MARIA Will you tell her in a nice way?

SON Yes, I will.

MOTHER Then I'll feel very happy [smiles and nods].

MARIA Mama, what else do you want to change between you and your son? He said he will talk to you when he comes back from school. What else?

MOTHER I'm willing to accept the way he asks me.

MARIA Is there anything else you want?

MOTHER Yes, it's very simple. You have pimples on your face. Don't keep asking me to take you to the hospital. Every time when he looks in the mirror, he complains that he has so many pimples, and he wants me to take him to the hospital. [Mother laughs; son is expressionless.]

MARIA What do you want him to do about the pimples? Accept them?

MOTHER It's not to the degree that he needs to go to the skin specialist. He always asks me to take him to the skin specialist.

MARIA Can you say something about what you want? I don't see any pimples.

SON [smiles and looks at Maria] It's all over my face.

MARIA At your age, everything is changing in your body. I wouldn't go to the hospital if I were you. [Son laughs.]

MOTHER Did you hear it?

MARIA Maybe some other people can give you some other ideas. I have one son and two grandsons. They all had pimples when they were fifteen. They don't have any now. They will go away.

MAMA [to son] Don't smoke.

MARIA [looking shocked] He smokes?

MOTHER Yes, he started smoking last year. He will have two packets of cigarette on Friday night and Saturday night.

MARIA [to son] I'm sorry to tell you, your mother is right. I'm telling you from my experience. Don't get used to it. You know, when I was 17, I started smoking for the only reason that my friends were smoking. I thought that I would fit in better with my friends. It is very hard to give it up. I did smoke for many years.

And then, one day, two years ago, I found out that I had cancer. It was for no other reason but smoking. You cannot get away with smoking without being punished. Now when I see cigarettes, especially when I care for somebody, I see them as poison. So if you can avoid smoking, do it for your body, for your health, even if your friends are smoking.

SON [to Maria] Actually, I already smoke less. I'm gradually quitting smoking.

MARIA So Mama, two right points for you. Now I want to suggest something for you. Your son is grown up enough to buy his own clothes and even make mistakes. That's hard, you know, because he is no longer a baby. Can you accept that?

COMMENTARY *The discussion then turned from buying clothes and smoking to the parents' concern about how he spends money irresponsibly. He has used money intended for food and transportation to buy items off the internet. I change the subject by asking the son if there is anything else he wants to change in the relationship.*

MARIA Is there anything else you want to change in your relationship with Mama? We know now that she will tell you how she loves you. What will you promise, in return, when you get home? If Mama asks you something when you come home, what will you do differently?

SON I will try my best to come back home early. Then I will try my best to have dinner together. And I will also leave some time for us to interact.

MARIA Good. I see you [therapist] are writing this down. Mama, I appreciate you because you did not learn growing up that you could make an effort to put words to your feelings. I know you have it in your heart, but it's good for people to hear it. I think you are a very tough person and it is hard for you to express in words how you feel. Is that true?

MOTHER It's not difficult to put into words. I've been doing this already. Every Friday, I don't drive my taxi. I just stay home and cook for him. After I cook, he stays on the computer. I keep asking him to come to the dinner table, but he doesn't come.

MARIA [to son] Is that true?

SON It happened once.

MARIA Once only?

MOTHER No. More than once. We had dinner last night.

SON I told you last night, I was going out with my friends and did not come home.

MOTHER Two nights ago I had dinner with your father. We kept calling you for dinner but you didn't come until your father had finished. He left and you came over then and ate dinner by yourself at the table.

SON It's only once.

MARIA Papa, how do you see it?

FATHER Basically like what he said. It was once. Also once she did not come home. So it's fair.

MOTHER One time I couldn't make it. I called them to say that I couldn't come home.

MARIA So, is there anything you want to tell Papa that you want to change? What do you want? Your son said that he would like harmony. Mama, how could you have more harmony with Papa?

MOTHER I'm willing to change, but he [husband] has a bad temper. He talks with a loud voice and a serious face.

MARIA To you?

MOTHER Yes.

MARIA So, you would like him to talk differently? Tell him what you want. Talk to him. I will ask him, too.

MOTHER Just the way you talk with the neighbours, your friends, your colleagues, or even strangers. I want to be treated the same.

MARIA [to Papa] Do you hear what she said?

FATHER I heard. It's very simple. I can do that. [Starts speaking with a serious tone and serious face.] But I don't understand it. We often have conflict because once I say something I want to discuss with her calmly, but she seems not to hear me. So when I tried to communicate with her, and when she doesn't hear me, I become upset. She still doesn't hear me, she just keeps talking. When I want to remind her again, she is still the same.

COMMENTARY *I consistently ask Papa to speak directly to his wife, say-ing "you" rather than "she" or "her."*

MARIA What would be helpful for you?

FATHER When other people are talking, you do not listen. I pay a lot of attention to other people's feelings, then people can communicate. I'm using this with my son now. I did the same to her [pointing at Mama], but it's less effective with her. Nothing seems to work with her, so I just talk less.

COMMENTARY *In order to emphasize his opinion, Papa gives an exam-ple when they had a disagreement about parking the car. I then ask them to sculpt this scenario.*

MARIA We'll make an exaggerated picture. Let's stand up. [Everybody stands.] So you are all sitting in the car. Papa wants to back up. [Help-ers move chairs to set up a car scenario – two seats in front and one in the back.]

OK, who is sitting in the back, on the driver's side]? You [son] are in the back. Who is driving the car?

MARIE [translates] Mama is driving.

MARIA If Mama is the driver, how come Papa says to back up?

FATHER No, the person in the parking lot asked us to back up.

MARIA OK. [Invites a participant to role play the person at the park-ing lot.] Would you say "Back up?"

ROLE PLAYER Back up.

MARIA How did it happen?

FATHER No, no, no [stands and moves over behind the car]. I was standing outside the car. And I asked the person in the parking lot where I could park. The person said, "Park here." [Points behind him.] That's where he instructed us to park.

MOTHER I think they asked me to back up there. I wanted to turn around and then park there. [Marie asks Mama to confirm what she has just translated from Mama's dialect.] Yes. Yes. Yes.

[Papa corrects what Mama has just said. Mama interrupts. Mama and Papa talk at the same time. Chaos ensues. The group laughs, but not the family.]

FATHER [to Mama] Because you drove forward, you needed to back up a little bit. When you backed up, I said back up more, back up more, but you drove forward. I said to back up more and you drove forward. And then when you tried to correct the steering, but at the end, the car was not straight. [The group laughs.]

MARIA So, Mama, are you stubborn? Do you agree with what Papa said? That you don't listen to him?

MOTHER I couldn't hear him because the door was closed. I could only see him from the back mirror. I was just looking in the back mirror and following my sense.

MARIA It's very interesting. You all find this discussion very funny, but he [pointing at son] does not. You don't find this funny because maybe this is just symbolic of what's going on between your parents. I saw you very sad. So how did you feel when that happened?

SON They are always like this. They each insist on their own opinion, then they cannot meet. So they have conflicts.

MARIA So whether it's about how to park the car or how to deal with you or how to have dinner, it's the same story.

SON Yes, more or less.

MARIA [goes to Mama, holds her hand] So this is just one example. Would you like to stand up? I'll show you something.
    [To Papa] And you, please come here. [Papa and Mama face each other while son stands at a distance.] This is what you did. You both said, "I'm right!" Papa, would you say, "I'm right." [Papa points finger at Mama, blaming.]
    And you, Mama, say, "I'm right. You're wrong and I'm right." [Mama points her blaming finger half way out and laughs.]
    Mama, as loud as you can, say, "I'm right!"

MOTHER [points finger at Papa, laughing] I'm right!

FATHER Then I give up [puts down the blaming finger]. I don't want to fight with her.

MARIA [son looks at the sculpt and laughs] Both are saying, "I'm right. You are wrong." [Walks to Papa's side] Do it, point at your wife. That's how you feel. [Points a blaming finger at Mama to demonstrate] Say "I'm right. You are wrong."

FATHER I'm right.

MOTHER [points blaming finger at Papa] I'm right [laughs].

FATHER [looking serious] I'm right. I'm right.

MOTHER [laughs] I'm not wrong.

FATHER I give up [in a hopeless tone and puts blaming finger down].

MARIA And you turn away?

FATHER No, no, no. [Explains the parking incident] When I sat in the car …

MARIA No, any time.

MARIE [clarifying Maria's meaning to Papa] When you give up, you ignore her, don't you?

FATHER Yes.

MARIA When you feel that this is hopeless. [Points at Mama.]

FATHER Yes.

MARIA Just like turning away. It's symbolic. How do you feel then?

FATHER I didn't do this.

MARIA [goes to Papa's side] Tell her how you feel when that happens.

FATHER [to Mama, in serious tone] I gave up because you don't listen to what I said. [In a serious tone] The consequence will tell you that you are wrong.

MARIA Papa, would you like to change that? Would you start communicating with each other?

FATHER I allow reality to make her change. I know that I won't benefit from this, something is wrong with our family … but it's not a big deal.

MARIA I see. Would you like to change it? Yes or no?

FATHER Yes, I want to change it.

MARIA [to Mama] Would you like to change?

MOTHER Yes.

MARIA So, you are both willing to change. [To son] When that happens, how do you feel?

SON I feel … [looks helpless].

MARIA Tell your Papa.

SON I feel the dilemma.

FATHER I know.

SON I also feel sad. It happens so frequently, I'm already used to it.

FATHER Actually, I give in just because I want him to feel less sad.

MARIA [to son] In your heart, whose side are you on? Papa's side or Mama's?

SON I support my father more.

MARIA So you are on his side. [Signals son to father's side, then walks over to mother.] When this happens, Mama, how do you feel? You have a lot of feelings.

MOTHER That's OK with me.

MARIA But how do you feel?

MOTHER When my son stood next to my husband, I knew I was wrong.

MARIA Would you like to change that?

MOTHER I would.

MARIA I have an idea how you could change, but it will take some effort.

MOTHER OK.

MARIA Before I tell you what I am suggesting, I would like to ask you something. When you were a little girl and your parents argued, do you remember what was very similar? [Mother nods.] What was the picture? [Referring to the earlier sculpt of the couple blaming each other.]

COMMENTARY *I have an assumption that this picture, feeling alone and not heard, might remind mother of an earlier experience from her family of origin. I decide to sculpt this experience.*

MARIA [to mother, and gesturing to the group] Choose role players for your Papa and Mama. [To father] And you choose your Papa and Mama.

[Maria explains to mother with a warm and accepting attitude] I think you learned that in your family. We all repeat what we learned, and we can change it. [Goes to the son] When you grow up and get married, I hope you will not repeat your parents' pattern. [Son nods.] It is very easy to repeat what you learn from your parents. So, I would like you to see this and remember.

[To group] We will make a picture of mother's family when they had an argument.

[To mother] Choose somebody for your Mama and Papa. We'll just make a picture. Just for five minutes to be your Mama. Anybody can role play your mama by pointing out a blaming finger. [Puts an arm around her shoulders and accompanies her to look around for role players.]

COMMENTARY *Now that this conversation is about her, Mother seems very lost. She has difficulty understanding what a role player is and needs a lot of encouragement to find someone to play her own mother. I explain that everyone in the group knows about arguments and blaming, and that we are all good at it.*

MOTHER [chooses a female trainee] This is Mama.

MARIA And your choice for the Papa role player? [Chooses a male trainee.]

MARIA [to son] These are your grandparents, your Mama's family. Do you know them?

[To mother] When your Papa and Mama had arguments, what did Mama do? Did Mama do this [points a blaming finger]? Or did she do this [placating stance]? Did she do that [super-reasonable stance]? Or did she turn away [irrelevant stance]?

MOTHER She blames first, and then turns away. [Mama role player points blaming finger at Papa role player.]

MARIA So she did the same thing that you do and your husband does? She also turns away like your husband. What did Papa do?

MOTHER My father would have a tantrum, and threw and broke things. [Papa role player points at Mama role player. Both role players blame each other.]

MARIA [goes to mother] So that must be hard for you. Where are you? Whose side are you on? [A helper gives the Papa role player a bottle to throw on the floor.]

MOTHER I was afraid of being beaten, so I hid in a corner and cried because I was feeling sad.

MARIA So, that's the picture you grew up with. [Mother closes her eyes and tears appear.]

COMMENTARY *This was a significant turning point for the entire family. Both the son and father were deeply moved when they saw mother crying because she was rejected and felt helpless in her family.*

MARIA So, I'm not surprised that you know how to blame, because you learned it from your Mama. I'm glad that you chose a husband who is not like that [pointing to Papa role player, who is a blamer]. Mother, what happens inside?

[To son] I would like you to come here and see that mother grew up this way. She had to hide. So you, Mother, are scared. [Mother wipes tears.] And your mother learned to do this [points to role players blaming each other]. You know, we learn from our family, then we repeat what we learned without even knowing that we are doing this.

[Maria taps mother's chest] What's going on inside you now? How do you feel?

MOTHER I think when children learn this, they bring it to their family. It's very bad.

MARIA So maybe you don't want to do that anymore. Maybe you don't want your son to feel like you felt. [Mother nods in agreement.] A child seeing your blaming finger, becomes afraid like you were. [Mother keeps looking down and nods her head.]

Your son is not hiding like you were, but he feels the same. Would you tell him how you felt when you were in your family, so he can hear it from you? [Maria brings son to face mother; mother faces son.]

MOTHER [looks down and is silent for a while before she starts to speak.] Son, I felt bad when I was in my home. So I learned from them and I can't be OK with you. I didn't have a good family. I hope in the future you will point out if I ever make mistakes, or if we make mistakes.

MARIA Maybe you can tell your son that you will make an effort so he doesn't see this blaming. You can be different. He doesn't have to have the same experience. You don't want him to feel like you felt.

MOTHER I don't want him to. I hope this will not happen in my family in the future [wipes tears].

MARIA I very much appreciate your intention [strokes Mama's arm].

[To son] How do you feel hearing your mother and seeing this picture, the sculpt?

SON I wouldn't feel any warmth in this family and I would gradually become distant from them. I would try my best to run away from this home.

MARIA This is how your Mama felt. [Son nods.] So, can you understand her better now? She just repeats what she learned, but she also told you she no longer wants to do that. Would you believe her?

SON I believe it. [Faces mother] I believe you will do better than now. You won't argue without a reason. You will make this family more harmonious.

MARIA [to mother] It's not easy to change. Sometimes you will automatically start to do that [points blaming finger], but then you will remember, because you are very smart. Your son and husband can remind you. All you have to do is to do this [puts down the blaming finger].

MOTHER [nods] OK.

MARIA You will try?

MOTHER OK. I'll work hard on this.

MARIA I believe that.

[To father] Now let's look at your family. Would you choose your Mama and Papa? [Husband chooses role players immediately.] What did you see your parents doing?

FATHER [to father's Papa role player] You are very smart. You are very competent. You are No. 1 in your office. You are the best. You have five children, but you are the only person who is working.

[To father's Mama role player] You are a housewife. You look after five children at home. That's all. That's the background.

In an argument, you [Mama role player] couldn't blame. She could only talk. She had no right to blame.

COMMENTARY *After a long discussion father decides that his Papa was super-reasonable and his Mama was placating. As a boy, father stood by his Mama's side, in tears, protecting her. Through tears he begs, "Don't do this, Papa. I will try my best."*

FATHER [to Papa role player] Be No. 1 at school. I don't ... I'm on the floor. [In tears] You, don't bully my Mama.

MARIA So you protect your Mama. [Husband nods.]

FATHER So I will not be very mean to my wife [wipes tears and points to his wife]. So I'm quite acceptable to her. I was always No. 1 in school.

MARIA [guides wife to face her husband] I just want to show you something. When your wife blames [puts wife in blaming position] it's very easy for you [husband] to unconsciously remember your Papa blaming you.

FATHER [husband] Yes.

MARIA So, you do the same.

FATHER Yes, but I won't blame. I just count on my wife that something will go wrong. I will say it twice, but if it's useless, I give up.

MARIA So, then you do what Mama did [pointing at Mama role player].

FATHER No, I'm not like this. [To wife] It's not because I cannot win you over. It's not because I couldn't fight over you. As a man, I cannot blame you. I blame, but I don't blame so much.

MARIA You did what your Papa did but you didn't want to.

FATHER I definitely don't allow myself to do this [points finger]. Because I didn't allow my Papa to blame, I won't do it easily myself.

MARIA So you protected Mama?

FATHER Yes.

MARIA You felt bad about this blaming, so when your wife blames ... [Father interrupts.]

FATHER But, at same time, I admire my father. I was very close to my parents. I spent ten years' salary to help them. Later they had a good relationship. He [Papa role player] stopped blaming and she [Mama role player] stopped placating. [Both role players put their hands down.]

MARIA [to son] How do you feel hearing that? This is what your father learned. This is why he does not blame back.

FATHER [husband] Yes.

SON No wonder when mother blames, he gets very quiet. Because of this, mother assumed that he didn't care about her. I felt the same thing, too.

MARIA So, you have a better understanding now about both of them. [Son nods.] [To husband and wife] Now, I would like to know how you two met.

FATHER My colleague introduced us.

MARIA And who decided? What did you like about her? Tell her, "Three things I like about you ..." [Reminds husband to speak directly to his wife.]

FATHER [looking at wife and speaking seriously] I like you being simple. I like how you look. [Laughter from the group, but wife has no facial expression.] I like that you told me you are willing to face challenges with me. It is not easy for us to establish our relationship. [Wife begins to look at husband.] When we fell in love, we went through lots of trouble. Because the mutual friend who introduced us had a good relationship with both of us, we did not disconnect even though we had troubles. We finally got married because of our mutual friend.

MARIA [softly touches wife's hand] What do you like about him? Because I don't think you would have married him if you didn't like him.

MOTHER [nods] I like him …

MARIA Tell him, "I like you."

MOTHER At that time I liked you. You had steady work [looks down at the floor]. I liked that you were in a big city [laughs]. I liked that he was very honest.

MARIA Now you have been together for how many years?

FATHER We got married in 1993, so 18 years.

MARIA [to husband] OK? Now we start a new time, a new way of communicating today. Do you want to?

FATHER Yes.

MARIA A new way of learning.

FATHER That's what I'm looking for, a new way of communicating. This is great.

MARIA Everything that was in the past goes to the museum. [To wife] For you, too. [Wife nods.]

FATHER This is great.

MARIA So, very simply, you start hearing each other and listening to each other. Whenever she blames, you tell her how you feel. "I feel bad now." Or, "I feel afraid" or "I feel angry." [Husband nods] So you remind her.

[Maria goes to the wife] When he reminds you, you may automatically do like that [points a blaming finger] because you learned it from your parents for so many years. So when he says, "I feel bad," what can you say to him when he is blaming? What can he say so you put down your blaming finger?

COMMENTARY *I am teaching them, along with a demonstration, that they are both blaming each other. It is hard for them to let go of the blame because the anger continuously re-surfaces. Eventually, I move to expectations.*

MARIA So you want him to have a bigger heart for you? [Wife nods] Tell him exactly what that means. What do you really want? "If you had a big heart for me ..."

MOTHER I want him to be more accepting.

MARIA She wants you to be more accepting. Do you know what that means?

FATHER She often says this to me. I can be generous. I will pay for things from the market. You just drive the taxi.

MARIA [to wife] Is that what you want? Is that what you mean?

MOTHER Um ... This is only related to our financial situation.

FATHER I can do more. [Speaks very fast and seriously] Whenever you feel sick, you don't need to drive a taxi. You can rest. The only thing is, when you park the taxi at home, don't ask me to drive. For example, you drive 10 hours and I drive 10 hours, you can take a break, but you don't ask me to drive for you, because it's no good for you, for me or for the family.

MARIA How do you feel so far about what he says? He's trying to do his best to help. True?

MOTHER [nods] Yes.

MARIA How do you respond to him about this?

MOTHER [looks up and thinks for a while] He is taking care of me.

MARIA "You." How does that feel in your heart?

MOTHER [Maria brings son next to her and holds his arm. Son looks at mother.] I feel warm. I feel he is being considerate.

MARIA So, tell your husband.

MOTHER [softly] In this way, I feel thankful for your caring towards me.

MARIA Now tell him what you want, on the emotional level.

MOTHER Don't have a cold war with me just because of one thing I said.

FATHER I can do this. [Looks around the group] I commit to all of you.

MOTHER He's not facing me. This is the way he usually speaks to me.

MARIA I would like you to hold each other's hand. [They hold each other's right hand.]
    [To husband] What do you commit to? [Maria points to wife] She will do hers later.

FATHER [looks at wife and points finger while speaking in a firm tone] I commit that I love you. [Points at son] I love my child. Whatever you want, basically I can say yes to you if it's appropriate.

MARIA You don't have to say yes all the time. You can also say no. You can both say yes and no. "I will say yes when I feel yes. I still love you when I say no to you."

MARIA [touches husband's forearm] Do you love her?

FATHER Yes, I love her.

MARIA Tell her.

FATHER I did a lot of things for you.

MARIA Simply tell her you love her, if it is true. It is true.

FATHER I love you.

MOTHER Thank you [smiles].

MARIA [to wife] Would you like to tell him what you want from him now? This is a good moment to tell him, in addition to everything that you've already said. I am sure you want more.

MOTHER [softly] Husband, I wish when you talk, you would soften your voice. [Husband looks at wife with a serious face.]

MARIA [to wife] Look into his eyes when you talk.

MOTHER I didn't look at him for more than ten years, so it's hard for me to look at him. [She turns and cannot help laughing. Everybody breaks into laughter, including the husband, their son and the group. Wife holds her laughter and continues.]

MARIA Good. Try now. Look at his eyes. This is your husband, your companion. What do you feel? Tell him what you feel, from your heart.

FATHER [wife looks down, keeping a smile on her face. Husband is talking with a smiling face and soft tone] Believe me, your husband is not worse than others. Our son is not worse than others either. All three of us are well and we can unite together. Our son makes lots of effort at school. He still has a lot of potential. Just like the stock market, he will go up soon. [Group laughs and applauds.]

MOTHER [talks with a smile, looks up a bit more but still not looking directly at her husband] I believe our happiness starts at this moment.

FATHER Many times when I give up, it's also a way for me to show my caring. So a lot of time I just let my son do things his way. For example, he fell down on this carpet and that's OK. It's not so bad. He learned something.

MARIA OK [signals husband to stop talking]. I would like her to hear her voice. It sounds like a new wedding. We are all witnesses. [A cell phone rings at this moment.] This is the bell for the wedding. [Wife smiles and the group laughs. The son smiles slightly and looks at his father with concern.]

[To wife] What do you commit to? This is now starting a new life, a new relationship. You both can put all the anger in the museum. Everything that you learned from your parents, along with how to blame. You know now it's not good for health. You are a very smart woman. You can make a decision and tell him what you decide and what you commit to. [Wife keeps silent and looks down with a smile.]

Go to your heart and tell him what you want and what you commit to yourself. All you want is true for you. We will all witness it. This is your life. This is your family life, so you need to be true to yourself. [Maria goes from the wife's side to the husband's.] So after you open your eyes, you can look into his eyes.

MOTHER Husband ...

MARIA Open your eyes.

MOTHER [smiles and looks at husband while their son watches] I learned a lot here. After I go home, I will do well. [Husband looks at wife with a sweet smile and a relaxed expression.] I will treasure this family. To my son, to my husband, I'll be very nice to you. I'm willing to put the past ... my mistakes.

FATHER It's not mistakes. If we just listen to each other, sometimes we may need to push us to each other. I have a feeling, in the future it's like we are just playing a game. If one of us wants to throw a tantrum, we can just hold it for ten seconds.

MARIA Yes, good idea.

FATHER Yes. So give us some time.

MARIA [to son] Would you remind them? [He nods] How do you feel, seeing them talking to each other?

SON I'm very happy. I also wish them to have a good start.

FATHER AND MOTHER Thank you, son.

FATHER I commit that I will be the first to do things well, no matter how these two are doing.

MARIA So, each of you has a part in it. When you [son] see their blaming fingers, remind them of this commitment [points at the couple's clasped hands]. Not blaming. Say to them, "Papa and Mama, remember?" [Son nods.]

[To whole family] This change is not easy. It is a decision, a commitment. It's very easy to go back to the old ways. So don't blame or be upset if you start the old ways. Just remind each other, each of you, and yourselves, of this day when you promised to change. [Signals to the couple holding hands.]

MOTHER Yes. I will always remember this in my mind. I will remember [smiles].

MARIA I believe you.

MOTHER It will be always be in my mind.

MARIA And then, everything will find a place. I am sure you [son] will be much happier. Because when we started today, that's what you wanted – harmony.

Now show me your picture of how you would like this family to be. Where are you in this? [Points to father and mother holding hands.] Not taking anybody's side, right? You want to be here, or you want to be closer to them? Where is your place?

SON I want to be closer [steps toward his parents], but I will stay neutral.

FATHER [to son] It will be wonderful if you can be like this. To be honest, I think a child is a bridge for a family. You look at the picture when I was young, even though I blamed my father, I protected my mother, but behind … [Maria interrupts.]

MARIA In a way, your son is a bridge, but he is growing up. [Father agrees.] And this is a beautiful picture. He is connected but he is also on his own. He's going to be grown up very soon. You can all look at each other. You don't have to treat him as a baby anymore.

FATHER [nods] Yes. Yes.

MARIA And you both can be very proud of him. Whatever you did in the past, Mother, you did a good job because he is such a beautiful person. Are you proud of your son?

MOTHER I am.

MARIA What else do you want to say, Mama? I feel you want to say something.

MOTHER [looks at son] I was going to give up on this family, but after I had my son I really felt happy in my heart. He is such a beautiful person and so smart, I wish that in the future, you will understand me and I can care about you.

MARIA [to son] Do you believe that? Do you know?

SON Yes. I know.

MARIA Anything you want to say to Mama?

SON [to both parents] Actually, I always love you, both of you. I'm also proud of both of you. I also know you both work very hard. So I will change, too.

FATHER [smiles and speaks in a soft tone] I feel great that he speaks like this. I think he's moving towards ... that direction and developing. As long as the three of us, each of us, show more loving to each other, I think our family will become better, because basically we have good qualities [laughter from the group]. This is true.

MARIA Where is the therapist? [Holds her hand] So you continue to check it out. Please continue. [Therapist nods] You want to say something?

THERAPIST I wrote down all your commitments in my notebook. I will check how you follow through.

MOTHER [to therapist] I will do it.

MARIA [to therapist] They only need reminders from now on. You can remind them if things sometimes go in another direction. That is all old learning.

THERAPIST Yes [nods].

MOTHER Thank you.

MARIA So would you like to hear feedback from people in the group? We are all witness to your new life.

SON Last Saturday, there was a sports day in my school. I participated even though I am not very good at physical exercise. I insisted. So, I think I am the best. And this week, I already got my report card from my examinations. Even though I'm just fifth, I still think I am the best.

Wednesday, I did an examination paper from another school – a school that is better than my school – and I'm still improving in my scores. So I still think I am the best. I am proud of myself. [Everybody applauds.]

FATHER I'm also proud of you.

MOTHER My son, I am also proud of you. I have faith in you.

FATHER What you did is much higher than I expected. I know you are improving, but you are improving so fast. It's a surprise. We agreed that you would be in the top ten or top fifteen and now you are top five. I am proud of you.

MARIA I am proud of you all, because you are open to change. Let's sit down and listen to other people's feedback.

## Feedback from participants

COMMENTARY *I ask the role players to de-role, by stating their own name as they return their name card to the respective family member.*

MOTHER ROLE PLAYER When you chose people to role play your parents, I knew you would choose me. I wanted to avoid it and not be your role player, but still you chose me. I was just like you. I grew up in that same environment and I also learned to blame. When your husband described how you argued about the parking incident, I was laughing at myself. That happens so often between me and my husband. When he parks, he likes to have the front in first and I like to have the back in first. Your presentation reminded me of my pattern with my husband. That happened a few years ago, because we learned so much from Maria. Just like you, I learned to let go. It's very painful to the blamer to let go. But actually, after I really let go, it becomes beautiful. I saw that this process was just like my work with my husband. I learned a lot. I even learned how to apply this to my own family. Thank you for your sharing.

PARTICIPANT I'm from Hong Kong. In the whole process, I was feeling very touched and had lots of learning. I have a daughter who is 16 years old. We also have an issue because I have different ideas than my wife for dealing with our daughter. So your process offered me lots of insight. Thank you very much.

I really appreciate this family. In two hours, which is so short, you faced such a big issue and every one of you was willing to make some changes. It's not easy. I admire you. There is so much loving from the father, and you are willing to be responsible and you are willing to do everything because of this family. You have such a big heart.

Mother, because of your background, you did not know how to express your love. But in just one session, you made such a big change. You committed to expressing your love, to change yourself and admit the mistakes you made. You are great!

And this young man, the more I look at you, the more I appreciate you. You are handsome, you are beautiful. You are very up-to-date and trendy. Your father said you have potential like the stock market. I agree with your father. If it were me, I would be willing to invest money in this stock [everybody laughs]. Thank you and I appreciate you.

PARTICIPANT I had a similar feeling. I really appreciate the mother. When I saw a beautiful smile on her face I suddenly had a feeling, just like a shell. Before the shell opens, there is a hard shell outside. When it opens, I can see the beautiful, soft part inside. I really felt touched in that moment. I can see the father is willing to be responsible, doing so much for this family. So in this warm family, I can feel the tender part will increase and there will be more beautiful parts too. I was touched in that moment.

PARTICIPANT I really appreciate the openness, sensitivity and honesty of the son. I also appreciate the father's strong motivation for change and his willingness to contribute. I want to send my biggest appreciation to the mother. I saw the fear and the hurt from your growing up. I hope father will remember when the mother becomes tough, maybe that's her way to protect herself. Please remember her tears and her fear.

MARIA So I hope you have fun and you celebrate your new wedding and your new relationship. [Family members smile and everybody applauds.]

## Evaluation notes

### EXPERIENTIAL

In this interview, the sculpt of the mother's family of origin was the essential source of change for the whole family. The piece that led me to the sculpt was the father's blaming stance and the mother's reaction to it. At that moment, I wanted to check out whether her fear of blame and her suppressed anger went back to earlier experiences in her family. The sculpts of both parents' families of origin also provided an important education for all three family members, by helping them understand that the parents' current behaviour was related to their experiences in the past. For this family, it was very important to broaden the scope of understanding regarding each other's behaviour. It was very moving to see the son's compassion for his mother when he realized that she had been abused.

With this family, it was essential for me to help them learn how to communicate by demonstrating specifically what to say to each other and how to say it. People who have limited understanding of their internal processes learn more from demonstration than from words.

SYSTEMIC

I involved everyone, including the therapist. At the beginning, before the family arrived, I appreciated having a discussion with the therapist. It was unusual to have a second interview with a family. I was also appreciative that the family wanted to come back. The therapist, who follows up with the family, is part of our system, so our discussion was relevant and important to how I would proceed.

It seems that more attention was paid to the parents' relationship than to the son. Their relationship is essential for the son to integrate into this family. When I first met this family, there was no apparent system. There were three people who were related at the core level yet disconnected in terms of communication. In this interview, they took the first steps toward learning how to deal with their unmet expectations, as well as how to express their yearnings and their repressed anger.

POSITIVELY DIRECTIONAL

The process was positively directional by encouraging the son to share his expectations with his parents. The intention was to create a positive shift in their feelings for each other and their willingness to share more openly. The positive direction helped them to understand each other more by revealing their past, especially the mother.

FOCUS ON CHANGE

The son's perception of his parents changed when he became aware of their backgrounds. It also seemed that the son's feelings about his parents changed. In the end, his desired picture of his family represents a positive shift compared with the perception he had during the first interview. There was an additional change when the parents realized that they could agree on boundaries and consequences for their son's behaviour.

The understanding between the husband and wife changed when they became aware that there is the possibility of communicating differently. Teaching them how to change, step-by-step, was necessary to support them in making changes in their communication and in their relationship.

## THERAPIST'S USE OF SELF

In this interview, I had to be more directive. I also used more physical touch in order to express my support. It was important for me to be physically connected with the family in order to engage them in the process. At various points, I shared in the humour that the family and the group were amused by.

## ENCOURAGE SELF ESTEEM

There were moments in the interview when I thought that they were feeling better about themselves. Mother finally got attention from her husband. Father also experienced a higher sense of self when his wife agreed to make eye contact with him. The boy revealed high self-esteem at the end of the session, when he talked about all of his successes.

It's important to recognize that it takes time to experience signals of high self-esteem.

## FOSTERING SELF-RESPONSIBILITY AND CHOICE MAKING

In the dialogues, they seemed to learn that it was important to be responsible for each other as a family system, not just for themselves as individuals. They still need to learn more about responsibility for the other. In making their commitments they demonstrated responsibility.

## FAMILY OF ORIGIN

Exploring mother's and father's family of origin was a significant turning point in changing every members' perception and understanding of their present behaviour. Again, it convinced me how important it is for the therapist to be aware of family-of-origin issues regardless of whether we do a family-of-origin sculpt or not. As I reflect back on this case, I wish I had done the sculpt sooner. It expressed far more than any words could have.

FACILITATING CONGRUENCE

Being congruent was a steep learning curve for this family. There were several moments of congruence in this session. Examples included when mother and father shared their experiences in their family of origin, and when the son shared his compassion for his parents. As their collective awareness and willingness to express authentic feelings demonstrates, they are learning that being congruent helps them to become more connected as a family.

\*\*\*

## Third interview (summary)

Between the second interview (October 2011) and the third interview (November 2012), the therapist met with members of the family for 16 sessions. Eight of these sessions involved the whole family.

Although, the boy had ups and downs in the course of the year, his teacher liked him very much. In Grade 10, the teacher nominated him as a member of the student body. This is an honour for a high-school student in China.

The parents were willing to make changes. They regularly came to the therapy sessions and have let go of some of their high expectations for their son. The new semester started in August of 2012. The boy decided to go back to school and rejoined the therapy sessions. He studied very hard and performed well in the first month. He also got validation from the teacher and ranked fifth in the September exam. He talked about having a healthy life – going to sleep before 11 p.m, quitting smoking, and cooperating with his parents.

The therapist told the family that Maria was coming back to China in November and asked them if they wanted to meet with her again. The boy was very happy and intended to meet with Maria. He said he would do well and "show his new face" to Maria.

Both parents think they need to be consistent when educating their son. They are learning to discuss and negotiate. They still have arguments sometimes, but there is no more "cold war" and they come to agreement in the end. They have started to value themselves and care for each other, instead of always focusing on their son.

They have reflected on the changes the family made before November 2012. The parents were pleased about the changes the boy had made, even though there were still ups and downs. They thought the boy was making positive changes. The couple had become closer, too.

They expressed their appreciation for the opportunity to work with Maria and said they would definitely go to the third interview with her in Shanghai.

MEETING IN SHANGHAI: MARIA'S COMMENTS
I met with them in November 2012 in Shanghai. Mama spontaneously sat between the father and the son in the interview. She had a smile on her face. I facilitated a conversation with the parents, encouraging them to trust the boy more and to allow him more autonomy. I also encouraged the boy to be more responsible for himself so that he could earn the trust of his parents.

I was very happy to see the improvements in the family. The parents were closer, smiling a lot, and seemed to be connected. The boy demonstrated responsibility for himself. I observed a touching connection between father and son. Mother seemed to enjoy how this relationship had evolved. The whole interview focused on the positive changes they had made. The group gave them a lot of appreciation for what they had accomplished as a family. The climate of this interview was very different from the tension of the first one. They had definitely learned a lot and continued to make further commitments to each other.

FOLLOW-UP REPORT FROM THE THERAPIST
Twenty days after the third interview, the therapist reported that she called the father on the phone. The father said, "I learned a lot from the third interview. We have to communicate more and trust the boy more, allow him to learn to be more responsible." He said the boy also learned from the interview. He is going to school every day and studying very hard. Basically, he kept the commitment he made in the interview. He placed first in the mid-term examination. The whole family was happy.

From December 2012 to January 2013, the therapist met the family three more times. The therapist intended to anchor the family's learnings in the third interview with Maria, reinforcing the point that the parents must provide more trust and autonomy to their son and help him learn to be more responsible so that he can earn their trust. The therapist was preparing to close the case, which the parents agreed to. The boy wanted to meet with the therapist two or three months later. The therapist agreed.

From April to May 2013, the therapist met with the parents three times. They reviewed their learnings and made a summary to prepare for closure. The parents reviewed the DVD of the first two interviews together with the therapist. They were touched when they reviewed the DVDs, and they had deeper insights as well as more integration. Mother said, "It was not an easy journey. I am so grateful to Maria and the therapist. I am feeling very happy now. I was too negative in the past. I always criticized both of them. I have witnessed their improvement and change. I can appreciate them now."

Father said, "I thought I was higher than them, that I was always right, and I wanted them to obey me. I was angry when they did not, and I would stop talking to them. I learned they are not wrong when they do not follow what I say. We can still learn from a mistake, even it is a mistake. I thought we all had to work hard to make the family well. I know now, I need to make myself well before the family can get well."

Both parents were aware that they had missed showing appreciation and encouragement to their son. They did not have clear boundaries, either. They were willing to start over – to care about themselves, to care for and love each other, and care for and love their son, while also keeping some space and room for the boy so he can be more responsible for himself.

The family case was closed in May of 2013. The father sent a message to the therapist in December 2013. The couple is still very close, and the boy is becoming more mature. He did well in school and placed first in his class in the examination in December 2013.

## *Postscript*

### FROM MARIA

In November 2013 the foundation that sponsored this family therapy training program organized a celebration for the publication of the Mandarin-Chinese editions of this book, *The Elephant in The Room* and *Crossing The River*. I was surprised and delighted to meet this family and the therapist again at this gathering. In order to participate in the celebration, they came all the way from Nanjing, which was a seven-hour drive. They wanted to be there, to share their happiness and experience with other people. They were all smiles. I could hardly recognize the son, who had matured so much. He was finishing high school and was preparing for the entrance examination for university. As soon as he opened the book he looked for their story. I asked him "Why do you want to read it?" He said "I want to read to see if every word we said is accurate." The parents were proud of their son and smiled constantly. When we opened the session up for questions to the audience, the mother stood up and told everybody how their life changed because they had family therapy. The therapist spoke up with a testimony to the Satir Model, saying that this process had convinced her that change can happen.

It was a wonderful celebration and memory to see them again and to capture the moment in pictures.

### FROM THE THERAPIST

The family was invited to attend the book celebration in Shanghai on March 16th, 2014. They offered me a ride from Nanjing in their taxi. I had not seen them since the closure of the case in May 2013. During the seven-hour trip between the two cities, I had a chance to catch up with the family and was happily reassured by the positive changes I observed.

The boy appeared to be more settled and calm. I said to him, "You are so busy preparing for the university entrance examination. How did you make the decision to attend the book celebration? It's taking up your whole day!" He responded, "Maria has helped our whole family. We are happier now. I want to meet her. It is OK for me to take the whole day."

The mother said happily, "He goes to school on time everyday!" The parents eagerly updated me. The boy is helpful to his peers when they have problems. A boy who was one of their relatives had withdrawn from the school and his parents were anxious. Their son had a talk with that boy, who then decided to go back to school. I could sense how proud the parents were of their son.

The parents did not focus as much on their son's academic achievement and were satisfied to know he is trying his best. They respect the choices their son made for his preferred university.

I also discovered that the couple is willing to share their ideas and discuss decisions. They can also accept disagreement. For example, the wife drove the taxi to Shanghai even though she was not familiar with the route. Once in Shanghai, she appreciated that her husband would get out and ask for directions. The husband did it with pleasure. If the wife was not confident in the directions he got, she asked the husband to ask again. The husband expressed that he was reluctant and said, "I think it is clear enough. You can ask yourself if it is not clear for you!" The wife did it without argument. Both of them were calm.

## Chapter Seven
### LETTING GO: FROM CHILD TO MAN

This case concerns a 17-year-old boy with anger issues. He had had a positive experience in grammar school, where he had three close friends, but began having problems in Grade 8, after a teacher made some humiliating comments about him. He retaliated by hitting the teacher with a chair. Following this incident, his parents moved him into an apartment in Shanghai and asked his paternal grandparents to live with him. He did not know them well. He attended Grade 9 in a new school and only went home on holidays.

The boy had previously been diagnosed as having anxiety attacks. At school, he often ended up in the principal's office due to his poor study habits and problematic relationships with his peers. His mother took him to see the school counsellor five times. He expressed his fear and anger to the counsellor, and during the fifth session, the boy confessed that he took a knife to school daily for his own safety. He said he feared he would kill somebody and then commit suicide if he failed Grade 10.

The boy said he wanted to hurt the teachers when they beat their students, which triggered memories of his mother beating him and locking him out on the balcony at night. From that point on, he had been afraid to sleep alone. The school counsellor recommended further therapy.

The boy's father, 47, is the deputy head of a hospital. When his son was five years old, father was in graduate school and seldom at home. He is currently working on his PhD. Father and son have a distant relationship, and the boy thinks his father does not know how to express himself.

The father's parents live in the country. His mother is a housewife on the farm and his father is a cook at the local school. Before the move to Shanghai, the boy only saw his paternal grandparents once or twice a year. He does not know this side of the family well.

Mother is 42 and works as a translator in the police system. She feels lonely because her husband is always at work and her son now lives in Shanghai. The boy considers his mother controlling and seductive. He says that she cries frequently and wants him to comfort her. She is enmeshed with her son.

The mother's father is a judge and her mother is a medical doctor. Since birth, the boy has always had dinner at his maternal grandparents' home. He feels closer to them than to his paternal grandparents.

## Maria's preliminary comments

This boy may be at risk because of the way he is acting out with uncontrolled anger and violence. There is hope, however, because he has admitted that he needs help with his anger.

We can assume that the boy is enmeshed with his mother. He is conflicted about how to deal with her, and getting confusing messages from his father. I am concerned about the way he fears his anger. When I see the family, however, I will let go of all these assumptions and let the family members speak for themselves.

## The interview

COMMENTARY *I welcome every family member individually, then ask the group members to introduce themselves one by one. The interview includes father, mother, the boy, the paternal grandmother, and the therapist. After the introductions, I ask each family member what they want from this meeting.*

*I first address Grandma, with whom the boy lives. Grandma wishes that her grandson would learn how to deal with pressure and tension at school. I ask her if her son (the boy's father) experienced pressure when he was at school, hoping this will normalize the pressures that all adolescents face. Grandma answers that although the family had financial stress, her son did graduate from high school.*

GRANDMA Whenever we study, we often have pressure. Everybody has pressure. His parents had pressure, too. Whenever we go to school, everybody has pressure.

MARIA So how is it different? How did Papa, your son, deal with pressure and how does he, your grandson, deal with pressure?

GRANDMA [to son] He had his own pressures. [To grandson] His pressure is from school.

MARIA The school is putting pressure on him?

GRANDMA No. He puts pressure on himself.

MARIA I see. So you would like him to put less pressure on himself?

GRANDMA Yes.

MARIA Mama, what did you hope for when you came here?

MOTHER I wish my child could accomplish his studies in a relaxed way and feel happy. I always thought that my child was not very happy. When compared with his childhood, it seems like he is too stressed. I can see that from his facial expression and his eyes. As a parent, to see my child not being happy really worries me.

MARIA You would like him to be happy.

COMMENTARY *Mother describes her son as a sensitive child, appreciated for his talent in piano and his high grades in grammar school. She thinks he is not happy because his teachers don't appreciate him. I comment on mother consistently referring to her son as a child and ask her to treat him like a young man. Throughout the interview, I need to remind her many times to not call him a child. My first intervention is to teach her that she has a grown-up son and treating him like a baby has many implications. The boy's expression conveys to me a non-verbal message that he appreciates this. In placing this expectation on mother, I am also creating more connection and building trust with the boy. Mother acknowledges that she needs to make some changes.*

MOTHER He makes me feel he is suppressing a lot in his mind. I don't know how I can get into his mind. That is why I searched for psychological help one year ago.

MARIA I will tell you a secret. You won't get into his mind. He has his own mind. We can only know our children as much as we can. He is growing up.

COMMENTARY *I consistently comment that she is separate from her son. My intention is to deal with the enmeshment and help her recognize that he has a mind of his own.*

MOTHER As a parent, many times we don't know what they are thinking. I am very worried about this. I want to be his friend.

MARIA Did you ask him?

COMMENTARY *The question encourages more respect for, and distancing, from her son.*

MOTHER Ask him what?

MARIA What he is thinking.

MOTHER I did ask him.

MARIA And he tells you?

MOTHER He ignores me.

MARIA He doesn't tell you?

COMMENTARY *I am clarifying mother's interpretation.*

MARIA I want to ask Papa. Did you always tell everything to your Mama? Everything you were thinking?

COMMMENTARY *In response to my question, father says "No." I include father and ask the question to normalize the son's behaviour. Father was raised in a family where children fended for themselves. His mother was busy, so the children went to school and made their own decisions. It was a happier generation, with less stress. I am talking to father, but the message is intended for mother. By including him, I hope to get his support.*

MARIA How do you feel about your wife? She needs to know everything about him even if he doesn't want to tell. What do you think?

FATHER That's a bad habit of hers. I disagree with that. In my perception, as long as a child is healthy both physically and mentally, then he will be OK.

MARIA When you came here today, what did you hope for?

FATHER My hope is that he can be healthy, mentally and physically. He can be brighter and happier.

COMMENTARY *Father agrees with what mother and grandma have said and acknowledges that his son is not happy. At this point, mother interrupts my discussion with father, sharing her worry that the boy is under too much stress and might collapse. I ask if this is why she wants to know what he is thinking. She agrees and says she wants to share his burden about school and learning. At this point I turn to the son, asking him what he hopes for, giving a message to mother that she doesn't need to make up her own story about what her son is thinking. He can speak for himself.*

MARIA Let's ask him. I would like to ask you what you hoped for when you came here.

SON I did not think about it much. When I first came, I thought it was just conversations and nothing else.

MARIA And now what do you think?

SON Sometimes, I think a lot. Sometimes, I am just numb. And right now, I don't have any idea.

COMMENTARY *I return to the boy's yearning.*

MARIA Now that you are here and we have some time, is there anything you hope for and would like to change in your life?

SON Maybe about my parents. They always think that I am just a foolish child and that I haven't grown up yet. They do care about me very much, but in too much detail. I am 17 years old, but I haven't even had a chance to travel by myself. Even if I just want to do something by myself, my mother will be really worried. I feel distrusted. She doesn't trust me.

MARIA OK, I think what you are saying is very important. I would like you to tell your mother. Would you turn your chair to your mother?

SON I told her before, many times.

MARIA Well, tell her now. You can only talk to people if you look at them.

SON I know that.

MARIA Tell your mother. We are all listening. Today is different. She is listening much more now because there are so many witnesses and you are telling her something very important. Tell her now, "For example …"

SON [turns to his mother but does not look at her] Some things you should trust me about and let me do by myself. Whenever a little thing happens, you exaggerate it, make it a big thing.

MARIA Like what, for example. Give her three examples.

SON The first example is about my physical situation. My stomach is not very well. Actually, it's a small thing. I only need to take some medication, but I dare not tell her that something is wrong with my stomach because once I call her, she becomes anxious and even thinks I am pretending to have a stomach ache. She thinks I have too much pressure and don't want to go to school, so I pretend to be sick. So if I have a stomach ache, I always just try to tolerate it. I dare not tell the teachers unless I am really feeling pain.

MARIA What do you want from your mother? Do you want your mother to leave it to you to deal with the stomach ache?

COMMENTARY *I am teaching mother and supporting the son to stand on his own feet.*

SON I want her to let me do things alone rather than always commenting after I have done it. She is always trying to control me. I really don't like people ordering me to do anything. If you want me to do something, you can discuss it with me. If I am willing to do it, I will do it. But I don't want to be ordered to do something.

MARIA In other words, you don't want to be controlled. You are no longer a little boy.

COMMENTARY *This message is intended for mother, again, to remind her that her son is grown up. I interrupt the discussion and ask the boy's counsellor to make notes of everything that the boy wants from mother, such as letting him take care of a stomach ache on his own, to have freedom and to have friends.*

*My intention is to support the boy, to build trust and to identify his yearnings. I encourage the boy to talk directly to the counsellor as she takes notes. He wants to be left alone and trusted to ask for help if he can't handle something. He does not want to be watched 24 hours a day. His parents call him long distance every day, and check with grandma on how he is doing.*

*I wondered whether father was also controlling him, but the boy said, "Mostly mother."*

SON Yes. The difference I have with my peers is that they are at the same age as me but their parents really trust them. When there is a holiday, they can travel together or sometimes they just have fun in some place. Their parents think they are already grown up. The children have their own problems and their parents have their own amusements, so they don't interfere with each other. They just do their own things.

MARIA Now I want to tell you something. I agree with you that at your age you are no longer a child. You are almost fully grown up. You want to have more responsibility and more freedom. I am asking you, if you get your parents' trust, then can you take care of yourself? Would you tell them that you can be responsible, that you will take care of yourself, that you will go to school and that you will be safe? Can you take responsibility for that?

SON Of course.

MARIA Of course. You can make a commitment to that? I would like you to look at both of your parents. Tell them that you want your freedom, that you are growing up and want to take responsibility. It's a two-way street. If you don't want to be treated like a child, which I agree with, then you have to be responsible as a grown up. We can negotiate that. How does that sound to you? We can then make use of the time here, because what you mean by freedom, we have to talk about in more detail. Are you willing to take responsibility for yourself and find out what your parents want from you so that they don't worry about you? OK? [Son nods.]Trust has to be both ways, and the reason I asked your counsellor to write down everything is because you will meet again with her.

Mama, would you agree that you have a grown-up son rather than a child? [Mother nods repeatedly.] Can you make that big step? You look at him and you no longer treat him and see him as a little boy. Are you willing?

MOTHER I am willing as long as we can resolve the issue. Of course, I am willing to. Son looks down at the floor.]

MARIA Which issue? Grandma was talking about pressure and your son was saying that the biggest pressure is that he has no freedom. He is treated like a child. You see, if he is treated like a child in his family, then he will also behave as a child in school. If he is treated like a young man in his family, he will be a grown up in school. The family is the most important system to give a message to somebody. If you trust him, then he will know that he is trustworthy.

Papa, you said that in your family, your mama didn't have time to worry about everything. You had to learn to be grown up. You got a lot of trust. [To mother] How was it in your family? Were you treated as a little girl forever?

COMMENTARY *My intention is for mother to become more aware of her own experience growing up, so she can use her own personal experience to understand her son. In what follows I remind her that she is treating her son like a child and encourage her to call him her "son" rather than her "child."*

MOTHER I had a different family from his. Both of my parents graduated from university. They made demands of me. I was taught when I was very young that I had to get into a good university. I stayed with my paternal grandmother before I was in junior high. I also had some mental issues when I was the same age as my child.

MARIA No. Say your "son." I would like you to call him your son.

MOTHER I am sorry. I have to get used to it.

MARIA OK.

MOTHER I also had some issues, but my parents were busy at work. Other than having demands on me, they rarely spent time disciplining me.

MARIA How did you deal with your issues? Your parents didn't have the time.

MOTHER I did it by myself. I just overcame my issues.

MARIA Great. Do you think he can do that?

MOTHER But when I look back, I was suffering. I almost collapsed.

MARIA He is suffering because you are helping him too much.

COMMENTARY *I again remind mother that she is treating her son like a child.*

MOTHER I think if my parents had helped me, I would be different.

MARIA He is not saying that. He says, "I want to help myself."

MOTHER I am from a different generation than my son.

MARIA Yes.

MOTHER I am a girl. So I needed to be dependent, to be helped. I felt helpless because I didn't get that.

MARIA Right now. Do you feel helpless?

MOTHER It's different now. I have a family. I have a child.

MARIA No, you have a son.

MOTHER [nods] So it pushes me to be more responsible.

MARIA He wants to be responsible. You are somehow taking all the responsibility. [Son sits up straight.] A parent's job is to teach their children to be responsible for themselves, to believe in themselves and not to be a mama's boy. He is not a little girl like you were. It's different to be a son. I think for you, it is very difficult to go from having a child to having an adolescent son. [Mother nods.] What's going on with you?

MOTHER I don't understand you. [Puts finger of right hand on lower lip.]

MARIA OK, I will show you a picture.

MOTHER Yeah [wipes eyes with her scarf].

COMMENTARY *I believe the time is right for a sculpt because mother says she does not understand. There is no use talking any more as the issues have already been identified. Sculpting will be helpful to bring a new perspective. The purpose of sculpting is to create an experiential picture, to deal with mother's resistance, and to support the son.*

MARIA [to son] I want to ask you something. Do you have an imagination?

SON Yes.

MARIA Can you imagine a picture?

SON Yes.

MARIA I would like you to show your mother your picture of how you feel about not being trusted and also a picture about how you would like to be treated. I will ask you to choose somebody in this group to be you so that you can make a picture for us. That way, your mama can see your experience from your point of view. Can you help me to make that picture?

SON I had a feeling to just let things be.

MARIA No, no, no. I disagree with letting things be. You are here now for another hour.

SON I was saying the feeling I had was "Just give up."

MARIA I don't believe in that. We will not give up. I want Mama to learn, and the whole family to know how you feel.

SON Everything I do, they always object to. So that's why I said, "It doesn't really matter." That's how I feel.

MARIA I feel very sad. It does matter. Your feelings and your whole life are important. [To father] Does it matter to you how he feels, Papa?

FATHER The kind of feeling he has, I have this feeling too. I think I have a different perspective from my wife, from his mother. I often try to convince her. Maybe it relates to my experience. My mother told us that all children have their own journey.

COMMENTARY *Going forward, I will support the parents, reframing their concept of "help" and including the son in the dialogue.*

MARIA We are talking about his journey. I believe that what he is telling you is very important. "Parents, I want to have more responsibility. I am 17 years old." And, I tell you, Mama, I think this is difficult. I have a son, too. I had a very difficult time realizing that he was not my baby anymore. We all have difficulty as parents letting go, especially if you have only one child. So I am not judging you. I want to help you because the most help you can give him is to let him grow up. I want him to show you the picture of how he feels. [To son] Would you be interested in that?

SON How?

MARIA I'll guide you to make a picture based on your perception of how people communicate in this family and then you show me yours. We will choose somebody to be you. OK? [Son looks at Maria.] I would like you to choose somebody but if you don't, then I will.

SON You choose for me.

MARIA Can I choose for you?

SON [sits straight and watches what Maria does] Yes.

MARIA [invites a participant to role play the son] Would you be willing to be him?

COMMENTARY *I generally do not choose role players, but in this case I do because the boy and the parents do not yet understand the process involved in sculpting. Therefore, I choose participants to be role players for the son, the mother and the father. I ask the boy to show me his picture of his parents' relationship using the role players. I explain how to demonstrate closeness, distance, power, and control and turning their backs toward each other. The boy's picture was mother blaming father, and father just holding his hands up and sideways. I then ask the boy to position the role player representing himself. He places him far away, "doing his own thing" and leaving the parents alone.*

MARIA This is how you see it?

SON That was when I was young. When they had an argument, I would just shut the door and do my own things. [Role player turns his back to parents.]

MARIA OK. That's good.

SON I am used to it now, but it was difficult when I was young because they were very loud, especially mother.

MARIA What did she say? What were the major voices?

ROLE PLAYER MOTHER Should I be on the chair?

SON No, no, no.

MARIA If she's very powerful, she will be on the chair. To show power is to be on a chair. Is she controlling?

SON No. When mother throws a temper tantrum, she is very unique. She wouldn't let others know she was angry in the beginning. She doesn't yell. But she lets us know from her behaviour. She starts feeling resentful and shows us that she is very unhappy.

MARIA Does she cry?

SON Yes.

MARIA Let's have the Kleenex.

SON She doesn't need the whole box.

MARIA But this is representing your perception.

SON Before she expresses it, I'll sense it. Then I approach her. "Are you feeling resentful?" She would say, "Nothing, nothing".

MARIA OK. [To son role player] Would you ask her what's wrong?

ROLE PLAYER SON What have I done wrong?

ROLE PLAYER MOTHER Nothing. Nothing.

SON Exactly. She would be very impatient, just saying "Nothing, nothing." But it's just her words. If I continue to do something, the whole environment becomes very tense. I can see from her expression. For example, when she was weeping, she made a noise at the table. It showed you her attitude.

MARIA What did daddy do?

SON He avoided things in the room. [Father role player turns and walks away.]

MARIA [points to son role player] Is this how you felt?

SON No. I would throw a temper tantrum. I would hit the table and throw things on the floor.

MARIA [to son role player] You are very angry. [Son role player throws a book on the floor.]

SON Sometimes I would just rush in front of her and say, "Just tell me what you want to say."

MARIA [to son role player]. OK. Would you do that?

ROLE PLAYER SON Just tell me if you have anything to say. I can't tolerate it.

ROLE PLAYER MOTHER What do you want me to say?

ROLE PLAYER SON If you are angry, just tell me you are angry.

ROLE PLAYER MOTHER I am not angry.

SON She always says she is not angry, but when I am loud, she says I have an attitude. Then we start to have an argument.

COMMENTARY *I guide the son toward the possibility for change and ask him to show his desired picture.*

MARIA OK. We get the picture. What would you have liked? What kind of relationships do you want to have?

SON I wish the three of us would have our own lives.

MARIA OK. Show us.

SON I would rather she played mah-jong with her friends so that she'd have her own social circle, but she never goes. She spends all her time at home and watches me as much as she can. Sometimes I have said, "You just go ahead. Have your own business and have fun." She said no.

COMMENTARY *I ask the son to express his expectations of his parents. The sculpt makes it possible for the son to express this through a role player.*

MARIA What would you have liked when you were young?

SON [to mother role player] When I was young, I wished she…

MARIA "You." She represents your mom. OK. [Turns to mother role player] Tell her.

SON I wished you would do some of your own business and plan for yourself. Of course, I wished that you would care about me but not to the extent that you are doing now.

MARIA OK. What would you like to have from your papa?

SON I wished he talked more. Whenever they had an argument, after she blamed him, he would say, "Forget it," and he left the scene. I wished he would really fight back with her, because I felt even more disgusted when he avoided it himself.

MARIA Now we'll make a big jump. You are doing very well. Let's go to today. Show us your picture of how you would like the family to be now. We will invite your parents and have the role players behind them.

COMMENTARY *At this point I feel the parents are ready to participate in the sculpt. I ask the son again to sculpt his desired outcome picture, including his own parents.*

SON Here?

MARIA Yes. Right now with your parents. Do you want to show it first with the role players? I prefer you show the picture with your parents.

SON I don't have a picture now.

MARIA OK. [To mother role player] I would like to ask you how you feel being Mama?

MOTHER ROLE PLAYER I feel that in my heart I want to grab him. He runs so far. [The son role player moves to the end of the room.] Actually, I want to get a rope and get him back. When he was so far away, I felt a loss.

MARIA [to mother] Do you feel that?

MOTHER Yes.

MARIA [to father role player] How did you feel, Papa?

FATHER ROLE PLAYER I think it's too troublesome here. It's too much trouble to have affection. Can we be simpler? As long as we have freedom, it will be OK. But at the same time, I also want to have a good rest. I am tired too.

MARIA [to father] Do you agree with what the role player is saying? [Father shakes his head, "No."] How do you feel?

FATHER We have different backgrounds. I don't like arguments. I am not good at fighting. She just yelled a little bit. He [son] said he wanted me to speak more. Ever since I was young, I've never had lots of words to say. Later when I got into university and started working, I talked more. So after work, I still don't have many words to say.

COMMENTARY *The parents now seem to be ready to role play themselves. I first ask father to show us his picture. Father's picture is that in the present, mother is controlling and he positions her on the chair. He says that as the son got older, she got worse and abandoned her own interests and pastimes. When she was stressed she focused all her attention on her son, and on her husband as well. She put too much pressure on her son. Mother's hand, in the sculpt, is on the son's shoulder. The son comments that at times he feels his mother's pressure like this.*

*At this point I show my picture, which is as follows. The son is carrying mother on his back as he walks. She is leaning on his shoulders. Father laughs at this picture. I ask the son to continue to walk and feel the pressure as he walks. The son agrees with this picture.*

*At this point, I ask mother to let the son go, but she will not let go.*

SON I cannot run away from her.

MARIA OK. That's how you feel. That's the picture of how father feels. [To mother] What's your picture?

FATHER That's how I feel about the present situation.

MARIA [to mother] Your picture now.

MOTHER I agree with them. Other than work, I put all my energy into the family.

MARIA Into your son?

MOTHER And my husband. I worry for everybody.

MARIA OK, I will show you another picture of how I see it.

COMMENTARY *I ask the role player son to make himself very small by kneeling forward and down enough so his head touches the floor. I ask mother to sit on him and tell him, "Don't grow up. Be my little boy. Be my child. Stay like that." At this point, mother stands and says she doesn't think it is like this.*

*I ask the role player son how he feels. He reports that he wants to cry because he is so angry.*

*I then ask the role player son to choose someone to role play his anger and position Anger behind the role player son. I then turn to the son and say, "This is my picture of you with your mama sitting on you. Did you feel very angry?"*

SON Yes.

MARIA How do you feel, Anger?

ANGER ROLE PLAYER It seems like I am going to explode.

MARIA [to son] Tell mother how angry you can be.

SON I don't have the anger now.

MARIA Not now, but sometimes you might feel angry.

SON Sometimes, but very little. The feeling I have is more like being really frustrated.

MARIA You really cannot show your anger, so you hide your anger. [Places a blanket over Anger.] I think what can happen is that your Anger might show up in school or in other situations.

SON Yes, I agree with this.

MARIA Tell Anger that sometimes it shows up "because my mother doesn't let me grow up."

SON I don't know if the anger is towards my family or towards my school. I think I feel more frustrated and helpless at home. I do have anger in school. It's two different feelings for me. It's more obvious for me to show my anger in the school.

MARIA I would like you to look at your anger. Will you be willing to get your anger out right now? [Anger role player walks and stands in front of son.]

SON Now?

MARIA Tell Anger how angry you feel sometimes. You can be as angry as you want here.

SON Sometimes I want to use my knife to kill people.

MARIA I understand. [To son role player] How do you feel?

SON ROLE PLAYER I am very angry, but I don't know what I can do. Sometimes I feel uncomfortable. I want to kill. I want to fight.

MARIA [to son role player] Tell your parents. Anger can stand beside you. [To son] The role player who represents you will talk first and then you will talk. If he doesn't say what you feel, you can correct him.

SON ROLE PLAYER [to parents] When I watched your relationship with your son, I felt tingling in my head and numbness all over my body.

SON No, I don't feel so strong when I look at them. I said before I just really feel frustrated and helpless. I never thought about wanting to fight against them. I said, "Just let it be."

COMMENTARY *I hope that the role player's words will provoke and encourage the son to finally speak up and talk to his parents.*

MARIA [to son role player] Tell them what you really want to say now.

SON ROLE PLAYER I want you to let me go, to respect me and allow me to be myself. And I wish the two of you could talk more in this family.

SON No, it's different. I do want them to let me go, to allow me to do my things. They can support me. Whenever I mention something I want to do, they always object. They always have good reasons, such as my safety. I want them to really trust me because I am grown up now. They are so old now. I wish they had their own life. They can have fun and not always worry about me. I am not sad, so don't impose your sadness on me. And when they have conversations, I want them to not only talk about me and my school. Once they talk about this topic, they become really worried. My mother even worries about my father's work. I think my mother should be more relaxed and do her own things. My mother should be just like other people and not worry, but she is more anxious than other people. I think she could calm down more when there are issues. She could take care of herself and have her own stuff. She thinks if we are happy, she will be happy. But she doesn't know that if she is happy, then we'll be happy. Then I think because I am unhappy, she becomes really worried because she doesn't think the happiness I have is the happiness she wants me to have.

MARIA Tell her how you would be happy.

SON I think life is actually quite simple. I do have pressure. The pressure is quite big but not to the degree that I have to cry out. When I talk with them about my pressure, I just want to have some relief. I just want to tell them and have a conversation. But at the end, they are always very anxious. They keep reminding me that it's a very serious issue and they want me to think about it. A simple problem becomes a huge one. Then I dare not do anything. I am really afraid of making any mistake. I'll avoid them as much as I can.

MARIA You don't want grandma to report to your mother every day?

SON Yes.

MARIA What else do you want from grandma?

SON I think my grandma really cares about me, but I wish she also had some self-care because she takes care of me too much. As a high school student, I have a lot of homework. When I am doing homework, sometimes I work until midnight or one or two in the morning. This is normal because everybody at school is doing the same thing. She stays up with me every night. I ask her to go to sleep and she won't. I don't need her to sit beside me when I am doing my homework. What is it for? If she would care about herself, that would be enough.

A lot of things I could do by myself, but they object. They say, "This is not good for you as it's wasting your time. You need to spend your time in school." They say, "We have good intentions for you." And they don't want me to do something, so I don't do it. Even now, I need to get their approval to make friends. Even though my parents tell me I can have anybody for a friend, even though they tell me that some people have their strengths, they still dislike them. They object to my being friends with those people. I know they only want me to be friends with those who do well in school, but I can't do that. I have my own social circle. I don't like those bookworms.

MARIA Do you have your own friends?

SON I have no more friends now.

MARIA Do you want to have friends?

SON I want to.

MARIA That's good. Do you want to have a girlfriend, too?

SON Of course.

MARIA Well, this is going to be your homework. To find friends and a girlfriend.

SON I have fewer friends since I came to Shanghai. I had some close friends when I was in my hometown, but they are not good students in the eyes of our teachers. Even in the eyes of my parents, who think their parents are not good people. My parents will emphasize this to me. So when I make friends, there's some blockage and it makes me feel it's too distant. I have one very close friend. His parents work in the same unit with my parents. When the parents of my friend misbehave, my parents want me to cut him off as my friend. They are trying to tell me only the same quality of people should stay together. I don't think so. As friends, it's very simple to be friends without involving the parents. I am friends with him. That doesn't mean that I am friends with his parents. He's different from his parents. Even though in my parent's eyes he is a child who would fight in school, he is more real than my friends who do well in school. I want to be friends with him because he is real. I don't know how to describe that.

MARIA I understand what you are saying. [To the parents] I think you did a wonderful job. You have a wonderful grown-up son here who has his own plans and does his own thinking. I can tell that you are teaching him a lot of wonderful values. You can be very proud of him. Now I would like us to sit down to discuss how much freedom you are willing to give him based on his request, so from tomorrow on he will feel less pressure and can let go of his anger and really live like a 17-year-old young man. I know that would be very difficult for you, Mama, but I also know that you can do it because you know you didn't get much help when you were growing up but you still did it. You know that your son can do it. He has already talked like an adult. We will ask him whether he would also commit to you to be responsible in school and in his life and with his friends. [To son's counsellor] And you will write it down.

[To son] So now be very specific. What do you want? First of all, from grandma. We are talking about change now. What do you want from grandma? Tell her.

SON I want her to take care of herself. Sometimes, I feel unhappy in school. I might throw a temper tantrum at home, but when I throw a tantrum, it's not at them. I just close my door. I just hit some furniture in my own room. I just want to release my emotions. The reason I close my door is that I didn't want to bother them. Sometimes I may shout, but that causes them to become very anxious. They rush into my room. If I lock my door, they open it with their key.

MARIA So look at grandma and tell her, "Let me express my anger."

SON [moves towards his grandma] It's OK for me to be angry. I just want to throw things to show my anger.

MARIA That would frighten grandma. Is there any other way you can deal with your anger than by throwing things around?

SON Yes, I did frighten her. But if I suddenly shout, she'll also be frightened. So sometimes I have to suppress my temper at home.

MARIA Grandma, what do you say to that? Can you let him just be alone in his room and not worry about him?

GRANDMA OK. I still worry if he is doing …

MARIA You are worried but you cannot stop him.

GRANDMA I did not stop him. I know now.

MARIA [to son] You hear grandma? You remind her. You know what you can do? I will make a suggestion for you. You come home and you tell grandma, "I feel very angry now about something in school." You tell her, "I want to go to my room. Don't worry about me. I'll just be alone for half an hour." Can you do that? You give her information.

SON If I can inform her first, then I won't be angry anymore.

MARIA Maybe that's a good idea.

SON If I can tell her that, then I won't need to throw a temper tantrum.

MARIA You are saying something very important. The best way to deal with anger is to say to somebody, "I feel so angry because of what happened in school." Can you do that? You can tell her and the anger goes away.

SON No. I suppress too much in school. It happens every day. To be honest, those teachers are really lousy.

MARIA I know. Everybody knows.

SON For example, if you get angry and you slam your fist on the desk, they say you are destroying property.

MARIA You are spending too much energy being angry with the teachers. That will not change the teachers.

SON I don't want to be like this, but the teachers are just showing off. Whenever you reduce your anger towards them, they will suddenly come to you and irritate you even more.

MARIA I think you spend too much energy watching your teachers. I think it will change when you are less angry with your parents. When you have more friends and a girlfriend, you won't spend so much energy on your teachers.

COMMENTARY *The boy continues to express his frustration about his teachers. He comments on how the teachers like to humiliate the students. At one point he interrupts me and tries to keep the focus on the hopeless situation regarding the teachers' behaviour and the school. I acknowledge his frustration and turn the conversation back to the parents and the change within the family system.*

MARIA [to parents] Have you talked to the teachers about what's going on? [To the son] For the rest of the time, I would like you to talk with your parents more specifically about what's going to change. You tell your mama what you want to be different, what changes you want. Tell her what you want and what you don't want in the future. How would it be for you if your mother treated you as a grown-up 17-year-old? What specific freedom do you want?

SON I just want them to have their own lives. If they need to go to work, go to work and don't worry about me.

MARIA You cannot expect them to not worry about you. What they do with their lives is up to them. How will you know they aren't worrying about you?

SON I think if they have their own amusements, then they will not watch over me all the time.

MARIA OK. Mama, what do you want to say? Do you want to have more time and fun with your husband?

SON I think they are not happy. And I think they are unhappy because of me. Then I feel even more tired.

MARIA Do you want to hear from Mama? [Son passes the microphone to mother.]

MOTHER My son said that that he wants us to have our own life, not to put too much energy into him. Maybe it's quite difficult for me, but I think I have worked hard on this in the last few years. For example, I sent him to study in Shanghai. It was very difficult for me to make the decision that he would not be with me every day. Recently, I tried not to call him so often. I keep myself busy, for example, by learning how to drive. I am trying very hard to change. I don't know if my son can feel it. But I do worry about a lot of things.

MARIA In your heart, can you imagine trusting your son more, so he can be responsible and not need so much help? Can he really believe that?

MOTHER I am working hard on this.

MARIA I believe you. What can you do for yourself to really start to live your life more fully for you and not have him take up so much space in your life?

MOTHER It's my lifestyle. I cannot change in one or two days.

MARIA I know. What can you think about for changes in the future? Is there any hobby you like? Do you have friends?

MOTHER I have friends, but they are also busy with their own stuff. Other than work, I don't have other things.

MARIA Up to now, because he was a little child, all of your interest was on raising him. It's a new learning. You are a young woman. You can learn to worry less about him. Have more fun in your life, as he suggested. In my eyes, you are young and have plenty of energy.

MOTHER I will try.

MARIA Tell him that you will try to give him more freedom.

MOTHER Actually, I feel I am doing this now.

MARIA Look at him and tell him more details.

MOTHER Maybe he is not satisfied with what I am doing. I am working hard at this.

MARIA Do you believe she is working hard at this?

SON I know. I wish she could change happily. I don't like my mother being worried all the time. Whenever she mentions my name, she follows it with a sigh. It seems like I do everything wrong.

MARIA You cannot change the fact that mother worries. The worries belong to her. [Mother nods.] [To son] What you can change and what she can change is [to mother] that you think he does everything wrong. Do you think that he does everything wrong?

MOTHER This is my pattern, because I tend to think of things negatively. Then, as a mother I have the responsibility and obligation to tell him my negative thoughts. He interprets my reminders as distrust.

MARIA It is distrust for him.

MOTHER But as parents, do we have the right to remind them?

COMMENTARY *I turn my attention to the couple and encourage them to talk to each other. They resist.*

MARIA Do you tell your worries to your husband?

MOTHER I did and I explored them with him. Sometimes he disagrees with me.

MARIA OK. Can he disagree?

MOTHER I think he is being irresponsible. He just focuses more on his work, maybe because he trusts our son.

MARIA Tell him what you want from him.

MOTHER My husband?

MARIA Yes. Tell him what you want.

MOTHER What I want from him for me, or for my son?

MARIA No. Your husband is your partner, not your son's. Tell him what you want from him. Your son has his own life. He will have his own life more and more. He is going to have a girlfriend and later a wife. Your partner and priority is your husband. Your son wants that too. He said he wants his parents to have more time together. Tell your husband what you want with him. If you have worries, talk to him about that. If your relationship is stronger, it will be easier for you to let go of your son.

MOTHER My husband is very busy at work.

MARIA Talk to him.

MOTHER [to husband] You are too busy at work. You don't spend enough time with me. Compared with other men, I think you are quite responsible for your family. But for me, other than work, I only have my husband and my son in my mind. So I am also feeling pain. Our son doesn't want me to take care of him and my husband doesn't take care of me. I work very hard in my job. But after work, I need more caring. I need to do more things. My son wants me to have some amusement. I am a married woman. It is impossible for me to have activities always outside the family. It's OK to do this occasionally, but I want to have more family life. I wish my husband would communicate more with me. So if I have any thoughts or if I feel depressed, you would just listen to me.

MARIA I think you are doing wonderfully. You have to tell him that speech every day.

MOTHER He will think it's too annoying.

MARIA [to father] What do you have to say to her? What she wants is very normal.

FATHER After my son moved to Shanghai, we both changed. I told her we are also growing with our son.

To be honest, I am busy at work because I am in administration at a hospital. Right now, I am the deputy principal, so I have a lot of social activities. After the social activities, I try to walk with her after I get home. The lifestyle in our city is different from that in other large cities. It is a slower pace. There are a lot of activities after Chinese New Year, because my colleagues invite each other for dinner. She also wants me to have a good relationship with my colleagues, so I have to attend those parties. Sometimes we go as a family. I want her to come along. I feel it's kind of relaxing, but she doesn't like it because she doesn't like to play mah-jong. I usually get home by nine o'clock.

I wish we could all make some changes because my son is not with us. I wish she could be happier. Because we are living in a society, we all need to make some changes. When I go to a party, everybody comes along with family, except her. When people ask me, I can only lie about why my wife is not there. I understand my son. He was only trying to say she could be happier. She can distract herself and not always focus on her son.

MARIA [to mother] You don't like to go with him to social activities?

MOTHER I don't like him to do this every day.

FATHER It's on Saturdays and Sundays.

MARIA That's not every day.

MOTHER The parties are on Saturdays and Sundays, but he always has social activities related to work. We can only have meals together once or twice a week. I always call him after work to see where he is going to have dinner. If he says he will eat at home, I'm very happy and cook at home. Otherwise, I don't cook because I am alone.

MARIA Everybody in this family has difficulties. I am hearing that you miss your son and you would like to spend more time with your husband.

MOTHER Yes.

MARIA Your husband has a lot of work to do.

MOTHER Yes. He doesn't talk much but once he is home, I feel quite solid. Even though he does his own things, I feel very happy.

MARIA [to mother] Your situation is now different because your son is not at home. You now have a grown-up son. I really wish that you would somehow find a life for yourself, not based only on him or your husband. Maybe you can have more friends and more interests. In the life of a family, there are big changes to look at. It is a big change when the children grow up. It will be an even bigger change when he is married. These are changes a couple needs to deal with together. Your son wants more trust. This is what I hear. If you express less worry for him, then he knows that he is more trusted and that he can manage his life. Your worry and expressing your worries sounds to him like "You cannot do it." As you start to trust him more, he will feel more responsible for his own life. That cannot happen in one day. It happens a little bit more every day. I know you understand that.

MOTHER I understand this theory.

MARIA It's hard to do it.

MOTHER Yes.

MARIA Can you tell him that you will pay attention to it? Will you tell him that your intention is to give him more freedom? You can talk about it. If you express your worry, he can say, "Mama, you don't have to worry. I can do it."

MOTHER That's what I want.

MARIA Tell him what you can do and what you want.

MOTHER I wish my son could …

MARIA Tell him, "You …"

MOTHER [to son] If you want anything from me or if you have any thoughts, I want you to not worry about my feelings. Just tell me straight. From now on, I want to change myself, too. I need to trust my son; trust that you will handle everything well.

I also wish that we could share everything inside, even if it's a criticism or a blaming. When I saw the sculpt, you said you felt frustrated and helpless even though you understood the good intentions of your parents. I can understand that's why you stop the communication and you just give up. This kind of frustrated and helpless feeling is hard for me to accept. I feel I am helpless, too. At least I want you to tell me what you want me to do, what you want to do and your reason. I'll tell you my reason. Even if we cannot agree, at least we know each other's views. If we have some disagreement, maybe you need to convince me or I need to convince you. Right? Then I won't worry as much.

I am not worried about your personality and who you are. I just feel I am blind. I have no information. I really care about you. So, I become worried. If you have some thoughts, you need to trust me. Obviously, I am more highly educated. I am not like other parents. I am really concerned about your mental health. If you don't tell me, that means you don't trust me. What do you think?

MARIA I think that's very beautiful. I understand that you understand. Do you believe your mother?

SON I don't have much to tell them. I will just chat, complain to them, tell them what happens in school, and my mood. My purpose is only to inform them. They only need to listen. I don't want them to tell me about their thoughts.

MOTHER I said it's OK to express things. You don't need to accept my perception. We need to have discussions.

SON That's the reason we cannot be friends. After all, parents are adults. They are elders. With friends, we can say everything and they do not make comments or criticism.

MOTHER Maybe I did not notice that my reminders to my son are taken as criticism. Friends do not worry about your future the way parents do.

SON That's the point. I don't want mother to worry about my future.

MOTHER I do not talk about the future, but how things develop or evolve.

SON I think she exaggerates things. I was only complaining and then she exaggerates, like it will influence my future. It's only a small thing. I am not the only one that has the problem. It happens to many students. Many students have complaints about school, but not every student will necessarily tell their parents.

MOTHER I am not talking about the future. I am just talking about how these events evolve.

SON I just want to tell you. I don't really want to beat up my teacher.

MOTHER That's my worry. I am afraid that you'll hit him.

SON I do think of beating up my teacher, but I would not necessarily do it. The more she says it's a big deal if you hit the teacher, the more I want to hit him.

MOTHER After all, at this age, they are very impulsive.

SON If I can tell you over the phone with a calm voice, that means I won't hit them. If I really wanted to hit them, I wouldn't even make phone calls. I would just stand there and hit them.

MARIA Why do you have to tell that to your mother?

SON I told you I have no friends. I can only tell my mother.

MARIA You will have friends.

SON I don't want to be friends with those people.

MARIA It is a problem that you don't have friends. I wish you did. You don't have to discuss every thought with your mother. We are talking with your mother about not worrying about everything you do. If you really want your freedom, then you don't need to share everything with your mother. Your mother will start to worry.

SON The reason I tell my parents is because my teacher behaves differently in front of them. My purpose is just to tell them, so I can have some release. I want them to know the other face of my teacher.

MOTHER Now I understand. I did not know that and so I worried. I thought he wanted to hit his teacher. I was afraid he would commit an offence.

MARIA [to mother] He only wants to share his worries with you. He will do this as long as he doesn't have friends. [To son] I really wish you would find some friends because if you really want to be grown up, then your mother is not the only friend you should have. In a way, there is a funny game going on. You also provoke her worries because you tell her every worry you have. Then she worries. It's a vicious cycle.

SON She always wants me to tell her what's happening to me. I have nothing else happening to me. So those are the things she worries about. If I tell her everything is fine, she won't believe me.

MARIA You said that you wanted to have friends. Are you interested in finding friends for yourself? Your parents are not going to stop you.

SON I try to make friends, but it's a habit now.

MARIA Mother, can he make friends?

MOTHER Of course. I wish he had a lot of friends. I never stopped him from making friends. The problem he mentioned earlier was a fact. The friends he made in our home town, I agree, did not do well in school.

MARIA Can he have friends in the future?

MOTHER Yes. That's my wish.

MARIA You can have friends. If you want to be grown up, you will have your own friends.

SON It's my pattern now. When I am about to make friends with my peers or other people, I learned from my parents. I investigate their personality and I find out about their parents before I decide to make friends, so much that I observe them for a long time to make sure a person deserves to be my friend. It didn't use to be so complicated. It was very simple to make friends. If you think that he is your friend, he is. But now I do not.

MARIA Why?

SON Because I copy my parents, by considering how a friend behaves and what jobs his parents do.

MARIA That's your choice of how you will find your own friends. You can copy your parents. You can also make your own choice.

COMMENTARY *The boy claims he has lost interest in finding friends. He is repeating his parents' patterns. I refer back to the sculpt, reminding him of his mother sitting on his back. She would not be able to do this if he stood up. It is important for him to take the initiative. I also remind him that his mother made a commitment that he can have his freedom. This is why I want his commitment that he will be responsible and use his freedom to grow up. Only then will he be able to deal with his issues. Now I want to re-emphasize the importance of commitments.*

MARIA Will you make that commitment?

SON I am willing to.

MARIA Tell your mother.

SON I will handle my issues myself. You can show your caring to me, but do not intervene. Don't give me too much advice. Allow me to do it myself. If I need your help, I will ask.

MARIA Good. You can ask for help from your father, too. What do you commit to your father?

SON What commitment am I going to give my father?

MARIA Man to man.

SON If I feel uncomfortable, I'll let you know and you can tell me what kind of medicine I need to take. I only want your caring. I'll take care of myself, my physical body. If I need medication, I'll take it. You don't need to call me several times every day. I am not six or seven. Just because I have a stomach ache, everyone worries.

MARIA Good. What commitment do you make to grandma?

SON I will not explode with anger or show my temper suddenly. Don't worry that I will fight with people.

MARIA You hear him, grandma? You don't have to worry. Let him be angry. OK. We'll have to end somewhere. I hope you will continue to meet with this wonderful counsellor.

[To the counsellor] I also hope that you will see him, and hopefully meet with the family sometimes, too. How do you feel?

COUNSELLOR I had a nice surprise today. I discovered the son suddenly grew up today. When I heard his mother talking, I felt quite touched. I also am a mother. It's difficult to let go suddenly. I want to cheer for you.

MARIA We will end here. I want to thank you. [To mother] I want to tell you something. I had a hard time in letting go of my own son. I know how difficult it is. He went far away to study, and when I said to him, "It's OK. You are on your own. You don't have to call me every day," he said, "Oh, I feel so good. I was afraid you didn't trust me." I never forgot that. I suggest that you trust your son. You can trust yourself and your husband because you have already helped him grow. I wish you all the best.

[To son] Thank you for being a grown-up man and speaking for yourself. Grandma, thank you for being here. Don't worry when your grandson is angry. Let him be angry.

COMMENTARY *This interview happened in the context of a large group of participants. I ask the family if it's OK to spend a few minutes listening to feedback from the observers. I ask the role players and observers to share their experience. They are reminded not to give any advice or comment on the family issues, but only to share their own experience. The energy of the participants in their own sharing and understanding contributes in an important way to the family's process.*

*The role players report they could identify similarities between the role they played and their own life experience. The person who played the mother learned how to deal differently with her own son. The role-player who played the son had a similar experience in his youth. The person who role-played the father had similar issues with his mother. He also resonated with the perceptions of the father in this interview.*

*The most important learning the group reported was the need to work on their own personal growth and self-integration before practising as therapists. Participants who were observing the interview appreciated the learning as it related to their personal life experiences.*

## Questions and answers

QUESTION *Was there any transformation in this interview?*

MARIA Transformation is a process. The reason I ask for a commitment or contract, whenever I can, is that everything the family talked about will be anchored in the commitment. For me, that is the beginning of a transformation. It's a process that can take the next few years, because every day the mother may want to call him. If she doesn't call, that would be a little piece of transformation. Change is a process. For me, a commitment is the beginning of a transformation, and verbalizing it creates an anchor. Whatever happened in this interview is only the beginning of the transformation process. A choice, a decision, was made and then the next steps are practice, practice and more practice, leading to integration.

Another way I define transformation is that the boy is changing from a child to a grown up. The perception of the mother has to change. Of course, that is going to cause internal chaos for her, because while she's working on changing her perception, she has to hold back some feelings, expectations and yearnings. The real transformation happens internally.

Whichever book you read about the Satir Model, you will find that chaos accompanies every change. Change is difficult.

Integration and transformation only happen with practice. Each time you discover that the boy was more independent and the parents didn't interfere, you celebrate it. Each time there's a step back, you can explain that it's difficult, so they realize that chaos is part of change because they are moving from the old and predictable situation to a new and unpredictable one.

The most difficult process is letting go. In this family, there is a need for a lot of letting go. For the mother, this is very difficult. I believe that everything she said to her son came from her heart. She really understood. Whether she will do it is another question. It's difficult. It's an everyday process.

[Looking at the son's therapist] I think after this interview, when mother interferes, you tell her, "Remember, you promised." You can establish that kind of relationship. I suggest you see the whole family from time to time. I think the father needs to be involved.

The one thing I wanted to do but there was no time, was to connect the father and the son. I tried to do a little piece, connecting mother and father, and a lot between mother and son. I think it's very important, because as the son gets less involved with mother, hopefully he'll get more involved with his father. My sense is that it is not only mother who is enmeshed with the son. The son is also enmeshed with mother. He provokes her. He tells her things. He says there's nobody else who cares. He doesn't want her to get involved, yet he also wants and gets her involved. He has an ambivalent pattern. If she doesn't get involved, he will have to get used to it. He needs a lot of help to find friends. Remember that this boy was taken out of his environment, away from his friends and from his family. That's another aspect that was difficult for him.

QUESTION *At the beginning of the session from this morning, you didn't make much contact with the mother, but you challenged her to remember that "He's your son, he's not your child." Did you have enough rapport with the mother?*

MARIA That was my rapport. At the beginning, I didn't have much contact with the mother. I started with the grandmother. Somehow, maybe because of my age, I wanted to start with her, and because I wanted to show my respect to her. She's very helpful. She's now living with this child. I tried to use her to tap the family-of-origin questions. How did Papa grow up? I connected them with Papa. I found out a lot about their background. Then I talked to the mother. As soon as she said "child," her behaviour showed the enmeshment. My rapport with her was developed as I disagreed with her. She was talking about a child, and this is a young man. I wanted to give her very strong feedback. I think there was rapport. I don't think she was angry. Her facial expression became very serious. Later, I tried to give her some support in many different ways and by telling her how difficult it is to make changes.

QUESTION *At the end, when Mama gave feedback to her son, she talked for a long time. You thought that was great and that the mother did well. We were annoyed by the mother's talking. Would you explain what your intention was for doing that?*

MARIA Do you mean that I gave her too much positive feedback? She said other things, too. Did you not see any change in the mother? The mother talked for a long time. I was impressed with the talk of the mother. I think there was a change from her first statement to the last statement when she turned to her son. I heard her make a commitment that she would try to step back. Making that commitment, given where she was originally, and the way she turned to her son and spoke, was genuine. I think it came from her heart. She did say that she learned from the sculpting. She had an insight. She used the word "son" instead of "child." For me, it's significant because she made an effort. That indicates to me that she has a new direction she wants to take. I was also impressed that at the same time, she was able to tell her husband how lonely she is in this relationship. At the beginning, the mother really didn't understand what was going on. She is a very smart woman. She understood and she tried to make a very difficult commitment. I wanted her to know my appreciation for her for making the effort. I let her talk as much as she wanted because I think it was difficult for her. Just imagine making that decision in an hour. I said she's doing well and I wanted to acknowledge her intention. I think she did make the change. As a therapist you need to learn to listen carefully, with compassion.

QUESTION *How many sessions do you think are required to see a family?*

MARIA I suggest making appointments for four sessions. After four sessions, evaluate the situation and decide whether the family needs more sessions. Tell them that they have to do the homework. The family has to do the work.

How long a session lasts depends how you work. There's not much we can do in less than 90 minutes. I know there are some agencies where they will take 50 minutes, but family therapy cannot be done in 50 minutes. We have to give people a chance to talk, to express themselves. I like to do at least one sculpt in a session.

QUESTION *Is there any reason why you asked the role players to sculpt how this family was when the star was young, instead of asking him to sculpt the present situation?*

MARIA I wanted to show mother the enmeshment, and I wanted the son to use fewer words and have an experience through the sculpt. I was happy that he was willing to talk, but all that talk did not show anything to the family about what's going on within him. I wanted to go from the interactional to the intra-psychic.

In this family situation, my sense was that they needed to see the picture first in order to have their own experience. I think that happened when the boy spoke up to his parents. After the parents saw this picture, they got much more involved, especially when Anger was introduced to the sculpt. For me, the most important point was when the boy started to talk to his parents. The sculpt provided the opportunity for the boy to express himself. It conveyed what a thousand words could not.

QUESTION *How would you work with an enmeshed relationship?*

MARIA There are many ways to externalize enmeshment. I demonstrated some in the sculpt with mother on her son's back and not wanting to let go, and also with mother sitting on his back. Satir sometimes demonstrated it with ropes. With enmeshed families, she would tie 10 people together. Then when they are all roped together she said, "Now one person has to go to the bathroom." They all go together. She emphasized that there is no room for outsiders. She demonstrated, in a very exaggerated way, what enmeshment means. With all the people this close together, there is no room to breathe. There is not even room for caring, for loving, because if I'm so close to you [holding the translator very close], I don't see you.

I showed the enmeshment of the boy with the mother in a different way here. When I put the mother on his back, that portrayed enmeshment. A very controlling enmeshment was demonstrated when the son role player was on the floor and I told her to sit on him. I think the boy feels that heaviness in his body. I think the mother found out through the sculpting what she is actually doing. This is why I like sculpting so much.

QUESTION *You said that the son couldn't share his anger towards his parents so he expressed it in the school to his teachers. Why did you not focus on his anger toward his teachers? Instead, you let him express what he wanted to tell his parents.*

MARIA The son tried to change the subject twice to talk about the teacher and the school. When he wanted to talk so much about the teacher, the anger and school, I didn't want to go into that because there's a whole lot more to this. In addition, I did not want to be derailed from dealing with the family issues. I hope that when he's less angry with his mother, he will start to see the school more realistically.

QUESTION *Does the mother need individual counselling at the same time when there is family therapy? Would you recommend that she receive some individual counselling?*

MARIA No. The issue with the mother is her enmeshment with the son. I think she can learn to be de-enmeshed with the family in the family therapy session. I would continue to work with her son and the family.

[To the therapist] I know you cannot see the mother very often, but you can work with the mother through the son. Any time there's enmeshment, you can encourage the son to say "No." When it happens too much and too often, you can call the mother for an interview and reconnection. I have developed a connection with the parents based on today's interview. You can call her to remind her of her commitment to her son.

QUESTION *How do we know when we can close a family's case?*

MARIA I never close a case. I just say, "You learned a lot. You learned communication. Now you need to practice. If you have any trouble, phone." You don't close a case because life is a process. There will always be new issues that come up. If you think of life as a process, there's no closure. Sometimes somebody phones a year later if a new situation arises. Like with your children, you say, "You are on your own." That doesn't mean they don't come back to you when they need you. Let the family walk and grow.

QUESTION *How can we use the Satir Model effectively in a business setting? Sometimes it is very difficult to be congruent there.*

COMMENTARY *This question is not strictly relevant here, but I chose to answer, since I think it is an important topic.*

MARIA This is a good question. You can use the Satir Model in a business setting because an organization is just like a family. We even use it in government settings, but you use a different language. The CEO is the parent or the grandparent. They are the managers of the family. You can sculpt an internal experience of the business system. In one company, many people can have different perceptions, expectations and yearnings. Different departments can have different experiences and different understandings about the goal of the company. An employee can be contributing their best effort for the company, yet their behaviour is always influenced by what they learned in their family of origin. Every piece of the Satir Model can be utilized in a business setting. A company also has a past history, including how it started, how it grew, how it developed, how it is now, and its future direction.

QUESTION *You very calmly passed over the boy's angry disclosure that he sometimes wants to kill his teachers. Why did you not respond to this specifically? As a therapist is it not your responsibility to address this?*

MARIA This is a good question. First of all, we already knew about this as a presenting problem. I was very happy when the boy said it, because this indicated he feels safe to express himself and that he understands where his anger comes from. As a therapist I chose not to respond to this because I want him and the family to know that this is not the issue. This is only the symptom. The basic issue is systemic and belongs to the family as a whole. Furthermore, he does not yet know how to deal with his accumulated anger from so many aspects of his life, his family and his environment. The boy acknowledges his anger, which is the important point. In choosing a role player for his Anger, I acknowledge it and ask him to verbalize it in an acceptable way. This is when I suggest that he tells his parents what he wants and how he feels. He does it in a very clear manner. My message is that anger is OK. He will need to learn how to deal with it. Then I teach him to express his anger in an acceptable way when he comes home from school. He makes a commitment with his grandmother about how he will deal with his anger.

Why did I not worry about his threat to kill his teachers? I interpret this as a message that he does not know yet how to manage his anger. The whole issue is how he uses his anger. Killing is the outcome of uncontrolled anger. I chose to teach him how to deal with his anger. Choosing a role player for Anger is more than acknowledging. Rather, it is to assist him to get in touch with it; to express anger in the here and now instead of letting it pile up. That would be a problem. It is the unexpressed anger that leads to violence. Therapy is supposed to assist in the expression of repressed feelings and clear the air for a new way to deal with feelings. For this process, I created a safe environment and a container, including role players. My point is that it would be a therapeutic mistake to dwell on this issue and detract from the underlying and deeper issues.

## Evaluation notes

The following section is my assessment of whether this interview utilized goals, basic elements, and directives of the Satir Family Therapy Model as outlined earlier in this book.

### EXPERIENTIAL

The sculpt was intentionally shown in a dramatic fashion. It was developed for both mother and son to become more aware of their relationship. The main purpose was to demonstrate, in an extreme manner, the depth of enmeshment between mother and son.

I chose to use role players first to develop a picture of the family system because I didn't feel the parents and the boy were ready to stand up and do it themselves. Using role players helped them to connect and to feel more comfortable participating in the process, and sharing more openly later in the interview. The sculpt also provided an experience to externalize the boy's anger and the parents' unspoken feelings.

SYSTEMIC

The interview included the entire family system and involved every family member. People connected between themselves (inter-psychically) and within themselves (intra-psychically). Many internal changes occurred for the boy and the mother. Mother was invited – pushed, even – to change her perception about the son, which deeply affected her feelings and her expectations about herself and her son. As a result, this transition impacted her whole self.

The son received a lot of support to stand up for himself and learned to express his yearnings congruently, while accepting his fear. I hope he learned how to accept his anger and to cope with it in a new way.

As mentioned earlier, the father could have been included more. He did take part in the interview, but time constraints limited the opportunity to focus on his internal experience, other than inviting him to express his feelings and observations.

The grandmother was included as an important part of the change process. She committed to some changes of her own and also supported her grandson's desire for change. Everyone was involved, but the main focus was on the issue between the mother and son, and the son's own process.

POSITIVELY DIRECTIONAL

The interview process was positively directional in that every family member made a commitment for change and their relationships became stronger. The boy and his parents learned a new way to deal with their feelings and with each other.

FOCUS ON CHANGE

Throughout the interview, there was a consistent direction and actual movement toward change. For example, I asked everybody what they wanted to change, and reminded the mother that her son was not a child and to call him her son. I also supported and challenged the boy to express his true feelings. All the members in the family expressed themselves congruently by the end of the interview. Everyone made a commitment to change.

## THERAPIST'S USE OF SELF

I tried to create safety in many ways: greeting everyone at the entrance, shaking hands with everybody, introducing myself and the translator, using my own examples during the interview when they made a relevant point. I believe I was congruent. At times I may have been too directive with the mother. While I consistently disagreed with her, I also understood her and supported her. I feel I had connection with every one of them, especially the boy, who felt my support. I agreed openly with the boy that many teachers are not good enough. I also shared my own experiences as a mother, in order to encourage the parents to let their son grow and eventually let go.

## RAISE SELF-ESTEEM

The priority in this process was to help the boy to stand up in every way, especially when he expressed his reluctance to value himself. He had a tendency to give up in difficult situations. Rather than focusing on the identified issue related to his anger and behaviour, the intention was on raising his self-esteem and getting him to believe in himself. Once he can change his internal process, he can deal with his anger in a new way. Violence will no longer be an issue.

## RESPONSIBILITY AND CHOICE MAKING

Each person in the family was encouraged and willing to make a commitment to take on responsibility for themselves. For example, the mother committed to cooking dinner. The boy made many commitments, the most important of which was to go to school. He yearned for freedom and he realized that freedom included self-responsibility for the choices he made. He also committed to expressing his anger differently. The father committed to not moving out. These were all choices they made in the negotiations for more caring and responsibility within the family.

## FAMILY OF ORIGIN

I asked questions related to family-of-origin issues throughout the interview, when it was relevant. Helping the mother and father get in touch with their own experience as adolescents gave them more awareness and understanding of their son's position.

## CONGRUENCE

I taught and demonstrated congruent communication and repeatedly asked the family members to do the same. I directed them to talk to each other rather than through me. Everyone was involved in practising congruence with each other, which supported them in getting what they wanted.

## Postscript

The therapist did not see the boy after the session, but she followed up with the family several times by telephone. The boy told her he was OK and was continuing with high school. His father told the therapist that his son was doing fine in the third year and hadn't been absent from school since the session, except when sick. Now the boy wants to go to medical school, but his teacher and the family want him to go to art school. His mother has decided to stay with him for the examination time, which the father worries about. The father has on many occasions asked the therapist to say thank you to Maria.

## Chapter Eight
### PARENTING IN THE SHADOW OF FAMILY-OF-ORIGIN EXPERIENCES

### *Therapist's presentation*

A family with a 16-year-old boy, a father, a mother, a foster grandfather, a class teacher and a counsellor attended this session on March 19th 2011 in Nanjing.

The boy is a 16-year-old grade 9 student who is scheduled to take the senior high school entrance examination in three months. Although he is disinterested and does not get good grades, he is willing to go to school.

Because he is feeling very alone at home, he prefers to spend time with teachers and peers. In grammar school he was known as the class clown. In junior high he began to feel insecure and was distanced from by his peers.

The boy connects well with older people and volunteers at an animation shop and a street dance studio. He has developed friendships with the owners of these businesses as well as the owner of a snack shop.

In the first session, the boy was quiet and restless.He was accompanied by his foster grandfather, a retired vocational school principal. The foster grandfather did all the talking while the biological father was waiting outside the session room. The father has a close relationship with the foster grandfather, who is a support for the father and the boy.

The father was worried about the boy's entrance examination and mother was angry that he was not doing homework. He has been sent to tutoring classes after school, but there has been no improvement.

The counsellor, who interviewed them for 16 sessions, is a volunteer at a youth center in Nanjing. The boy came for all 16 sessions and the father started attending from the second session. The mother only came for 7 or 8 sessions. She said she was too busy to attend more.

The counsellor reported improvements after 16 sessions. The boy is communicating more with the therapist and the father, which makes the father happier. He has also started doing homework and his behaviour has improved. Mother still has very little involvement.

At one individual session with the counsellor, the boy told the counsellor that his mother physically abuses him and he is very lonely at home. The counsellor recommended family therapy.

## Family background

The boy is the only child of parents who are in their 40s. Both parents' family background is farming. Father is now an owner of a motorcycle mechanic shop. Mother is a homemaker. She cooks two meals a day for everybody, including the employees at the father's shop. Her hobbies include dancing and mah-jong. The relationship between the couple is distant. Talking to each other often turns into heated quarrels or even physical fights.

The father is very independent and quiet. He wakes his son every morning and buys breakfast for him at 6 a.m. Since the shop is located on the ground floor of their apartment, he goes between the shop and the apartment when the boy comes home from school.

The mother blames her son's behaviour on her in-laws, because they did not help out in raising him. Her parents raised her brother's children, who are well behaved.

The boy is introverted, quiet and attention seeking. He has a closer relationship with the father and is distant from mother. She often verbally abuses the boy and sometimes beats him severely. He never calls her "mother." At one time he thought about running away from home, but father talked him out of it. The boy complained about the education system in China, claiming the only focus is on academic achievement with no attention given to the emotional happiness of the kids. In spite of this, the boy has a very close relationship with his teacher. She invites the boy to her home and lets him stay for dinner. She wants him to be happy and puts only a small amount of pressure on him to do his homework. He is willing to share with her.

The boy requested the presence of this teacher in the first six counselling sessions, asking her to be his spokesperson. He also requested her presence at this family interview.

## *The interview*

COMMENTARY *I greet the family, foster grandfather, teacher, and counsellor, then invite them to sit down. I explain that the group of participants will be observing. In order to make it more comfortable for the family, I ask each individual to introduce themselves and where they come from.*

MARIA Please sit down. Thank you very much for coming. I would especially like to thank the teacher for coming. I know you are busy.

TEACHER I think I should be here.

MARIA OK. Thank you. I would like to apologize for keeping you waiting a long time. I want to hear from the teacher about her experience with you. [To the son] I understand that you have seen your counsellor many times and that she really cares for you a lot. You really have a good sense of humour. You are very creative, and your teacher likes you and she has said a lot of very interesting things about you.

[To the father] We know that father has his own work.

[To the mother] You, Mama, you like to do a lot a cooking for the family.

[To the grandfather] I also hear that you are a grandfather who has been adopted into this family. Sometimes we have grandfathers who are not chosen. You are chosen, though you are not a member of this family [laughter]. This is a loving family. You have an important position in this family. I would like to hear what you are hoping for that would help this family to do better.

GRANDPA I came here today mainly to learn from Maria. I have been working in the education field for about 40 years. I would not let go of this opportunity. Today, I am already 67 years old. I still want to contribute to the education profession. My biggest mission is to bring help to young people. Thank you.

MARIA What do you think would be helpful to this family, to make everybody's life better?

GRANDPA Looking at the present moment, the biggest hope is that this boy could make some changes.

MARIA What changes do you want to see in this boy?

GRANDPA He needs to be more independent, motivate himself and be confident.

MARIA It seems to me from what I hear that he is motivated and he knows how to find friends.

GRANDPA Yes. But the key point is he has not found the right place for himself yet. Therefore, I wish that in this precious opportunity we can let him find his own place.

MARIA Do you have an idea what his right place should be, more specifically? What do people wish of him?

GRANDPA I cannot tell you clearly in one or two statements.

MARIA Can you tell him?

GRANDPA I have often told him but we cannot find a good way to help him understand.

MARIA [to the boy] Do you know what your grandpa is talking about? I will just call him grandpa.

SON I know.

MARIA You know his wish for you?

SON I know.

MARIA Would you like to share it with me?

SON I'm kind of willing.

MARIA OK. Share it.

[Son pauses, with apparent changes in eye movements, eyebrows, forehead and facial expression.]

MARIA Is that a difficult question.

SON [nodding, eyes closed] Yes, it is.

MARIA What would help your life to be better?

SON I don't have high expectations.

MARIA If we had some magic, what would you wish for? Anything could happen.

SON My life would be happier.

MARIA Do you know what makes you happy? I really like your answer. Tell me two things that would make you happier.

SON To be with the friends I like. To go out to do the things I like.

MARIA You want to meet with the friends you like? You cannot do that?

SON It's not so bad.

MARIA You have friends and you want to be with them. That's what I hear.

SON Yes. I have friends.

MARIA Yes. At home, what would make you happier?

SON Eh … [eyebrows tightened, eyes closed] I don't know.

MARIA OK. While you think about it, I will ask Papa. What did you hope for when you came here? What do you want?

PAPA I also want him to have some changes.

MARIA What would make you happy?

PAPA I spend a lot of energy on him but he doesn't make any changes.

MARIA What changes do you wish to see in him?

PAPA He could have some changes about his studies and about his feelings.

MARIA Feelings?

PAPA Yes. He has no energy when he goes to school. I want him to be more energetic. He is not aware that he is not doing well at school.

MARIA How did you do in school when you were his age?

PAPA I didn't do well in school, either.

MARIA You know about it. You want your son to do better.

PAPA I put a lot of energy and material into him changing and doing better in school.

MARIA You want him to do better than you did?

PAPA Yes.

MARIA [to the son] Did you know that?

SON Yeah. I know.

MARIA What would you like to tell your father about that? Do you appreciate that? He wants things to be better for you than what he experienced in school. Look at your father and tell him how you feel about what he said.

SON [pauses while looking at his father. It appears hard for the boy to speak.] You work too hard.

MARIA Does your father work too hard today?

SON Harder than before.

MARIA What does that mean for you?

SON I don't know.

MARIA How about telling him that?

SON I know father has already given a lot to me.

MARIA You appreciate that?

SON OK. Yes.

COMMENTARY *My intention is to connect father and son on a more personal level.*

MARIA Mother, when you came here today what did you hope for?

MOTHER I have similar wishes to his father.

MARIA I was asking what your wishes are.

MOTHER His father has already said that. That is also my wish.

MARIA Yes, that he would change?

MOTHER I want him to change and I want him to be independent and improve academically.

MARIA Both your parents have the same wish for you. [To the mother] Do you always want the same thing your husband wants?

MOTHER It is mainly me who looks after our son when he makes mistakes.

MARIA [to the translator, Marie] Who is "he" she is talking about?

MARIE "He" means the son.

MARIA When he does something wrong?

MOTHER Yes.

MARIA How do you look after him? How do you help him?

MOTHER Maybe I use the wrong methods?

MARIA Like what?

MOTHER I push him. If he doesn't listen to me, I beat him.

MARIA You beat him. Does that help?

MOTHER No.

MARIA Was that your experience when you grew up?

MOTHER Yes. It was.

MARIA Who beat you?

MOTHER My parents beat me.

MARIA They beat you when you didn't do what they wanted you to do?

MOTHER Yes.

MARIA How did you feel when they beat you? Did they help you?

MOTHER No.

MARIA How did you feel inside when they beat you?

MOTHER I felt very painful.

MARIA Can you imagine your son feels the same way when you beat him?

MOTHER I have not thought of that.

MARIA [to the son] Would you tell your mother how you feel when she beats you? [To the teacher and mother] Can you change places so the son can talk to mother?

MARIA Tell your mother how you feel. You may feel the same way she felt. Take a look at your mother. Tell your mother how you feel. Maybe we can do it the other way around. Will you, Mama, tell him how you felt? Tell him.

MOTHER I beat him because he did not behave.

MARIA How did you feel when your parents beat you? I can see your tears. I just want you to put words to how you felt. He may feel the same way.

MOTHER I did not know that.

MARIA Know what?

MOTHER I did not think about this when I beat him.

MARIA Now when you think about it how do you feel? What comes to your mind? Tell him. Tell him now what you think about it. [To son] Would you look at your mother?

MOTHER He was wrong when he misbehaved. I was wrong when I beat him.

COMMENTARY *I have been trying to make a connection between the boy and his parents. When the mother admits to beating her son, I hope for an opening. At this point I make an assumption that the only people the boy has a connection with are the foster grandfather, the teacher and some friends. As I move forward, I plan to include the teacher.*

MARIA [to the mother] Can you say "you" when you talk to him, instead of "he"? [To the son] You notice mother is talking to you. What did she say? What is mother saying to you? I want to know in your words what you heard mother say. It is very important.

SON I heard her.

MARIA Now you tell her how you felt. When she beat you, what was your body feeling? [The son shakes his head.] You don't want to tell her? You don't want to talk to your mother?

SON I do not want to review that painful experience.

MARIA It was very painful. Mama, now that you know that it was very painful for him and it did not make much change, can you imagine that you would use another way to deal with him?

MOTHER I've stopped blaming him and beating him now.

MARIA I am very happy to hear that. [To son] Do you believe that? Mother does not blame you and will not beat you anymore.

[To mother] Mama, I think that beating and blaming do not help people do their homework. It's not helpful. I am very glad you've made that decision not to beat him and blame him anymore.

[To the teacher] I would like to thank you for coming. I understand that he really likes you and appreciates your support for him. How do you feel about what's going on in this family? What do you see that would be helpful?

TEACHER I am very sympathetic. I have heart for the father as well as the son.

MARIA You are a big support for the family.

TEACHER I should be. As a teacher, I am supposed to be.

MARIA Papa, do you believe her?

PAPA I know he is really willing to share everything with his teacher.

MARIA Yes, I think that is very helpful.

TEACHER I want to offer more help to him.

MARIA How could you help him?

TEACHER In every stage along the way, I offered him help any time he needed me. Sometimes I have also felt confused, and couldn't find a very good or more effective way to help him.

MARIA What do you think could help him in the family? You have an opportunity here to tell Mama and Papa and Grandpa, since you know him well. What I hear is that everybody wants him to change. How could they help him to change? I know you are helping Papa. I know you are supporting the son and maybe even love him. Do you believe he gets support in this family?

TEACHER First of all, I believe he should be able to get support from the family because his Papa, Mama and his Grandpa have been trying hard. They all are trying hard to change themselves. How does this family help their son? I feel he was not taught to have good habits when he was young. This boy, from what I've understood, is very smart, humorous, and has his own interests and habits. But psychologically he likes to be dependent on others and he wants to have freedom. He is not willing to accept discipline. He hasn't been able to persist in the things that he wants to do. In the area of study, his foundation is comparatively weak. Therefore, I wish his parents could, first of all, change their hopes and wishes about this boy.

MARIA In what way specifically should they change? Tell Papa in what way you think he should change?

TEACHER OK. I think Papa and Mama should not ask too much about his studies. You could guide him to spend more energy forming his interest and habits. He has said that he likes to do the things he likes to do. He likes to make friends. If he does violate your principles, you can try your best to satisfy him. Secondly, I feel that you parents have to supervise his behaviour and his habits. Help him develop himself to be more independent and overcome his tendency to be dependent. You must have sufficient patience because it is not easy to change a habit or a pattern. He needs a lot of encouragement and persistence.

I want to check with you [Maria] if you asked me what I thought the family needed to change for the boy.

MARIA Yes. You have just done very well.

TEACHER I wish that the family would change their expectation of the boy, and not only focus on how he should do better in his school work.

COMMENTARY *This teacher is a very important resource for me and for the family. It is rather unusual that the teacher recommends more freedom and fun for the boy. The father still sees school performance as a priority.*

MARIA I agree with you, absolutely. Thank you. Thank you. [To father] How do you feel about what the teacher has just said?

FATHER I already knew this through the communication I have had with the counsellor and the teacher. I used to only focus on his school work. I only worried about whether he could get into a good senior high school, but not anymore. Now I no longer ask him to get into a particular high school. I leave it to him. After communicating with the counsellor, we only want him to try his best. We do not ask him to get into a so called reputable high school anymore.

MARIA [to the son] Did you know that? Did Papa tell you that?

SON [nods his head.]

MARIA Yes. [To Papa] You told him.

PAPA I did.

MARIA The teacher also knows that you have a relationship with your son, which is not only related to school work. [To the teacher] That was what you meant. You support him to make friends.

TEACHER Correct. As long as he doesn't violate principles, and he is still young, he can make the kind of friends he likes to make.

MARIA [to the Father] Do you support what the teacher has said?

PAPA I support it basically, but I still wish that he would show a little bit of improvement in school.

MARIA I understand that he already has and that he is doing his homework.

PAPA Yes, I know he has some improvement.

MARIA Never good enough?

PAPA No, because within a few days he is going to have examinations for getting into senior high school. I wish he would go out to play with his friends less and focus more on his studies.

MARIA I know this is very important to you. Every parent thinks this is important. However, for me, his happiness is also important. He said he wanted to be happier. What do you think, Papa? How happy is your son? Do you think he is a happy boy?

PAPA We talked about this in the previous session, that after school, he just goes to the studios to do street dance. What I ask is that he doesn't go there so frequently. Maybe just once a week. I disagree with him going to the studio to dance every day, right after school. I ask him to dance only once a week.

MARIA What would you like him to do instead?

PAPA I want him to study because he is going to have examinations soon. I want him to go there less.

MARIA I don't know whether this is right or wrong. I think it is more important that he be happy about his life and himself. I support what the teacher has said, to help him to feel good and build a good life.

PAPA I am sure he is happy in the studio, but if he goes to the studio every day, he will forget about his school work. Should we discipline him somehow or let him be? Maybe we need to have some limits on what he wants to do.

MARIA [to the teacher] You want limitations on him from his father. What limitations do you suggest from Mama?.

TEACHER [to Mama] I am a mother, too. As a mother, I feel we have to have patience when we are educating our children. We need to pay more attention to our children's life, especially the psychological change of adolescents. Timely guidance, whether your child listens or not, you have to tell him the right thing. You cannot stop giving him feedback.

MARIA Do you agree with him getting beaten by Mama?

TEACHER I disagree with the beating.

MARIA Tell Mama.

TEACHER [to Mama] Your beating your child is not effective. But this is in the past. You are not doing it any more. Even though you made mistakes in the past, you don't need to be afraid and stop teaching him. We need to correct the mistakes we make. We need to be persistent in educating our children.

MARIA Well, Mama, do you want to respond?

MAMA I will change.

MARIA Will you make a commitment that you won't beat him?

MAMA I am willing to give my commitment not to beat him now and in the future.

MARIA Mama, I am very happy to hear that. Thank you for making the commitment, because I do believe that beating is not helpful. Now instead of beating, can you talk to him?

MAMA I will talk to him.

PAPA Basically they cannot talk. Once they talk, they begin to argue.

MARIA They are not communicating.

PAPA She has a quick temper. When they talk about something, we get into a quarrel.

MARIA Tell her. Tell your wife.

PAPA I told her. Between us, we never quarrel. But we get into physical fights because of our son. We have different ideas about disciplining our son, so we often fight, either verbally or physically, because of this.

MARIA Do you disagree with how mother treats him?

PAPA Yes. And we even get into physical fights because of this.

MARIA You protect your son!

PAPA Yes.

MARIA [to son] Do you know that Papa protects you? It's very sad that Papa has to protect you from mother. [To mother] How was it when you were a child, Mama? Was there anyone to protect you?

MAMA My mother protected me.

MARIA You needed protection from Mama against Papa beating you?

MAMA Yes.

MARIA It's a similar situation here. Your son needs his father to protect him from you. Would you like to change that?

MAMA I am willing to.

MARIA How would you change that? Maybe you would like to spend more time with him. Would you like to?

MAMA Now I just leave him alone. He can do anything he likes. I don't need any commitment, not regarding the school work.

MARIA Do you love him?

MAMA Of course I love him.

MARIA Of course. How does he know that? How do you show it? Look at him and tell him. Can you tell him? [To son] Look at your mother.

MAMA There is no mother who would dislike her son.

MARIA Can you talk directly and say, "I love you"?

MAMA I love you.

MARIA [to son] Do you believe that? Can you talk? Do you believe that your mother loves you, but she doesn't know how to show you?

SON I've already discovered this.

MARIA Tell your mom how you notice that she loves you. Look at her. You cannot talk to your mother without looking at her. Could you look at your mother? You don't want to look at her? Is that it? Because that is the only way you can find out whether she means what she said. We talk about people talking to each other. If I don't look at her, I don't know whether I believe what she says. When she said she loves you, I believe her because I looked at her. I also understand that you have difficulty believing that, because she beat you. At that time, Papa had to protect you. That has changed. Would you like to change that? I know you are very smart. Everybody has been saying something about how they can be helpful to you. Now I want to hear from you. Are you willing to cooperate?

SON Yes.

MARIA [to the translator, Marie] He said "Yes" in English?

MARIE Yes.

MARIA You understand English. Are you willing to talk to me?

SON [sighing and nodding] Yes.

COMMENTARY *Up to this point I try to connect son with each of his parents. It is obvious that the son is not ready. He will not even look at mother. She has been abusive and the son does not believe she will change. I am supporting the boy to express what he wants. I ask him to communicate first with the people he trusts. I hope that later he will have more courage to face his parents. I utilize the support of the teacher and hope that the parents learn from the teacher.*

*I ask the boy to stand up. Hopefully, standing on his feet will literally give him more courage and he will feel more empowered to say what he wants. I hope that the support of the teacher, the counsellor, and myself, will encourage him to speak up to his father, and later to his mother.*

*The issue with his father is based on disagreement between home-work and play. The issue with the mother is based on mistrust because she has beaten him.*

*Later we hear more about the parents' family-of-origin experiences, which have a significant influence in their current role as parents. The father could not continue his own studies in senior high school, and so he is pushing his son to achieve in school. My intention is to connect the son to his father first because the issue with mother is loaded and complex. The son is not even willing to look at her at this point. As a child, mother was abused by her mother and protected by her father. She is repeating the same pattern now with her son.*

MARIA OK. I would like to ask you to do something. I want you to stand up and stand here [in front of father]. Your teacher and counsellor are supporting you. You know that. You will feel comfortable standing here. They support you. They care for you and they are here for you. Do you know that?

SON I know.

MARIA You feel their support. You can say anything you want. They will support you, and I will too. I think both Mama, Papa, and Grandpa want the best for you. That's why they are here. Do you know that? Do you believe that?

SON I believe that.

MARIA What I am asking you to tell them, first Papa, is what you want that would make your life better. You know that he would like you to do better in school work. But I don't think he knows what you want from him. I think if you can get from him, from Grandpa and from Mama what you want, then your school work will be OK. But we're not talking about school work today. We're talking about you. How your life, in their home and outside, will be better. This is an opportunity to tell Papa. You can say anything you want. These two [teacher and counsellor] will support you.

Will you tell Papa what you've never, never told him, and also what you don't want? What do you want that would make your life better and what you don't want? I know this is hard. But it is useful, believe me. I will support you, not only me, everybody here. Tell Papa what you want.

I'll support Papa. Would you come closer? [Maria moves closer to Papa.]

TEACHER Use your courage.

MARIA Yes. She knows you have courage. [To teacher] What do you want to tell him? What can he use?

TEACHER Your father wants to hear what you want and what you don't want.

GRANDPA Just put it in simple words, the kind of life you want. Just say it.

TEACHER Don't make it so complicated.

MARIA Yes, keep it simple. Maybe you want more time to play. Maybe you want to play with father. Maybe you want to talk to him more. Or maybe you don't want that.

COUNSELLOR You can say anything you want.

MARIA When I asked what you wanted, you said you wanted to be happier. Tell your father how you could be happier. It's very simple.

SON I want to play more.

FATHER More?

MARIA Good!

SON I want more pocket money.

MARIA OK. What else? Will you find out what Papa would say to that? This is a big chance to say anything you want. You said you wanted more pocket money. That's very good. I want that, too. Everybody wants that. What do you want specifically for you?

COUNSELLOR What are the things you like to do.

SON You allow me to go to three dances.

MARIA You know how to have fun.

TEACHER You need to answer to Maria, not only say mmmm.

MARIA OK, more.

SON I will make a list when I go home.

MARIA Well, I would like to hear it now, specifically what you want for you. I am serious. We have to negotiate, because Papa wants something, too. You see it is up for negotiation. If you could play more, have more fun, have more pocket money, would you do more of what Papa wants, like, more homework? Would that be true for you? You ask Papa what you want and you also make a commitment to what you can do to get what you want.

SON I want to exchange terms with him. If I accept his terms and he gets what he wants, I will also get my terms and what I want.

MARIA That's exactly what I am talking about. Good thinking. Let's talk about terms. Are you willing to discuss that Papa?

PAPA I can.

MARIA OK. [To the son] You know his terms?

SON Yes.

MARIA What are his terms?

SON Work hard on my studies.

MARIA Now would you accept that if you could play more?

SON There is no such thing as a free lunch. If we do something, we get something in return.

MARIA So you know it. Would you tell your teacher and your counsellor what you want from Papa, so they can hear it?

FATHER Basically like this. That is what he wants.

MARIA Well, I don't know whether everybody wants to play the way you want to play. Papa said you can go to that place once a week and you want to do it every day?

SON Once a week.

MARIA OK?

SON Yes.

MARIA That's OK. Tell him. So, is that OK? Ask him.

SON Can I?

FATHER You can. You can go on Saturdays.

MARIA Is that what you want?

SON I want to go there on Sundays and Saturdays.

MARIA Ask him.

FATHER If you go both on Saturdays and Sundays, you won't have time for homework. If you want to go on Saturdays and Sundays, you need to arrange your schedule well. After all, you are a student. You need to do your homework.

SON OK.

MARIA Can you commit to do your homework, seriously, so that you get Saturdays and Sundays?

SON That's OK.

MARIA Now tell Papa, so that he can believe it. Look at him.

SON I guarantee it. [He raises three fingers to make a solemn promise.]

FATHER If you really guarantee it, you may go.

MARIA We all believe you.

SON I will do it. [Everybody claps.]

MARIA How do you feel? Everybody is on your side. You know why? Because everybody who is here remembers when they were 16 years old. We all know about it – that we want to have fun, as well as do homework. I wish Papa would remember. Papa, I'd like to ask you how much fun you had when you were 16.

PAPA I did have fun.

MARIA Did you like to play?

PAPA Yes, I wanted to play.

MARIA Tell him. Let your son know how it was when you were 16.

PAPA When I was 16, I finished my homework. I was in grade 9 when I was 16, too. I even got a scholarship.

MARIA So that is why you have high expectations for your son.

PAPA Later I didn't have a chance to go to senior high. I really wish he could go. I don't want him to experience the same thing as I did. I invest a lot in him.

MARIA Do you hear that? Papa wants better for you, even better than he did.

SON [to loud laughter from the group.] A good man …

MARIA It's important to know that. You knew about him when he was 16?

254 SATIR FAMILY THERAPY IN ACTION

SON No, not until now.

MARIA So what's your commitment, about play and homework? What is the deal here?

FATHER Homework, then play. You finish your homework and you can play.

SON I need to arrange it first.

MARIA You can?

SON I can.

FATHER You made a commitment here, you have to keep it.

MARIA Yes. I believe he can keep it. There are many witnesses here.

FATHER Teacher Maria is here. She heard you.

SON We have evidence here. The video recording.

MARIA All evidence goes into history books.

SON Save it in a file!

MARIA I am a funny person. I hear people make a commitment. I check it out. From time to time I check out when people make a commitment, and my experience with young people like you, here in China, is that when they make a commitment, they keep it. I think you are not different. I finally can see your eyes now and I believe you. Yes, I believe you that you will keep the commitment.

SON Hmm.

TEACHER I was also a witness, and I can ask the supervisor every day.

MARIA They are all witnesses here. Now, OK, I would like to ask whether there is anything else you would like from Papa. How do you like to have fun with Papa? How do you two play together? It's nice to play with Papa. Is there anything, any ideas?

FATHER My shop is very busy. I don't get into that very often.

TEACHER We are talking about going out to play, not going on the internet.

MARIA I am not talking about the internet. I am talking about going for a walk, or going to a movie. Are you willing to do that?

FATHER I will.

MARIA Now look at him and tell him about how you want to do it. It's nice that father and son do something together. What would you like to do with Papa? I know you like to play. But when you are with Papa, what interesting things could you do together? What could you play with Papa? Do you like to go to the movies? Do you like to walk? I don't know whether you two people would go fishing. Anything that two men can do. Papa, do you have any ideas? What did you do with your Papa? What do you want to do with your son together?

FATHER We usually go to the supermarket and do window shopping together.

MARIA Do you like to do that?

SON Hmm.

MARIA Papa is offering that.

SON Yes.

MARIA Thank you. I won't be here. Don't just talk to me. You need to tell Papa, "I'd like to do that."

SON I am willing to.

MARIA Will you commit, Papa, to sometimes going out with your son to play?

FATHER OK.

MARIA I want to see that in the video.

SON There are also human witnesses.

MARIA I would like you to look at Mama. I know that would be a big change that Mama committed to, not beating you. Do you believe it?

SON I believe it.

COMMENTARY *Now that Mama has witnessed the father and son negotiating and making a commitment, she has an example of what is possible for her. As well, the son now has an experience of negotiation.*

MARIA What would you like from Mama when you are at home and Mama is at home? Do you think that there is anything that the two of you could do together happily? Or maybe you want nothing. Tell her whatever is good for you.

SON Add a piece of meat to each meal.

MARIA You want to eat more meat? Tell Mama.

MAMA I am willing to cook whatever you like to eat. I can add more meat. I am willing to satisfy whatever you tell me. But you don't eat vegetables. You only eat meat.

MARIA He likes meat. Mama, you are thinking that he has to eat vegetables in order to eat meat?

MAMA He needs to eat both.

MARIA Can you do that?

SON Yes.

MARIA I don't like vegetables either. See Mama, I am 90 years old, so I don't think it is so important. But if you want him to eat vegetables I think it is a good idea. Now I have a big question. Mama, I hear from Papa that you have a temper. Sometimes we all have a temper, but how can you deal with your temper with him without beating him? What could you do? That could be a big change. Can I suggest something when you have temper? You just tell him, "I feel angry now." I want you [Marie] to translate to her not to say "You make me angry" but "I feel angry." When I say "I feel angry," something changes in me. My temper goes away when I can express it. But it's helpful for the relationship if you own your anger and do not say it is his fault. Also you know, in that case, he can feel better in knowing that your temper has nothing to do with him. You can even do that with your husband. Just the same, "I feel so angry." Can you do that?

COMMENTARY *Rather than focusing on mother's negative behaviour from the past, I am suggesting how she can make some positive changes going forward. I deal with mother and father differently. Mother needs education and support to deal with her own feelings. Father needs to learn how to negotiate with the son. It seems that my approach with mother and father is giving the son some confidence to speak up.*

MAMA Yes.

MARIA Would that help you if Mama just tells you, "I feel angry"?

SON Yes.

MARIA Actually it's very helpful for everybody in the family to say how they feel. Do you have a temper sometimes? Do you feel angry sometimes?

SON Not much.

MARIA But when you do, can you just say it, rather than holding it?

SON I don't suppress my anger. I just distract myself from it. I'll go out and walk.

MARIA Good idea. So you know how to deal with your anger. Mama did not know. But everybody can learn.

SON I am surprised how I've learned it in ten years.

MARIA You are not so angry.

SON That's OK, if I've learned how to release it.

MARIA So you have learned how to release it. You said you went out for a walk. What do you do, Papa, when you feel anger?

PAPA When I am angry, I throw my temper at objects, not at people.

MARIA You break something?

PAPA Yes, I do.

MARIA That's expensive!

PAPA I don't break expensive things.

MARIA So you see everybody has to learn how to deal with anger, not only Mama. Papa breaks things and you go out for a walk. Mama is it OK for you if you just say so?

MAMA Yes, I can.

COMMENTARY *I am normalizing anger and helping them to recognize that anger is OK. Each family member needs to learn how to cope with the feeling. The next step is anchoring the commitment by associating their feelings with their commitment. When people become aware of their internal experience it strengthens the commitment.*

MARIA So you all have commitments. [To Grandpa] How do you deal with anger?

GRANDPA I don't have too much anger. I was an obedient child when I was young. I was always a good student when I was at school. It was easy for me to get into the best university in Shanghai. So I don't have much anger in my life.

MARIA Now how do you feel about these new commitments here in this family?

GRANDPA I feel this opportunity is very good. If everyone has made a commitment, the family will change. My best wish for this boy is that he can grow happily and I think the goal is already achieved. I am very thankful to Maria.

MARIA [to son] I think you said something very important. You see, I understand school is important, study is important. I love studying myself. But I would not be able to study if I was not happy with myself and having fun. Therefore, I think it's important for you to have support from Mama, Papa, and Grandpa. You already have support from these people. I want to give you a suggestion. You ask for what you want. You may not always get it. I think you have a Papa here who really, really wants to support you. Do you know that? Do you believe that?

SON I believe that.

MARIA You have lots of support here. You have Grandpa to support you. You have Mama who really, I believe, has the intention to support you. She will learn more how to do it. The only thing they want for you is to be more serious at what you do. My understanding is, from what I heard from your counsellor, that you have a great ability to make friends and to find people who can support you. I think that is a great treasure for life. I also think you try to do that because you haven't found much happiness at home. Is that true?

SON Yes.

MARIA My last question for you is, what would have to change for you to be more willing to be at home? Is it that there be more fun at home? What would you need to be at home more? What would make a difference?

SON Maybe more warmth in the family.

COMMENTARY *I feel that at this point the boy is ready to be more vulnerable and willing to share his needs. I encourage him to be more open. When he says that he wants more warmth in the family, I feel this is a significant turning point in the interview. This is what's been missing in the family – an expression of feelings. When he expresses his deep yearning, I know that I have arrived at the essence. I experience this as a very beautiful part of this whole interview.*

MARIA That's very important. How could there be more warmth from Papa and Mama? How do you know when there is warmth?

SON It is too late. I don't know how to explain it.

MARIA I can show you. Would you like to stand up? You have to help me. If there are no worries to keep people distant from each other in the family, you see, for me, warmth looks like this [Maria walks close to Marie and puts her left arm round her back. She then steps away from Marie and looks at her from a distance.] Now there is no warmth. Show me your picture with the three of you. What does warmth mean and feel like for you? How much closeness or distance is in the family?

COMMENTARY *Using myself with the translator, I am showing how we can physically express feelings by being close or distant with our bodies.*

SON One metre.

MARIA I don't know how much one metre is. Show me.

SON They are like this. [The son moves his parents an arms length apart from each other, with him standing in between them. Then he walks away from them and stands face to face with Maria.]

MARIA Where are you? Are you on this side [Papa's]? Or are you close to this side [Mama's]? Where are you? [The son walks to Papa's side with his back facing Papa.] So you are here.

What is your picture Grandpa? [Grandpa moves parents side by side very close and then puts the son in the middle between them, hugging them.] Oh, that is Grandpa's picture.

[To Grandpa] That's your picture. That's what Grandpa wants. So, Grandpa, you understand what I am talking about.

[To the son] Is that what you want?

SON I want to put down my arms, Grandpa.

MARIA [to the son] So that is Grandpa's picture. What is your picture? Is it like that?

SON I agree. [Son stands between the parents, nobody touches each other.]

MARIA So this is warmth with Mama and with Papa. Now I would like to make a suggestion. You see, warmth has to be expressed and the way we express it is in talking. You can look at each other. [Helps Papa to turn and look at son.] You can see Papa, and Mama. And you can start talking. So warmth is relationship. Sometimes you want really to talk to Papa seriously.

[Turns to Marie to demonstrate.] You can reach out to his hand. "Marie, I want to say something very serious. I really want to talk to you." So, in this way, we have a connection. Can you try holding Papa's hand? Tell him something while looking at him.

How do you want to have warmth from him? [The son turns to Papa and spontaneously moves to hug his Papa.]

COMMENTARY *The son spontaneously hugging Papa is an important turning point in the interview. The son has expressed himself without words. I draw a personal conclusion that the parents need to learn how to express their feelings in both words and body language.*

MARIA That is a beautiful. Do you, Papa, sometimes hug him?

PAPA Not much.

MARIA Would you want to?

PAPA Yes, I want to.

MARIA [to the son] Would you want to have a hug each day … one hug when you meet him at night or when he comes home? That is not so unusual. Would you like that? That is warmth. It's a good step forward. Mama, can you hug? Yes?

MAMA Yes.

MARIA Do you ever hug your son?

MAMA [shaking her head and looking down] No.

MARIA Would you like to?

MAMA Yes, I hugged him when he was young.

MARIA Well, he's still your son, even though he is 16. [To the son] Would you like to have a hug from her? It's a new beginning.

SON [more relaxed and smiling] Hmm.

MARIA [to son] Well, you initiate it. You cannot hug her from there.

[Son looks reluctant but steps toward Mama, reaching for her hand, and hugs her.]

MARIE [translator to Maria] Grandpa suggested that he should hug both.

[Son hugs both parents, standing between them with arms around them. There is clapping from the group.]

MARIA That is real warmth and I encourage you to continue. That's very important. You know it is not enough to have it in the video and talk about it. You need to practice it. Every day a hug here [Papa and son]. Every second day a hug here to begin with [Mama and son]. OK? [Papa nods his head.]

COMMENTARY *The son appeared reluctant to hug his mother, and I did not push him further. The grandfather, however, encouraged him, and the group applauded. I was not convinced in this moment, but I did encourage them to continue working on this.*

MARIA OK. Now we are not going to leave you out, Grandpa. Do you like hugs, too? Do you hug him [son] sometimes? He also needs hugs from Grandpa.

GRANDPA I did before.

SON He is too tall to hug.

MARIA No, try it.

SON I want to do it stronger. [The son hugs Grandpa comfortably. They stay together for a while.]

MARIA OK. Let's sit down and see what we've learned here, today. I think there are many feelings in this family. It's just not expressed. How do you feel, teacher?

TEACHER I feel very happy. I see the hope here and I also understand how I could follow up.

MARIA Could you do follow up?

COMMENTARY *It is very important for this family to have follow up and support. Getting feedback about their commitments to express feelings and to learn a new body language is new and very difficult. They need support from the counsellor and teacher so they can be encouraged to continue this positive direction.*

TEACHER Sometimes I was also angry with him, the boy, but I knew I shouldn't be angry. I learned today, Maria told me, I should say, "I am angry."

MARIA I think that we can't say we shouldn't be angry because that's not being human. If I say to myself, "I shouldn't," it goes into my stomach and then I'll have more and more stomach ache. But I can feel and just say "I feel angry." We do not say, "You made me angry."

TEACHER I know. Thank you very much.

MARIA Well, I thank you for being here today, and your commitment to follow up. That's important because this is only a new beginning, a new decision. I think that everything else will fall into place when there is more happiness, love, and more warmth in the family. How do you feel [teacher and counsellor]?

TEACHER I have met the boy 16 times and met Papa and Mama many times. I witnessed that the boy was improving and growing. Now I can see a big change in the family, especially in the relationship with the father and mother. I feel that's great. I also see the effect and function of family therapy. We will have two counsellors working with the boy in the future and with his mother and father. I am sure that he will move on with his new goals.

MARIA They've made wonderful decisions and I believe them. His intention to study is very, very wonderful. They need support to change. Follow up is important. To change old patterns is difficult. A decision and a commitment are very important. Everyone has to practice and integrate. Grandpa, how do you feel?

GRANDPA Yes, it's very difficult to change an old pattern. Sometimes, it's even painful. But for a better life in the future, when we need to change, we have to change. Thank you, Maria.

MARIA Papa?

PAPA I feel I believe that my son will change and I am sure I will change with my son.

MARIA Thank you. Mama?

MAMA Yes, I am sure I will change my really bad habit, that I beat him. I also want to appreciate my counsellor.

MARIA I know you are sincere. I hope you can find ways to show him. For example, if you give him more meat, that shows your love for him. Very interesting. Children know in their own peculiar ways that they are loved.
[To the son] How do you feel?

SON As long I get meat, that's great. Everything will be alright. I will be strong in my commitment.

MARIA And everything else that we talked about?

SON As long as I have that, it will be best.

MARIA I will check out whether you do your homework. Can you commit to that, too?

SON Yes, yes.

MARIA OK. Good. I believe you. Is it OK to invite people to share what they want to say?

## Group comments

There were many appreciations for the family from the participants, who shared how closely this interview process reflected their own family experiences. They also appreciated having the teacher and counsellor involved.

One participant had a very important teacher in her own life. This teacher had conveyed a 'mother's love' toward her. Another participant shared his story of being beaten by his mother and felt compassion toward the boy in this family. Another male participant was reminded of how much he loved meat as a child. As an adult he recognized that mother cooking meat for him represented love.

One participant shared with the boy's father that he himself as a father did not know how to express love to his son. He shared with the boy that now, as an adult, he experiences hugging as a gift. He encouraged the boy to continue hugging his parents. Another participant expressed warmth and appreciation for the extent of change that happened within a relatively short time.

## Group discussion

As in other sessions, the larger group was divided into groups of ten. These small groups were given guidelines for their discussion of the interview. To convey my appreciation for the groups' learnings and questions, I decided to include here the group leaders' summaries as originally presented. They are included in place of my own evaluation of the interview process at the end of each of the previous cases.

In this specific case, I decided to give the group an additional task. Each group had 15 minutes to present a sculpt of the process and how they would conduct the next interview with this family. I did not give them any specific instructions, because there are so many ways of doing this. I wanted them to practice the art of using the Satir Model and utilizing their own creativity. I appreciated the creativity and variety expressed in each group.

GROUP LEADER 1

We observed Maria's different ways of using herself to establish safety and trust. She raised each person's self-esteem and created connections between them. For example, Maria validated everyone using the information she got from the counsellor, especially appreciating the boy for his creativity and humour. We noticed the boy became more relaxed.

The group members said that the mother was the biggest challenge, because the father described her as a monster. We could not find anything in the presentation that we could appreciate about her. She only had one facial expression during the whole session. Yet Maria acknowledged her for doing a lot of cooking at home, even though she did not like to stay home. Maria reframed it so mother became more relaxed.

In the process, Maria included other reframes, such as saying to the boy, "Your mother loves you. She just doesn't know how to show it." The boy agreed and was touched. In addition, Maria asked the mother to commit to not beating the boy. When talking about the mother beating the boy, Maria asked if she had had the experience of being beaten when she was young. Maria thus connected the boy and the mother at the level of pain, both having been beaten by their mothers, and both having been protected by their fathers.

Maria also explored what the boy wanted in coming here. It was difficult for him to know and say what he wanted. Maria used the metaphor of magic to help the family members feel safe in saying what they wanted. This connected them at the yearning level.

Another thing that impressed us was how Maria taught them to be more congruent. She demonstrated first. She looked at the boy's eyes and also invited him to look at her eyes. When the boy began to look at Maria's eyes, Maria said with excitement, "Oh, I finally can look at your eyes!" Other than this, Maria also helped the boy to stand up. Before he stood up, Maria had the mother and the teacher exchange seats, so that they could talk to each other, even though it was difficult. She also let the boy have a conversation with the father. We thought the most powerful part was when the boy finally stood up to tell his parents what he wanted from each of them. One of our members said this could have been very stressful for the boy. At this point,

Maria utilized the teacher and the counsellor as resources to support him.

As to the teaching of congruence, it included negotiating what they wanted. The boy wanted to street dance and the parents wanted him to study more. After the discussion, they came to an agreement or a contract. Another teaching of congruence was helping them to deal with their anger. These pieces offered a lot of learning.

We discussed what we might have done if we had been the therapists. We thought we would probably tell them that happiness was most important so the boy did not have to study hard, despite the expressed expectations of the parents. We might try to tell the boy that graduating from high school was not enough. He should aim at getting into university. All these reflect the values that belong to our individual selves. Maria remained neutral. She really thought about what everyone in the family wanted. It is important to notice that Maria was constantly working on the internal experience of each member in the family. The boy yearned for love. For him, the mother's promise to give him one more piece of meat at each meal would mean love. Father's love was expressed in the expectation that he would go out with his son for fun.

In addition to the internal experiences of the father, the mother and the son, we observed that Maria was also working on the whole family system. This included the relationships between the father and the son, the mother and the son, the grandpa with the family, and the resources in the community, such as the teacher. In addition, Maria included the mother and her own parents. Some of us therapists might have been side-tracked by the mother and fallen into the trap of her past painful experiences and violence. Maria knew where she would stop, where she would repeat and where she would come back to the whole family experience.

Another highlight is that Maria really focused on the positive in the entire process. I feel most touched by the loving amongst them, accepting of differences and different needs and also the expression of loving and hugging. Those are the things that we feel clear about and are impressed by. The whole process was experiential, including for us, the audience.

There were a few ideas and questions from our small group. One member said she would do the integration of resources of the boy, including his self-esteem. She believed that Maria would do this in the following session. Another member said that since the boy had difficulty expressing his feelings, we might invite somebody to role-play him and do a small sculpt of the primary triad. In this way, the parents could see the boy's pain and the reason why he wanted to run away. The role-players could express the feelings for them.

One question is why, towards the end, did Maria not encourage the boy to hug his mother and the mother to hug the boy? We are afraid since they didn't hug here in the session they probably would not when they went home.

Another question: Maria asked the father to hold hands with his son when talking to him. In some cultures, only women would do this. Our group member wanted to know if this fits for the culture.

We have a recommendation about the feedback to the family. Our suggestion is that when we give feedback, we only share our experience and not give suggestions, criticisms and analyze.

GROUP LEADER 2

We learned from Maria how to use the iceberg metaphor by weaving between the intra-psychic system and inter-personal system in order to work at a deeper lever. Maria got in touch with the boy's yearning at the very beginning.

In response to the expectations of the parents for the boy to do better in his studies, Maria reframed this that he needed to be happy first, before he could do better in his studies. From the very beginning, Maria taught them that only when our yearnings were met could we fulfill our expectations. Even better work is found in the dialogue between the father and the son. Maria put expectations and yearning together so that the son could be responsible for his choices and learn to be a choice maker. She had him ask his parents about what he wanted in order to meet his yearnings. Maria changed the boy's perception of his mother from unsafe to safe. The boy used to feel unsafe, but now he could feel safe.

If we were to work more on the basis of this session, we might work more on parenting. We might also utilize the teacher, as she has already been part of the parenting. She could be a model to the parents in concrete situations, showing them how they could help and discipline their child. This was also the expectation Maria had for the teacher today.

We have a question related to the position of the mother. When she walked into the room, she was identified as the abuser in this family system. We observed that most of the time today the mother was outside of the family circle, and Maria didn't do anything about it. We think this was based on her assessment. We want to ask Maria this question: Did she keep the mother at a distance in order to reduce her negative impact on the family, not allowing her to become the focus of this unit?

GROUP LEADER 3

We focused on discussing the process. How did Maria use her creativity to make contact, to build safety, and achieve therapeutic goals, including using herself and her resources to raise individual levels of self-esteem and encourage congruent communication? How did Maria anchor changes? I will follow this sequence in my report.

In the very beginning, Maria used information she got from the counsellor's presentation of the case to express appreciations to the boy and the grandfather for maintaining contact with the family. In fact, in the whole process, there was a lot of encouragement and appreciation shown to each member of the family. The special thing in the process was that everybody received lots of positive appreciation and encouragement. We saw that Maria's positively directional goals were to create better connection between the boy and his family members and for the boy to be understood. This then helped them to have better communication, stop violence in the family, help the boy to be more responsible, and help each member learn how to deal with his or her own anger. Those are the goals that Maria had in the process that we have discussed.

We saw that Maria met the grandfather first and asked what he wanted for the family. She took care of everybody. Maria asked the boy what he would like to see happen in the family today. When he said he didn't know, Maria asked if he could play magic to discover what he might want. This was great, as that is how teenagers usually answer. In addition to asking what the boy wished, Maria also asked what he really wanted. On the interpersonal level, Maria did a lot of work, whether it was between the son and the father or the son

PARENTING IN THE SHADOW OF FAMILY-OF-ORIGIN EXPERIENCES 269

and the mother, on mutual understanding and connection or using father's and mother's experience. Maria had the father share how he was when he was 16, and the mother shared her experience of being beaten by her parents when she was young. All this was used to help them communicate congruently and be more connected.

Maria not only worked on the family systems, but also used the resources in the bigger systems, such as that of the community, and the grandfather. Maria utilized all this in the process.

There was a beautiful moment when Maria asked the teacher and the counsellor to support the boy to talk to his parents about what he wanted. Maria went to sit next to the father, saying, "I sit here because I want to support you." Maria was using every issue and every moment to support everybody. I personally appreciate how Maria utilized resources in the whole process and followed everyone's pace. When one person was not able to respond, Maria would ask another person rather than pushing that person.

## GROUP LEADER 4

We appreciate what you have done to educate this family, especially on how they can manage their anger better. Most interesting is that you taught each person to manage his or her anger. In this way, you actually gave every person a few choices, not just one. I will only say things that are different from the other groups. You validated the parents' temper and that each one may have a different way of managing his or her own temper. This became their homework. If we were Maria, we would do a family reconstruction for the mother in the future as well as for the father. We would validate each member of the family more and surface more of their inner resources. If we were Maria in this interview, we would have utilized the incident of the boy handing the box of tissue to his mother. We wanted the mother to see that her son was expressing his care for her in a subtle way. Then we would have used this incident to ask the mother to find ways to express her care for her son. We would have worked more on the mother-son relationship, asking them to put their past pains into a museum and start afresh to build a new, loving relationship.

If we were to give homework, for example, father could go to the supermarket with his son or they could go to a movie together. We may have done a little more to find out what kind of movie they each liked. We have an assumption that the son likes to see animated cartoon movies. He might feel bored seeing a movie that his father liked. We would have worked more to find out their common interest.

## Questions and answers

QUESTION *Why did you repeatedly go back to ask mother for her commitment to stop beating her son?*

MARIA I asked her so many times because I wanted to make sure the mother had a commitment. I heard from the counsellor it was more than beating. It was cruelty. I wanted to give her the message and that was my congruence. I wanted to be clear about the message between the mother and me. I wanted her to understand that it was important for me that she be committed. I think it was a huge commitment on her part since she used to beat him in a cruel way. So I later used the time to talk about how she could deal with her anger. I cannot just say to somebody, "Don't do this." I also provided another opportunity, for her to learn to deal with her anger. I think that recognizing that she had been beaten herself didn't change her behaviour. I felt that deep inside her she knew the beating was not working for her. The boy's tears told me that he was touched by mother's acknowledgement that she had been beaten. I think there was a lot in this message for the boy. He can understand it and, if he wishes, he can forgive Mama. Maybe he was happy to know that she had also been beaten. I didn't know what he would do with it. He surely would do something, because he was touched. This was a question from many of you. I am glad you noticed that.

QUESTION *Mother repeatedly said she had behaved wrongly and acknowledged she would not do it anymore. Could we have asked the mother what else she could do now that she was no longer going to beat her son?*

MARIA Yes, this is a good suggestion.

QUESTION *Why not encourage the boy to hug his mother?*

MARIA I feel asking something like that too soon is not helpful. He was very happy to hug. He himself went to his father. After everything the mother had done to the boy, for me, to ask him to hug her would really diminish the cruelty she had done to him and would not be genuine. The mother has to work for it. She now has all the opportunity. If the boy had moved on his own to the mother to hug her, that would be different. He didn't. I was observing him. You know, I am not going to value a happy ending. That is for the movies. This is serious stuff. I respected how far the boy would go. I really would like you to be careful about that. Watch whether the boy wants that. Of course, it would be a nice ending. But it may not mean anything and it can be damaging, in that he might feel that I didn't understand his painful past experience. It is difficult to forgive years of beating in an hour. I want the mother to feel she has to do a lot of change if she wants her son to hug her. I gave him a choice. The boy could have responded to that choice I gave him, but he didn't.

Now about holding hands. I watched them. You hold hands when you talk to somebody who you feel very connected to. If it didn't fit them or the culture, I wouldn't do it. Neither would they. I noticed that it was not OK. I agree with you that we have to be careful and we can ask, is it OK for you? I don't know, at least I have not noticed here that people don't shake hands. I didn't question that much. Is there something in your culture that you cannot shake hands?

PARTICIPANT We can.

MARIA I have seen people touching each other in your culture. This is a good point. A therapist needs to be aware of cultural ways.

QUESTION *This interview ended without you asking them to share their appreciations for each other. Why?*

I have been thinking about that. I like to end a family session with appreciation. I often ask everybody to give a piece of appreciation. The reason I didn't do it this time was simply because of the timing. I really wish I had done it because, if I had, it would have been nice for the mother to get appreciation from everybody.

I also was conscious of time because it was already more than two hours and, for me, a hug was a nice ending. My choice was to provide an opportunity to have an experience in hugging. This made it concrete. To put it in words again is a consideration. There are always more choice points. I think this is related to your own sense of security.

I think that sequence and timing are very important – what you do and when you do it – not only in therapy, but also in workshops. How much can people absorb? This time and situation is the only time I am here to see this family, once. I try to do one closure for one experience. All the other things can be followed up by the counsellor.

QUESTION *Did you purposefully not invite mother in?*

MARIA Regarding the mother. You said mother identified herself as an abuser and I purposely put her at a distance. I didn't put her at a distance. She chose to sit at a distance.

Yes. I purposefully accepted and respected where she was sitting because I did not want to spend a long process trying to get her back into the family. I did not want to get her back into the family in this way. That is a whole other piece. If she only moved her chair closer, that would not have much meaning. She would have done it if I had asked her. But I wanted her to be closer to herself in the rest of the session. When she came in, I would watch where she would want to sit.

She is an abuser. The teacher and the counsellor assumed the role of mothering in order to nurture the boy. Two other women took her role. I can imagine how bad and difficult this is for her to realize as a mother. I think where she put herself fit her. I found it very positive that she was sitting on the side where her son was sitting. I don't know whether it was the only chair available. I don't remember, but that's where she felt like sitting. Did I purposefully leave her at a distance? Yes. I think I gave her acknowledgement and some support. I think it was realistic that she belonged there, because the other three belonged together.

QUESTION *We noticed that you did not allow mother to be the focus. Why?*

MARIA I find this is a very good observation. I wanted to give her some recognition. I did not want the beating to become the focus of the session. It could be the focus of a session dealing with her family of origin. At the same time, not talking about it took away the chance for her to be labeled. I was thinking about this a lot when the counsellor was talking about her abuse. My opinion from what I heard about her abusing is really horrible. I did not want to emphasize it too much. In the Satir Model we do not go back to the trauma. The healing process is not talking about this traumatizing event but to focus on the change and her willingness to change, which is most important.

QUESTION *Why did you leave the negotiation to the end?*

MARIA The negotiation was the outcome of the whole process. I don't think the boy was ready at the beginning, even to talk. I asked him many times what he wanted. He had very interesting body language, moving his body and his head around. His body language didn't give me the impression that I would be able to talk to him, but I wanted him to talk to his parents to say what he wanted. He needed first of all a lot of support in the session from the two people, and he used them also as resources. I saw that he would talk to the father. The negotiations meant that he would become aware that things could change.

As well, I did not want to make the school problem a focus. The teacher could help him with that. The father learned that in a negotiation he had to give something in order to get something. I wanted the father to understand from his own experience that playing is important and happiness is important. From what I understand the father is a workaholic. He works very hard. He expects the same from his child. Therefore I also wanted a commitment that they would play together. I will always leave negotiations to a time when people are ready for it. I waited until the father became more open to it.

QUESTION *What would you do in the next session with the parents' family of origin?*

MARIA You suggested mother's family of origin in the next session, to sculpt the mother's family so that the son could understand the mother better. I would also be curious about the father's family of origin. It is always nice for children to hear about their parents' background. I think it would be therapeutic for the family.

I would explore father's family of origin, mother's family of origin and, if possible, do a family reconstruction. Definitely not in the first session. In the first session, you set the context. We need to know people's internal experience and what their expectations are, and what their yearnings are. We don't do family therapy and family reconstruction as a textbook. We wait for the appropriate opportunity to work with the family of origin. As I told you earlier, we know all these processes are available, but the timing is very important. The family is coming here with a lot of anxiety. Everybody here would have anxiety to bring their family here in front of 60 people, especially when a son has difficulty and the teacher is also present. Do I want to talk about my family of origin, especially I if I have been abused? You always set the context first. What is the context? Building their trust, their safety, relationship and connection with the therapist. Sometimes, if you have five hours, you can do a lot. But first you still have to set the context.

I want to respond to your suggestions. One was to "explore the boy's internal resources." I think we explored, to a certain degree, everybody's internal resources. Another suggestion was to sculpt his resources. Of course, this is always a possibility. It can be very helpful. You saw it the other day, yesterday. For the family today, the priority for me was for them to connect. Another thing is that the boy had two wonderful resources here with his teacher and counsellor being present. The teacher put forward all the boy's resources as a message to the parents that the boy was OK. The teacher talked in support of the boy. Is there anything nicer for a parent then to hear good things from a teacher? In addition the counsellor told us about his resources, and I mentioned a few. If I focused this first session on the boy's resources, it probably would connect the father more. Maybe it could have led to the negotiation but I wanted to work on the whole system, rather than just on the boy's. Again, timing is important.

Of course we could have sculpted the family in the present time so the mother could learn more. Yes, if that is what you chose, I think that would be fine, but you would have less time to do other things. All these ideas are here in our pockets. What you do and when depends on your priorities in the moment.

QUESTION *The boy was standing when he was talking to his father, while father was sitting. Do you find meaning in this?*

MARIA Yes, I wanted to empower the boy standing. Also you know the congruent position is standing. I think there is a respect for the father to sit, and in addition here we have a situation I wanted to create so that the boy feels empowered and can also be congruent.

QUESTION *What is your reason for asking the participants to say their names at the beginning of the interview?*

MARIA I have a reason for asking people to say their names, especially because of the grandfather. I don't know how he felt. I had an assumption that he would feel more comfortable hearing who you all are. The son was giving me the message with body language that he wanted that. Maybe he was very anxious. This gave him time to breathe and to get himself here. So I was willing to spend time doing that.

QUESTION *Why did you talk with the grandfather first?*

MARIA Well there were many reasons in my head. One is he is the oldest. He is not connected to the family by blood yet he made an effort to come here. He was very supportive to this family. I wanted to give special respect by asking him to talk first.

QUESTION *How could we do the follow-up sessions given that we already have two co-therapists for the family and told the family that this counsellor would join them. Would the three see the family together or two?*

MARIA The boy has a strong relationship with the counsellor. I don't think you can take this away from the boy. I think that it will be helpful, at least in the beginning, at the transition, to have the counsellor there, for a few sessions. Then discuss with him how long he wants to get her support in the transition. For the boy this is very important. Just as important as to have the teacher here.

QUESTION *Do you think there needs to be follow-up work on the couple's relationship?*

MARIA Yes. Definitely a need to work on the couple's relationship. I would even work on the couple's relationship two times separately. I think that was a very good comment.

QUESTION *The teacher is a wonderful resource. I am afraid if the teacher does too much, would she become a substitute for the mother, replacing the mother?*

MARIA No one can be a substitute for the mother. So she is very important, but she cannot take the place of the mother. I don't understand your question. She probably provides a lot of attention and love he misses from his mother. My picture is that he got so much from his teacher, compared to so little from his mother.

QUESTION *We have a hypothetical question. The boy admitted to feeling very pained when the mother beat him. But he said he did not want to talk about this anymore. Our experience with adolescent cases is that they usually do not talk about their pain. How do we work with them when they refuse to talk about their pain? We also would like to ask if it is possible that, in insisting that they talk about their pain, we may have them re-experience it and re-traumatize them?*

MARIA I would not push anybody, especially an adolescent, to talk and share. As a therapist you have many ways to connect verbally or non-verbally. An adolescent gets the message, non-verbally. They also respond, sometimes, to sculpting. Pushing them creates resistance because they have to protect themselves. You need patience, acceptance and understanding to work with adolescents. They respond to your non-verbal compassion. In the Satir Model, we do not re-visit the trauma because it is not positively directional.

# Chapter Nine
## THREE SISTERS AND AN ATTEMPTED SUICIDE: BREAKING THE SILENCE

## *Therapist's presentation*

The family in this interview comprises three sisters, aged 22, 26 and 34, their mother, her husband (the girls' stepfather), and the 26-year-old's husband.

The sisters' biological parents were married for 21 years but lived apart for 18 years. While they lived together they always had conflict.

When the youngest sister was born, her parents were disappointed because they wanted a boy. For four years she was raised by relatives of the mother. When she returned to her biological family she was not registered as a permanent resident. She felt rejected and without an identity, never having experienced belonging and acceptance by the family. The young girl felt close to the relative who raised her, but mother had negative feelings towards this person.

The biological father is described as irresponsible and a "bad guy." He doubted whether the young girl was his in fact his daughter, and divorced his wife and left the family when she was six years old.

The youngest, 22-year-old, sister is seen as the problem in the family. The 26-year-old is married and lives with her husband. The 34-year-old is married, with two children. She supported her whole family in a move from the country to Shanghai. They all live in one housing complex that the 34-year-old and her husband own. She and her husband provide financial support for the whole family.

The 22-year-old lives with her mother and stepfather. She adopted a wandering cat, with whom she closely identified. The cat reminded her of her own life of not belonging anywhere. When she was babysitting for her older sister, one child became allergic to the cat. Her mother insisted she had to get rid of the cat. This precipitated a suicide attempt and conflict within the family. The 26-year-old sister looked after her and took her to the therapist. This was the reason for the initial referral.

The therapist's hope was that I could help the 22-year-old in her relationship with her mother. The therapist shared that she herself had difficulty in communicating with this mother because she experienced her as strong and controlling.

## *The first interview*

COMMENTARY *I greet the family and tell them about the group's learning process. I also explain that we are aware of the previous interviews with their therapist. I invite them to sit down on the chairs provided for them. Mama sits between her husband and her oldest daughter. The 22-year-old and 26-year-old sit together, along with the 26-year-old's husband. I start by asking Mama what she wants.*

MOTHER I wish we had more harmony when we are together, and that we could work and live more happily in our daily life.

MARIA That's what you want?

MOTHER Yes, yes. Just like this.

MARIA Families have lots of similarities but every family is also unique. In your perception, what specifically needs to be changed in your family?

MOTHER I think my family is always quite good. I was a high-school teacher. My husband was also a high-school teacher. Our three daughters are all university graduates and make a good living in Shanghai. My sons-in-law are outstanding too. My family was in harmony but there was an issue. The therapist helped us and we worked together and we are now beyond this issue. I know we were lacking communication. We now can communicate better and we make everything clear, so we have re-established our relationship in the family.

MARIA [to the therapist] That's wonderful. I am proud of you. I am proud of you too, Mama. You have a close relationship with everybody in your family now.

MOTHER Basically, yes.

MARIA There is nothing more you want?

MOTHER No, not like this.

MARIA Then, I need to know what would make you feel even better, otherwise I cannot help you.

MOTHER "The issue" happened not long ago. Basically it is all resolved but in the future a similar "issue" could arise. I'd like you to give us some guidance so we can do better.

MARIA I hope this is not going to happen again. I believe if you resolve one issue, you can learn how to resolve it again in the future.

MOTHER After we learn from you we will be able to use a professional way to solve our little issues and we will have less trouble in the future.

MARIA I am happy to know that you feel like everything is resolved in this family. That's your perception, and this must be a good feeling for you.

MOTHER We will still have different issues in the future. We wish for more guidance and theory.

MARIA I understand. You are teachers [mother and father nodding], and I am also a teacher. When I see a family, I do not teach. I like you people to have an experience, because we learn from experience. From whatever you tell me I will try to help you to have an experience.

MOTHER We want experience too.

MARIA Good!

MOTHER We have the same wishes.

MARIA Good. You are open to new experience.

MOTHER Yes.

MARIA Good, I am happy to hear this. [Faces stepfather] Papa, is there anything you wish for?

PAPA She represents me, so I do not need to put it in more words. I agree with her. We wish to learn so in the future we can have your model to solve our problems.

MARIA Do you always agree with everything that Mama says?

PAPA Basically, yes.

MARIA Mama, life is easy for you because he agrees with you on everything.

MAMA Oh, it's not like this. He just agreed about what I just said.

MARIA He just agrees, he does not always agree with everything?

MAMA He does not. He only agreed with what I just said to you earlier.

MARIA But Papa just said he always agreed with you.

PAPA Only in the family perspective like this. Of course we have differences in other areas.

COMMENTARY *I now ask the other family members to comment. Everyone confirms that Papa usually agrees with whatever Mama says. When I say "Mama, you have it easy" I imply that she is in control. It is also obvious that Mama tries to paint a picture of them being a "good family" and clearly avoids mentioning the real issues; for example, the daughter's suicide attempt.*

MARIA [to the oldest sister] What were you looking for when you came here today?

34 SISTER I came here for my youngest sister. She had "an issue" lately. She received some therapy and she has made some good changes, but I don't know if she will be like this in the future because I have heard that this kind of situation could repeat itself. The patterns can go up and down.

MARIA What is your perception about her patterns? What are you concerned about?

34 SISTER Did the therapist tell you what happened to her in the past? She had a "certain behaviour." Maybe she had traumatic experiences in the family when she was young. I wonder if there is a better way for her to resolve her internal issues so she can be more grounded and it won't happen to her again?

MARIA You are worried about your sister.

34 SISTER Yes. I also think our family should be able to be united and in harmony, because we care for each other, but we don't know how to express ourselves emotionally. We only know how to be responsible behaviourally, but we never express ourselves. From this interview I hope we can solve some basic issues.

MARIA You would like to feel more open to say how you feel?

34 SISTER Yes. If this can help us to resolve the issue, I can do it.

MARIA What stops you saying to Mama how you feel right now? Is there any feeling you can share with Mama that you never said? Just try.

34 SISTER I am always thankful to my mother because she has done so many things for us.

COMMENTARY *By this point I recognize that everyone is talking around "the issue." The family does not know how to communicate clearly. I now intervene by asking the 34-year-old daughter to talk directly to mother.*

MARIA Tell her. Look at her. When you express appreciation to a person you must look at her.

34 SISTER [looking at the mother directly] I do appreciate everything you did mother, and our stepfather is a pretty nice person too.

MARIA Is this hard for you, when you express your feelings?

34 SISTER It's not too hard, but I am not used to doing this.

MARIA I really appreciate that you make an effort. Mama, how do you feel when you hear that?

MAMA All my daughters show very much respect to me, especially the eldest one. She was so helpful.

MARIA Turn to her and look at her.

MAMA [speaks to eldest daughter face to face] In the beginning, at the time when she got married, my two daughters were still young and studied at the university. Financially my eldest daughter helped me a lot and did lots for her sisters. [Maria reminds Mama to say "you."] When we moved from my hometown to Shanghai, I felt like we were upgraded.

MARIA Papa do you want to say something to her?

PAPA Similar. What she said represents me.

MARIA I see. You agree.

PAPA I won't say any more. Time is treasure.

MARIA [to the 34-year-old sister] What would you like to say to your youngest sister? What are your worries about her? Look at her.

34 SISTER I feel she has lots of strengths in her.

MARIA Say "you."

34 SISTER You have lots of strength in you. Maybe we have high expectations of you and maybe we didn't encourage you much. [Youngest sister starts crying.] We think she is very kind and pure. We validate her.

MARIA Can you say "you" directly to your sister?

34 SISTER We wish you have a good life, like me and like your other sister. We have a good family and a good life.

MARIA Can you simply say "I love you"?

34 SISTER I love you very much. We all love you very much.

MARIA Just say "I," not "we."

34 SISTER I wish you could live well. Sometimes I told you when I noticed that you are missing something, but I did not mean that I don't validate you. [26-year-old sister starts crying. Her husband is holding her hands.] Maybe you felt like our expectations were a pressure for you. But I really care about you. I love you and want you to live well.

MARIA [to youngest sister] Do you believe that she cares about you and loves you? [Youngest sister nods] What do you hope for today?

22 SISTER I wish we all would feel better when we are together.

MARIA How would you feel better? What do you need to feel better?

22 SISTER I don't know how to say it.

MARIA What do you need in order to feel you belong to this family? What do you need to know so you feel accepted? Everybody here wants to help you. I think it is very important to let them know how you feel and what is important for you. This is a good chance for you to let them know what really is important to you. Tell me. Is it hard to say? You are 22, so you are grown up. Do you feel you are grown up?

22 SISTER I am not really.

MARIA Not yet? Everybody has a dream. What's yours?

22 SISTER To have a good job and live well.

MARIA You don't have a good job now?

22 SISTER Not so smooth.

MARIA A good job is not the only thing in the life. What did you say just now, Mama?

MAMA She doesn't mean that she does not have a good job. She doesn't have enough experience to do a good job at her post.

MARIA That's your opinion.

MAMA Yes. She wants to do things well. She is hard working. She is now really working harder on this. She is quite positive in her life. After work, she goes to the gym, dancing, plays the piano and goes swimming. She had some issues before, because I did not have good communication with her. I did not communicate clearly to her. [Maria reminds mother to use "you" and to tell the daughter directly.] Actually we all love you very much and wish you could live well. As a mother, I was too strict on her and maybe I was not tender enough. In the future I will offer her some help so she will have less pressure.

MARIA Do you think that you have put too much pressure on her?

MAMA In the past I always had demands on her.

MARIA On every daughter or only her?

MAMA The same with all of them.

MARIA [to eldest sister] Did you have the same pressure?

34 SISTER Yes. My mother communicated with us less. Maybe she didn't have the time or knowledge to communicate with us when we had emotional problems. In our situation, my mother was almost a single parent looking after us and at the same time going to work. Maybe she did not have enough time.

MARIA I understand. You are the eldest one so you really understand your mother had a lot of things to do.

34 SISTER Especially after I had my own children.

MARIA Yes. Mama, you feel you have put too much pressure on your youngest daughter?

MAMA Not only her. I made the same demands of all three children.

MARIA And now? Now they are all grown up, you can relax.

MAMA My youngest one is not totally independent. She is not married yet, so I cannot relax yet.

MARIA You want her to get married?

MAMA I just wish she could do her job well and be totally independent. Of course I wish she could have her own family, then I would have less burden.

MARIA [To youngest sister] Mama is still worried about you and your job. What do you want? Do you want her to continue to worry about you or do you want her to leave you alone? When I was 22, I wanted my mother to leave me alone. My mother wasn't very happy to hear that, but I insisted on it. How about you?

22 SISTER I'd rather that she didn't control me so much.

MARIA I understand that. How does your mother control you? When we talk about control, there are two sides to this. She can control you only if you allow it. The other person has something to do with it. You see, if anyone wants to control me it is up to me whether I allow the control. You are 22. How do you allow Mama to control you? How do you do it?

22 SISTER I don't like that she tells me how to do everything, and how I should not do it. I don't respond. I just let her say whatever she wants to say and I just won't obey.

MARIA Good, that sounds good to me. You stand up for yourself. Tell Mama, "I don't want you to control me, and I can take care of myself." Would you tell her? I support you. Then I would like to know how Mama will respond to you.

22 SISTER I want to go out and make friends with people. That does

not mean I want to develop a deeper relationship with them. I always have a chance to grow when I am with people. I don't have to be only together with excellent people. I think everyone's life or perspectives are helpful to me.

MARIA You want to have freedom to make friends? That's something you want?

22 SISTER Yes.

MARIA Mama, how do you want to respond to that?

MAMA I want this. She can handle her own things well. I'd be very happy. I want this too.

MARIA Something we can talk about more today is how that can happen. Once this becomes her responsibility, the burden can be taken off your shoulder.

MAMA Yes!

MARIA I know. I am a mother too and I am a grandmother and great grandmother. As long as we have children we always worry about them.

MAMA All parents are the same.

MARIA Yes. But we have to learn to let go. She can make mistakes. People can learn from their mistakes. If you control her too much then she has no opportunity to learn.

MAMA Yes, we have to make mistakes and then we can be more successful.

MARIA Yes, that's true. This means wisdom. So let her fail. Let her go out with a bad boy, and then she can learn something from that.

MAMA She did not make friends with bad boys.

MARIA Then what do you worry about?

MAMA I always wish she made friends with better boys. Maybe that's a shared wish of parents. I will give her more freedom in the future. I did not control her. I just gave her some recommendations.

MARIA She feels controlled. You see the question is how you communicate. The communication is important, Mama. How did you give her your recommendation? How about your voice, and what did you add to your recommendations? It can easily become a demand rather than a recommendation.

MAMA Maybe that's how she feels. Actually I do not chatter like other old people. I don't have many demands on her. I often offer some recommendation when it is necessary. To a child, the adult will give advice. Any recommendation with good intention is to make her life better. It's not being selfish. As a mother I always want my children to live better.

MARIA [to 22-year-old sister] Do you want recommendations from her?

22 SISTER No.

MARIA She said no.

MAMA Then I will not give you recommendations anymore.

MARIA That's great, Mama. Congratulations!

MAMA Thank you.

MARIA You know, everybody heard it. Mama will no longer control or recommend. Is it difficult for you to do that? I really appreciate that.

MAMA It's not so difficult for me. If she doesn't want me to give her any recommendations, that means she's already grown up. At her age she should be independent and leave her parents and live by herself in another country.

MARIA [to 22-year-old] Very good, that's great. Now how do you feel with this freedom? This is a present. You just got this big present from Mama. How do you feel? Do you believe it?

22 SISTER At first I feel much more relaxed. I think there are two things: what you said, and you actually putting your words into action.

MARIA Yes, you are absolutely right. You know what I suggest to you? You have to give a little space to Mama. Because the old patterns will come back, she may forget about this deal and give you recommendations or use control. Anytime when she goes back to the old pattern, rather than getting upset about it you can stand up and say, "Mama I can take care of myself," to remind her what she just promised. Would you try to do that?

22 SISTER I think she is already lightened. I think it's a big change. It will be very helpful for our communication in the future.

MARIA Yes. I'll tell you more about communication. It seems to me you are all very smart and very fast learners. We will get back to this later. How about your elder sister? Have you heard everybody else's wishes? What would you like?

26 SISTER I often feel puzzled in daily life, because it looks OK from the outside, but I often feel pain inside. I want to explore why I feel pain. That's why I learn a lot of different approaches. I have learned a little but I am not able to be totally clear about it.

MARIA You feel some pain inside?

26 SISTER Yes.

MARIA What kind of picture can you give to that pain? How would that look?

26 SISTER Talking about my body sensation, I have some fear of losing my security and my family. If you ask me about the picture, I feel about 7 or 8 years old and can still vividly see the picture of my parents arguing. Even in daily life, whenever there is difference or argument in our family then I feel pain [starts crying and the youngest sister holds her hand]. When I see some people suffering from pain, or they hurt each other, then my pain is something I cannot overcome.

MARIA Right now whose pain are you worried about in this family?

26 SISTER I am worried about the picture I see of my younger sister, for one. My mother has another picture, and maybe my elder sister saw another picture.

MARIA You can look at everybody's picture right now. Are your tears for your pain or for your younger sister's pain?

26 SISTER For my pain.

MARIA You feel pain when somebody is hurting in the family?

26 SISTER Yes.

MARIA What is hurting you when somebody else is hurting?

26 SISTER I've been feeling insecure for a long time. There's nobody there for me when I am in the most difficult situations. That makes me feel that life could change negatively and might be destructive to my life. That's my fear.

MARIA You are in charge of your life. Who else do you think is in charge of your life?

26 SISTER If you are talking about the present time, it is when I have my own ideas, or my perceptions. They are different from my mother's and my elder sister's, yet I try so hard to satisfy them. This will cause big conflict within me and I don't know which choice is the right one.

MARIA You are grown up and you are married. You still feel that you have to live up to their expectations?

26 SISTER Yes.

COMMENTARY *She is still trying to live up to others' expectations of her. I encourage her to be responsible for her own choices.*

MARIA That means that you are still not grown up. In my thinking, being grown up means that you live up to your own expectations. Of course you can take their expectations into consideration, and you can believe in yourself, your own expectations, and be responsible for yourself. When we are children we want to live up to mother's expectations. We have to, but when we are grown up we know our own wishes and hopes. Do you worry that you didn't live up to Mama's expectation?

26 SISTER Are you asking which of my mother's expectation I did not live up to? I want to double check with you.

MARIA Yes. Tell your mother and sister that you have a perception that you did not live up to their expectations. Could you please be more specific? In other words, you feel that you are not good enough and in your perception you did not live up to their expectations.

26 SISTER Do you want me to tell them which one of their expectations I did not live up to?

MARIA Yes.

26 SISTER I need to have some courage to do this.

MARIA Yes.

26 SISTER I will try.

MARIA OK. Can he help you [pointing to her husband]? He can be your courage.

26 SISTER Yes.

MARIA Ask him to give you courage. [She holds her husband's hand.]

MARIA [to husband] Do you want to say something?

HUSBAND I have my own perceptions and my feelings. Because you are all senior therapists here, I am willing to speak this openly and frankly. From my personal perspective, I respect and love everyone here from my heart. I am willing to contribute everything I can to this family from my heart. So I start with the negative part first. There's a particular unique thing in this family. Usually we obey most of the opinions of my mother-in-law. When we resist what she wants, most of the time we fail. So can I say it more, Mama? [Mother-in-law says yes.] After I got married, the first two-plus years we lived with my mother-in-law. Later as we looked back, we felt it was the newly wed experience. For 18 months we lived together. We expressed what we wanted, but we failed. I just say the truth [looks at mother-in-law].

MARIA So what do you want? You say you failed?

HUSBAND We rented an apartment. We wanted to live there so we could have our own life privately. We tried very hard to meet their expectations so they wouldn't be sad or resentful. We could not express our thoughts or feelings. For me, I have to repress any negative comments. I have a strong reaction if they comment that I did not do well.

26 SISTER My husband is trying to say, there is a unique quality in my family members, including myself. It's difficult for us to disagree. For example, when he disagrees about my perception, then I think he does not care about me.

HUSBAND So for me to express different ideas in this family is a headache for me.

MARIA So there is a rule which is not verbalized. "Do not disagree with Mama." Is that true? You are afraid to disagree, right?

HUSBAND Yes.

MARIA [to husband] That's not only in your family; that's universal. The question is, who in the family are you afraid to disagree with? [Husband points to his wife and mother-in-law. Maria faces the 26-year-old sister] So you are learning from your Mama?

HUSBAND Now she has a big change. We can criticize each other and criticize ourselves now.

MARIA Did you move out?

HUSBAND Eighteen months ago.

MARIA How did you do that?

HUSBAND I bought a flat.

MARIA And then Mama agreed?

HUSBAND She agreed. She bought the house for us. Because I am just the son-in-law, inside of me I wasn't strong enough. From outside people thought this was a wonderful family, but something happened on August 1st to the youngest sister. That's a big bomb for us. Nobody expected it and we are still in panic over the "issue." I also have some concern about my wife. She is still impacted by what happened in the early years for her. It's not finished yet, but whatever was unfinished in the past still has influence on her in the present. She often feels pain and insecurity.

MARIA Do you have any suggestion?

HUSBAND I don't know how to deal with her pain and insecurity. In the past I tried to help her to get rid of it. Her parents had some conflict when she was young and later they divorced. She was transferred to different schools six times. Those events still have an impact on her now. I don't know how to deal with it.

MARIA I understand. [Turns to the 26-year-old sister] You said before you can't tell your mother and your sister how you feel in relation to their expectations about you, and that you feel you are not good enough in their perception. Tell them.

26 SISTER Not only then. I still feel the same thing now.

MARIA Tell them now. Tell them that you feel you are not good enough for them. Is that true? What do you think they expect from you?

26 SISTER [faces Mama and elder sister] I always feel I didn't do things well enough, especially when you make a comment to me. I feel painful.

MAMA What kind of comment?

26 SISTER For example, I feel hurt when my elder sister tells me that I am not grateful enough to her. She asks me how I can be concerned about what other people say about her. I said, "Because I love you." Whenever I wake up in the night I am not able to sleep, when I feel very painful, I will often remember what my sister said to me. For example, Mama arranges some traveling and I try to express my thoughts, but Mama does not value it. Then I feel painful.

MARIA Look at Mama and tell her, "You did not validate my plans."

26 SISTER [crying] Actually I really want to say I love you too much.

MARIA [stands up and goes to her] I will help you. It is easier when you stand up. Tell Mama. [Maria helps her stand in front of the mother, and mother also stands up.]

MAMA I want to know clearly.

MARIA Listen to her first. She has more to say. [Turns to 26-year-old sister] Look at Mama.

26 SISTER But I am grown up now.

MARIA [standing beside her] "I want to be grown up."

26 SISTER I feel I never AM myself. I only have you in my mind, including your family. Right now I want to have a clear boundary. I want to find myself.

MARIA "I want to feel I am grown up, and you can help me."

MAMA You have your own family now, and you live independently. I never get involved in your family.

MARIA [to Mama] She feels you did not support her growing up. That's her feeling.

MAMA That's her feeling. I really appreciate this daughter. She does well at work, and she has a good relationship with her husband.

MARIA Can you say "you"?

MAMA You can make a good life for yourself. [Maria puts their hands together.] I am growing older now. I cannot get involved so much. I'd rather you take care of your own things. Actually you are all grown up. You learned a lot of new things and you can follow your own ideas to arrange your own life.

MARIA Mama, I believe you. I believe what you are saying. I don't know whether your daughter believes you. Do you believe what mother was saying?

26 SISTER No, I don't.

MARIA I would like you to tell Mama what you don't believe. Mama says words, but words need to have meaning to you. Tell Mama what you need in order for you to believe that she really accepts your freedom. I believe her, and I want to share with you that you will only believe her when you start believing in yourself. You know, you cannot expect Mama to give you belief in yourself.

At this moment I would like you to close your eyes [she closes her eyes]. Go inside and check within yourself if you can value yourself, because only if you can value yourself and love yourself, then you can let Mama know. She can trust you. She has a grown-up girl, and will respect you being grown up. Check out what you feel. You can be responsible for yourself if you want to. [She nods.] You know you can value yourself and the self of you is now standing here with all your energy. Look at Mama and tell her, "I want to be responsible for me. I do not need your approval. If I get it I will be happy, but I will do my best to live my own life." Say it in your own way.

26 SISTER I am worried if I say things like this she will be angry.

MAMA Don't worry, I won't be angry.

MARIA Don't worry, I will take care of her. She can be angry but she can do nothing to you. You are not helpless.

26 SISTER I want her to be happy and not angry.

MARIA Do you feel angry now?

MAMA No, I am not. I am very happy to see she is grown up.

MARIA You see your Papa is smiling. [Looks at Mama] I don't see that she is angry. [Mama smiles.]

MAMA I am not angry. I won't be angry too. I tell you how I feel now. I am almost 70 years old. When I was young, I was busy at work as a single mother. I raised all three of them by myself. After work I had to take care of three children. When I got home, I never had my own life. Now I really have the life for myself. I really want to let go of my burden, so I am doing this now. When I was young, I liked swimming, playing piano, and lots of other physical activities that I liked to do, but I did not have time to do it. I am now trying to fulfill my own dreams, I am learning piano and dance.

MARIA [to 26-year-old sister] I believe her. I think your grown-up self can hear her, but the little child in you can't hear her. I would like you to believe what she said. You know there's a problem here. This is not easy, because Mama is letting you go. To be a grown up means you can no longer make her responsible for you. You can no longer be a victim. How about that?

26 SISTER Yes, I understand [nods and smiles.]

MARIA I believe you.

26 SISTER Thank you.

MARIA When I look into your eyes I really believe that you understand. Now as a grown-up person I want you to tell your Mama that you hear her and you will take that responsibility. I understand your Mama wants to have her own life.

MAMA Yes, I can't be responsible any more. It's too much for me. I am almost 70 years old. I just want to be healthy and not cause trouble for my children. To be honest, I am not able to take care of them anymore.

MARIA Mama you already did your job well. [Turns to 26-year-old sister] From now, you will be responsible for yourself. Feeling grown up means that you are OK to use your own eyes. Even if you are not totally OK in her eyes, you are still responsible for you and your life with your husband. It's a new beginning. Both of you are part of it, because it's easy to go back. Your therapist will help you. Can you make a commitment to yourself? First of all, you will be a 26-year-old grown-up woman? Tell your husband, so he doesn't have to worry about you and carry you on his back.

26 SISTER [holds husband's hands] From now on I will learn to be responsible for myself. I will not try to get approval from you, my mother, or others to do anything.

MARIA I have a warning; you are a partner. I don't want you to learn to control him like your mother controlled you. That was your experience with mother. It's easy to learn, because you have a "good" example. Mama needed to control. She was raising three children as a single mother. She needed that control, and now [turns to Mama] you needn't control, because you are free.

MAMA Yes, I do need freedom.

MARIA Yes, everybody in this family needs freedom. Even the freedom to say how you feel, because there's a rule in this family not to say how you feel. [To the husband] You know it well.

HUSBAND Actually, I do think my mother-in-law is very nice to us. She has lots of consideration for us.

MARIA Yes, you don't need to placate anymore.

HUSBAND We feel guilty if we disagree with her.

MARIA Ask her, "Can I sometimes disagree with you without guilt?"

MAMA It shouldn't be like this. They learn a lot and they see a lot. They are more advanced than me and they can have their own life.

MARIA Mama, there is interesting communication in this family. [To 26-year-old sister] You don't look at each other when you talk. [To Mama] You do not use "you" and often use "they" when you talk. [Three of them all laugh.] If you use "you" directly and look at each other when you talk, there's more connection.

MAMA Yes. [To 26-year-old daughter] In the future you can live your own life in your own way, I will not interrupt you. I wish to let go the burdens.

MARIA Mama, even if you say you won't interrupt, you will interrupt because you can't change overnight. When you interrupt, I want them to stand up and say, "Do you remember, Mama? We all have freedom in this family?" and not dropping on your knees and say OK. [Stepfather laughing, Maria turns to him] So you agree with that?

MAMA I want to share some of my perceptions. Sometimes I have some recommendations and that's my way to show my love. I wouldn't interrupt if I was just a stranger. I care for them, so I give recommendations.

MARIA I heard you. Will you also expect them to stand up for themselves?

MAMA I stopped recommending for a long time, because they have their own family now.

MARIA [22-year-old sister wants to say something] OK, it's your turn. Wait a moment. I just make a short conclusion. [Turns to 26-year-old sister and her husband] You can learn to stand up for yourself and not placate Mama. [Stepfather laughs.] You, Papa you like this, and it also related to you. Do you want to say something?

PAPA I have nothing to say.

MARIA So you agree?

PAPA Yes, I agree.

MARIA What do you agree to? I want you to verbalize.

PAPA They are grown up so they are just like a kite to fly off by themselves.

COMMMENTARY *It was a long process for the 26-year-old sister to stand up for herself and make this commitment. Later in the interview, I will encourage her to practice her commitment to value herself.*

MARIA [to 26-year-old sister] Can you make your commitment?

26 SISTER Yes, I do.

MARIA What's that? For you, it's a beginning. What is the commitment you need to practice? Tell me and all of your family. Put words to what you promise to yourself and to us.

26 SISTER I commit from now on. I believe my own value, and I am not going to judge myself. I won't be a crying little girl any more. I don't want to be a victim anymore. I will try very hard to be grown up and to be responsible for myself.

MARIA I am really proud of you. [To husband] Are you proud of her?

HUSBAND Yes.

MARIA [to the therapist] You remember that, and remember to remind them. [Holds 22-year-old sister's hand] You want to say something and I want to hear from you now. What do you want to say to Mama?

22 SISTER Mama, you said because you love us you give us lots of recommendations, but we should have a right to choose whether we want to obey or not.

MARIA Good! You see your Papa agrees with you.

22 SISTER Maybe because he is the person who has needed to obey my mother most.

MARIA I notice that. But that's his business and their business between them. Now I want to talk with you. How do you feel right now?

22 SISTER Very good.

MARIA Now tell Mama what you want for you?

22 SISTER First of all, from the perspective of my work, I'll try very hard to overcome my difficulties so I can get to a higher level. When I make friends, I only consider them as friends. They don't have to be my husband in the future, because I am still young. I don't want to get involved in any intimate relationship. So when I go out for fun I just want to be a friend with them, and won't marry them yet.

MARIA Do you want to be grown up like your elder sister and take responsibility for yourself totally?

22 SISTER I have always been very clear about this, because when I was young I did not live with my mother, so I often had to make decisions for myself. So I have different experiences than my elder sister.

MARIA You really learned to make decisions for yourself.

22 SISTER Yes.

PAPA She is more rebellious than her elder sister.

MARIA What do you call rebellious Papa? Saying "No"?

PAPA Yes, she did.

MARIA You like that.

PAPA Yes, I like it.

MARIA Other people don't say no to Mama. Do you ever say no to your wife?

PAPA Sometimes, but not much. I don't rebel so strongly.

MARIA You like her rebelling.

PAPA No. I say she has her own principles. It's good when the children have their own principles.

MARIA [to 22-year-old sister] You have a big support from Papa. Did you know that?

22 SISTER Now I know.

MARIA Mama, you did a great job, raising all these people, including your husband. Now you can let it go.

MAMA I feel relaxed. Finally I can put down my burdens.

MARIA You are like an army officer taking care of everyone in the family, so you learned to control very well. You can imagine when you let go you can do anything you like.

MAMA I've been thinking this every day, and wish all this to happen.

MARIA Good.

MAMA So much burden was on my back so my lower back became bent. I was always looking for how to let go of all these burdens. I am happy to see them all growing up.

MARIA They all want to be grown up. Mama, you used your energy to control. You can use your energy to be free now.

MAMA I will have my own life.

MARIA With him? [Points to stepfather.]

MAMA Yes.

MARIA Yes, good. Tell him how you will use your energy.

MAMA How can I have any energy? I am almost 70 years old. I am just teasing.

MARIA You can have lots of fun.

MAMA I will enjoy the later part of my life.

MARIA I am almost 92 years old and I like to have fun.

MAMA Yes, I like to have fun and I want to learn from you. I want longevity and to be healthy.

MARIA Sometime I really don't like what my children are doing. It's hard for me to say nothing. I try to do what I believe and they are very well without me. They can learn from their mistakes. I do not want to control them.

MAMA Yes, thank you.

MARIA [turns to 22-year-old sister] Now I am back to you. What do you want now? Your sister got freedom. Your brother-in-law is beginning to stand up and to say what he wants to say. Papa is starting to say what he wants to say. You can be happy to see that everybody is getting free. [She nods.] [To eldest sister] So how do you feel?

34 SISTER I have different feelings from them. Even though my mother is quite dominant, she is quite democratic in big issues. For example regarding our marriage, she will respect our choice even if she thinks it doesn't fit. Like my sister said, she felt pain because I said she was not grateful. Actually my version is that at that time we had an argument. My mother was there too. Sometimes when I communicated with my sister, she said she was feeling heavy. Other people think our three sisters are excellent. As for my second sister, I think she has a good job and good family. People envy her, and her parents-in-law are very nice to her. I think she should be very happy. Anytime when I have a conversation with her I sense she is feeling very heavy.

MARIA Yes, I feel that too, but she won't be like this anymore. What do you think of her commitment?

34 SISTER I am not sure if she can make it, because of her childhood experience.

MARIA That is in the museum, you know. I believe the experience in her early childhood was very painful. I suggest to you we don't need to carry it on our backs. [Turns to 26-year-old sister and 22-year-old sister] I want to say to both of you that we can put the past in the museum. [26-year-old sister nods and smiles.]

34 SISTER I want to say that I talked with my second sister. I told her a lot. She is often quite negative when she looks at things.

MARIA You didn't hear anything that has happened here right now? What you said is about yesterday. Tell me. Are you a lawyer or the judge in this family?

34 SISTER I am just thinking she needs to change her thinking.

MARIA No, she shouldn't do anything. She is on her own. You no longer need to worry about her. Would you let her be on her own without judgement?

34 SISTER She made the statement that I was hurtful to her.

MARIA It's hurtful to me too, because you did not listen to what is happening right now. She made a decision, a big one and you don't believe it?

34 SISTER I want to help her to find the reason she feels so painful. From the few things she told me, I analysed it, and I discover she has high expectations for people around her.

MARIA [to 26-year-old sister] OK, would you like to respond to her? She is like your judge. Do you need her to judge you? Will you stand up to her? This will be a good exercise, right?

34 SISTER [26-year-old sister stands in front of 34-year-old sister] I want to say I am not a judge. It's too serious. I am coming with good intention.

MARIA I believe you, but when you talk to her it sounds judgemental. Now tell her your good intention without judgement. I believe you have a good intention.

34 SISTER I don't understand how you can suffer so much pain. I want to help you to get out of the pain. Sometimes you ask people to do 100 per cent. If the person can't live up to your criteria 100 per cent, you will totally exclude that person.

MARIA What do you want right now with her?

34 SISTER Nobody can do 100 per cent.

MARIA Would you be able to talk about your feeling rather than giving her a lecture. You are good, excellent in lecturing, but we are not at the university. Tell her how you're feeling and what you want with her, your intention.

34 SISTER I wish you would appreciate how others are doing, rather than what they did not do.

MARIA OK, does that make sense for you?

26 SISTER I understand, but I disagree.

MARIA Would you tell her what you want in the relationship between the two of you?

26 SISTER I feel you totally misunderstood me. From your description I don't think you were talking about me but to somebody else. I am really working hard and I was very giving and loving. I wish you or Mama could just see it. That's enough, because I can take good care of myself.

COMMENTARY *Up to this time my intention has been to promote communication in this family. It is clear they protect themselves by avoidance and covering up. No one has used the word "suicide." It is referred to as "the issue." It becomes clear in the interview that feelings are not expressed. It is apparent there is love in the family and they want to be connected. However, they do not know how to express their feelings. Fear is a factor in holding back feelings and expectations. Everyone wanted to live up to Mama's expectations yet nobody felt good enough. Mama wanted a perfect family and worked hard for it. As a result, nobody felt perfect and everybody had low self-esteem. I believe that Mama understands that she needs to give up control.*

*I focused on communication and encouraged each person to stand up for themselves to say what they want. This was the very beginning of change, therefore it was difficult for all of them. In summary, I tried to engage them in what Satir called The Third Birth, that is, becoming a responsible choice-maker, valuing self and accepting their parents as people rather than as roles.*

*I thought that the 26-year-old was now in a better place, and we had spent most of the interview helping her to express her feelings and hopes. I knew that the 34-year-old wanted more clarification with her younger sister. I had two concerns at this point. One was that I didn't want to go a step back in the process with the 26-year-old. There was no time to discuss the relationship between the 26-year-old and the 34-year-old. My greater concern was to include the youngest sister, who, to this point, had not received much attention in the interview.*

*I realized later that the oldest sister felt that I had cut her off and that she had had no opportunity to deal with her feelings. My assumption was that she, as the oldest, was more mature, and would have understood that the youngest sister needed time to work. Later, I found out that the older sister felt left out and was hurt. I also realized that I did not explain to her what my intention was in stopping the dialogue with her. After the interview I knew there was unfinished business between myself and the oldest sister. Moreover, there was more work to be done with the entire family. Following the interview, I asked the therapist to send a message to the family, inviting them for a second interview.*

MARIA OK, I would like to stop this right now because I will get back to the youngest sister. [To the 22-year-old] I am concerned about your feelings right now. How do you feel about everything? Do you believe that Mama will give you freedom?

22 SISTER I believe it.

MARIA Will you take your freedom and be responsible for yourself?

22 SISTER Actually I am always free, because Mama will tell me what to do and I will listen but I won't obey. That's the difference between me and my elder sister.

MARIA You say that you won't obey, because you are grown up, but you should be responsible for yourself.

22 SISTER Yes, I understand.

MARIA I think they are all worried about you because everybody was suffering from the "event" on August 1st, including you.

22 SISTER It is a very complicated event. It's only a result.

MARIA I understand it's only a result. It's only a symptom. Your suicide attempt conveyed the message to everybody that you are unhappy.

22 SISTER Actually, it was only an intention. I didn't actually commit suicide. It was just an attempt.

COMMENTARY *My intention now is to teach the family how to express their unspoken painful feelings rather than hurting themselves. To support the youngest sister in expressing herself, I guide her to discover and own her internal resources.*

MARIA I am really happy to hear that. Now I want you to tell Mama, Papa and your sisters too. What was the message you wanted to convey. Rather than doing it, you can talk about it. Mama, do you want to know? [Mama nods.]

[To 22-year-old sister] I'll support you, and I think everybody else will support you too. Tell Mama what you never told her before, so you can get rid of your pain. I can imagine it's painful for you to think about it ... [she looks down] ... that you couldn't always be a member in this family. But you are now. I think Mama tried to take care of you, because she wanted to make up for all those years. [22-year-old starts crying and 26-year-old stands behind her.] You tell her what kind of hurt is in your heart and you no longer need to give them your message in that funny way. You see your elder sister supports you, and you told me you have lots of resources. Tell Mama what resources you've learned. I want you to look at me [22-year-old sister nods and looks at Maria. Maria looks into her eyes]. I believe absolutely that when children have difficult times they learn to survive and develop many resources. Tell me, how did you survive? What resources did you have? You already told me about freedom [22-year-old sister nods]. I want to hear you.

22 SISTER Yes, I made decisions for myself and I stuck to my decisions.

MARIA I like to make pictures that help us to understand ourselves. I want you to choose somebody to role play each of your resources. You needed to survive, and you were not always in this family when you were young, so choose somebody as your Freedom.

22 SISTER Are you talking about a person?

MARIA Yes. The people who will represent your resources, so you can really feel and touch all those wonderful resources you have. Then you introduce them to your family. Choose somebody to act as your Freedom. [22-year-old sister points to a man.]

COMMENTARY *My hope is for the youngest sister to access and appreciate her resources. I make the assumption that she has many resources because she survived. I also want the family to see her resources so they can develop an appreciation for her. She chose Freedom, Decision Making, Hardworking, Optimistic, Strength, Learning. These are resources which helped her to survive. I suggested that she also has resources which helped her to survive, but may no longer be necessary. We could transform the energy of those resources to become more helpful in the present.*

*When she chose her mother to role play Loving I suggested selecting*
*someone else because I wanted her to communicate with her mother*
*later. She also added Hope as her foundation, because she wanted to*
*build her life in a different way. She also commented that she can make*
*good decisions.*

22 SISTER Because I can make many decisions quickly I think I am
very strong.

MARIA This can sometimes include even wrong decisions.

22 SISTER I don't think I made any wrong decision.

MARIA OK, OK, I believe you. How about your strength?

22 SISTER Just because I am so strong, I can survive.

MARIA Yes, you did. So would you be proud of yourself?

22 SISTER I am quite proud of myself.

MARIA I think you can be. And hardworking?

22 SISTER The hardworking can help me to have a better life.

MARIA You are hardworking?

22 SISTER Yes.

MARIA Then continue. Learning.

22 SISTER I always try very hard to learn.

MARIA [points to Loving] This is another foundation?

22 SISTER Lots of people love me. They may not use the right method,
but I know that they do love me.

MARIA Don't you love yourself?

22 SISTER I love myself more now, but in the past I think I was miserable. Right now I feel I am very confident.

MARIA Can you be proud of yourself?

22 SISTER Yes.

MARIA I think you have every reason to be proud of yourself, because you have all these resources. Your family members probably didn't see all this and worried about you, because they do not know you. I am doing this to let them know who you are, so they can stop worrying about you. Would you like that?

22 SISTER Yes.

MARIA You are no longer the scapegoat in this family, because people worry about the scapegoat. A very strong family like this one would need to worry about someone. You need to let them know they no longer need to worry about you. I want you to talk to your Mama first, who you love so much. Mama, I would ask you to listen first, and then you can say what you want to say.

22 SISTER I never told you I love you very much. Actually I knew when I was young, because you gave so much to us. [Crying and 26-year-old sister supporting her] You went through lots of difficult and painful times.

[Maria asks Hope and Strength role players to put their hands on her shoulders.]

22 SISTER I am thankful to you. Actually I am already grown up. I can make decisions well. I can be responsible for myself, and actually, you don't need to worry about me so much. I think I can handle lots of things well.

MAMA [tears in eyes] I believe what you said, I believe you. I always had confidence in you. You have lots of resources and that event happened because of some reasons there. I understand about this.

[To all participants] I would thank all of you to support our family. I believe this daughter is grown up and will become more mature from this event. I wish you can really keep your commitment and manage yourself much better so we won't worry.

MARIA Can she have freedom?

MAMA I'll give her enough freedom. I always respect her.

MARIA Do you feel she will give you enough freedom?

22 SISTER I will ask for it.

MARIA OK. You will always stand up to Mama.

22 SISTER I will.

MAMA I know this daughter loves me. All my three daughters love me and I love them very much too. They were everything for me. I almost forgot myself in the past. I am very happy I can let go all the burden. I always wished to be myself and live for myself. That's the wish I always have in my mind. I wish my children would also return my freedom back to me. At the same time I was controlling you and you were controlling me too. Actually I feel like I am bound by you too. I have my own ideal and my dreams, but I kept telling myself I had better live for my children. I would be very thankful if you give my freedom back to me. Thank you for this Maria. Thank you everybody for your support to our family. I sincerely thank you.

MARIA [points to 34-year-old sister] What do you want to say to this sister?

22 SISTER Before I got sick, we didn't communicate much, but I sense the changes between us. I feel it's already very good now. I love you very much and I also know that you love me very much.

MARIA [points to 26-year-old sister] What do you want to say to your other sister? Now both of you are grown up.

22 SISTER [They hug each other and Mama hugs them at the same time.] You offered me the biggest support in this period of time. I am thankful both of us are mature people now.

MARIA And to Papa.

22 SISTER You are a very important person for our family because you, Papa, supported us. We love you very much too.

PAPA I love all of you too.

MARIA Now I would like you to do one more thing. I will ask each of you. I will start with you first [to the 22-year-old]. You sculpt the picture of how you want this family to be, how close, how far, and how you want to connect, because everybody in this family is standing on their own feet, nobody down, nobody up, that's what you hope for.

Now I ask everyone to stand up to sculpt your picture. Each of you may have a different one. How do you want to show your connection? Who do you want to be closest to?

COMMENTARY *The 22-year-old sculpts her family members as follows: The 26-year-old sister stands close beside her and the 34-year-old stands on the other side. The brother-in-law stands behind the 26-year-old sister, Mama and Papa stand in front of her, facing her.*

MARIA [Mama approached them too closely] Not too close, not too close. So that is your picture?

22 SISTER Yes.

MARIA When Mama forgets her commitment, she tries to control. Each of you remember to stand up instead of going down on your knees and placating.

22 SISTER I don't know how to placate.

MARIA Good. [Points to the 26-year-old sister and 34-year-old sister] She knows how to placate and she knows how to placate too. You each need to communicate in a new way in the family. Mama knows how to blame, but don't worry. She won't do that anymore. If she does, then discuss it. [Turns to 26-year-old sister] Now how about your picture? What kind of connection do you want? [To the husband] You stand behind her.

COMMENTARY *The 26-year-old sister sculpts her family. They all stand holding hands, with everyone connected and equal. She puts her husband in front of her.*

MARIA It's nice, so you want everybody to be connected.

26 SISTER Yes. And we are all equal.

MARIA Equality is very important, nobody kneeling on the floor. In my picture of you earlier, you were kneeling down on the floor, being small.

26 SISTER What if somebody gets angry?

MARIA You just say, "I feel angry." Your therapist will teach you more about communication. [To therapist] They all need to learn communication tools, looking into each other's eyes and when they are talking

308 SATIR FAMILY THERAPY IN ACTION

to each other using "you" not "her." [To 34-year-old sister] How about your picture? How close and how far do you see people in the family?

COMMENTARY *The 34-year-old sister sculpts her picture as the three sisters standing side by side and close to the parents.*

MARIA [points to the 26-year-old sister's husband] Where is he? You forgot about him.

34 SISTER Put husband standing behind my sister.

MARIA OK, Mama, it's your turn. What's your picture?

MAMA It's just like this [points to the 34-year-old's sculpt].

MARIA How about Papa?

PAPA I agree. It's so good.

MARIA It's very interesting. In this family there has to be at least one person to agree with everybody and that's Papa. Thank you for sharing about yourself. I hope you learned something and you will use it. [22-year-old sister nods.] Your therapist will continue to help you. I wish that sometimes you would see your therapist all together. [Asks the therapist] How do you feel about seeing them together from time to time? They need to learn to talk to each other. They love each other; they just don't know how to express their love to each other. What would you like to tell them?

THERAPIST I want to congratulate you because you made a great decision coming here together. I feel touched by you in the process, because I have been working with you for the past two months. This was the first time that you all came together. I can see lots of positive resources in each one of you and lots of good intentions. I feel certain places got unblocked today. I am willing to work together with you.

COMMENTARY *The 26-year-old sister took pictures of the resources role players. They were then de-roled. I then asked the family if they would like to hear feedback from the group. The participants offered their feedback and we concluded as follows.*

MARIA I'd like to thank you for coming. I was very touched by your honesty and your willingness, and using every possible way to get what you want and what you need. I'd like to ask you, "Do you believe that change can happen now for everybody in this family?" [To the son-in-law] Because you are like an observer, will you feel free to speak up when you notice they are not congruent with each other?

HUSBAND Yes, I will.

MARIA Yes. Even to Mama?

HUSBAND Yes.

MARIA Good. Even to your wife?

HUSBAND Yes. We have no problem now. I think sometimes the issue is not an issue anymore.

MARIA I wish you well and I know you will continue to see your therapist. You requested a copy of this video and you can get it when it's finished. I think it is a very good idea. It's very good learning to see it again. Thank you Mama [shaking hands with Mama].

MAMA Thank you Maria.

MARIA [shaking hands with Papa] Thank you Papa. [Shaking hands with 34-year-old sister] Thank you. I hope you have more faith. Things can be changed. I understand that you are really concerned and really love them. Give them more space.

34 SISTER I believe that, because after the therapy I already see some changes here.

MARIA Good.

34 SISTER Thank you.

MARIA [shaking hands with 22-year-old sister] Thank you. You remember all your resources.

22 SISTER I will. I am also very grateful to you. I feel I grew up a lot today. Thank you.

MARIA Continue to grow up. [Shaking hands with 26-year-old sister] You too, I believe you will. [Shaking hands with her husband] You remember to speak up.

HUSBAND I will. Thank you.

MARIA [shaking hands with therapist] Thank you. This only happened because you've done a lot of good work with them. You made all the steps to make this possible. Let me clap for them.

COMMENTARY *After this interview I felt incomplete with the older sister. I requested to meet the family again so we could complete the unfinished business. I asked the therapist to approach the family to set up another interview. This took a fair bit of negotiation. I understood that Mama agreed to come back but the oldest sister felt misunderstood and hurt and hesitated to come back. I insisted that the whole family needed to come back. This negotiation became part of the process with the family. We did see the family a second and third time.*

## Evaluation notes

Following is my assessment of whether this interview utilized the goals, basic elements, and directives of the Satir Family Therapy Model as outlined earlier in this book.

EXPERIENTIAL
Throughout the interview I consistently taught the family to talk directly to each other and freely express what they want. I used sculpting to help the youngest sister to access and appreciate her resources, and for the family to recognize them.

SYSTEMIC
This is a very complicated system. At one level they are enmeshed. Everybody worries about the others, especially about living up to Mama's expectations. On another level, they are disconnected because they are afraid to communicate and put words to their real feelings and yearnings. Everybody has good intentions. Mama had to prove that this is a "good" family. She used control to make sure that the system functioned well. Each child paid the price in order to be perfect. The oldest sister was Mama's support and helped them financially, if not emotionally. She became Mama's assistant. As a result, the 26-year-old had two mothers to report to and couldn't be

good enough. After being rejected by the family, the 22-year-old had to develop survival resources. Through her suicide attempt, she was the one who gave the signal that the family needed help. I experienced the 22-year-old as being the healthiest one in the family. There is no doubt that love and yearning for connection are there at a deep level. Their lack of skills in communication creates internal stress and unhappiness.

## POSITIVELY DIRECTIONAL

I acknowledged and appreciated what Mama has already done for the family and that she now deserves to build her own life. I support everyone to talk openly about what they want to change rather than going to past examples where there is controversy. The most important thing here is that we are not discussing the specific negative circumstances such as suicide, divorce, Mama's difficulties and all the other challenges they have experienced. I reframe these into positive energy, available resources and focus for future connection.

## FOCUS ON CHANGE

Everyone in the family wanted change, but they were not aware that the change would need to happen within themselves. They also were not aware that change would require learning congruent communication and expressing their feelings. I believe that change happened with Mama when she realized that she had done her work in raising her daughters, and has the right to "freedom" and to live her own life. Theoretically she gave herself that permission, but in practice, she will have to learn how to let go of control. In this family the tool for change is to learn congruent communication and to function from a level of high self-esteem.

## THERAPIST'S USE OF SELF

Throughout the interview I offered examples from my own life to connect with and educate the family members. For example, I shared with the 22-year-old my own experience that at 22, I didn't want my mother telling me what to do. Another example is when I shared with Mama that I was also a mother, a grandmother and great grandmother. I often used physical touch and holding hands to make contact and support. I was congruent with the oldest sister when I shared that it was hurtful to me when she didn't believe her sister. I was also congruent in recognizing that the older sister might have been hurt because she felt ignored in the session. In my message to them after the interview, I acknowledged this by letting them know I was aware there was unfinished business between the oldest sister and me, and would like to meet with them again.

RAISING SELF-ESTEEM

In this interview I put a lot of energy into encouraging the 26-year-old to value herself. With the 22-year-old, my intention was for her to value herself through experiencing her resources and I encouraged her to speak up with what she wants. Unfortunately, I did not help the oldest sister to validate herself more, since I did not give her the time and opportunity to express herself as she wanted to. Mama did validate herself for raising her children as a single mother and working a full-time job. However, she didn't value herself for who she was. I encouraged her to pay attention to her own needs for the rest of her life. I think she got the message. The husband of the 26-year-old sister had high self-esteem. He was congruent and could see the issues resulting from lack of communication. He felt secure enough to speak up congruently. Papa's survival is placating and keeping the peace in the family. It is possible that his choice might come from high self-esteem if he is congruently aware of his placating stance.

FOSTERING SELF-RESPONSIBILITY AND CHOICE MAKING

This is the intended direction in every intervention. What we did in this interview is only the beginning of awareness that each person can be responsible for themselves and make their own choices, even if someone else disagrees. I hope that self-responsibility will increase as they become more secure in themselves. Some examples of fostering self-responsibility and choice making include encouraging Mama to live her own life, supporting the 22-year-old to share her expectations with Mama, encouraging the 26-year-old to value herself and encouraging the 34-year-old to recognize that she was being judgmental and expecting people to change according to her opinions.

FAMILY OF ORIGIN

I did not focus specifically on family of origin, but it is apparent that the sisters have all been impacted by their biological parents' relationship, which was filled with conflict and abandonment.

FACILITATING CONGRUENCE

I demonstrated congruence by challenging Mama, at the beginning of the interview, to be genuine about what she wanted. By challenging her in this way, I opened up the possibility for everyone to express themselves more freely. I welcomed and utilized the son-in-law's congruent feedback, in helping his wife to express herself. When it was difficult for her I used my presence in connecting with her to encourage her to communicate directly.

At various points in the session, I felt comfortable in sharing my thoughts and feelings. I encouraged the family to be free and happy rather than trying to live up to expectations of perfection.

I was congruent within myself when I recognized that the older sister might have been hurt because she felt ignored in the session. I acknowledged this by letting the family know I was aware of unfinished business between the oldest sister and me, and that I would like to meet with them again.

***

*Second interview*

COMMENTARY *Before the family came into the room, I shared with the group that there was unfinished business between myself and the oldest sister. At the end of the first interview, I observed that she looked sad and concerned but I could not spend more time with her then. I asked the therapist to invite the family for a second interview to continue the process. Initially there was some hesitation from mother and the 34-year-old sister. There were several exchanges between the therapist and the family before they decided to come back. The 22-year-old and 26-year-old expressed their appreciation. The 34-year-old had been unable to sleep and felt sad.*

*After I greeted the family and they sat down, I shared my feelings.*

MARIA After you left I had two feelings. One was that I felt very good about your family and the changes you want to make. The other was that I felt unfinished and concerned.

[Talking to and facing 34-year-old sister] I did not have more time to continue to talk with you. I very much appreciate that you came back. I also would like to tell you something I believe. When change happens, especially when the change relates to our internal feelings, we make decisions for change and something happens within us. We call that chaos. If any of you feel chaotic, I am sorry to say be happy about it and stay with it, because out of chaos comes change. There is no change without chaos. There are old ways to look at things, and old patterns we have used to relate to each other. The new way has to be integrated, and this integration feels uncomfortable and chaotic. There is a lot of anxiety, because we go from a known place to an unknown place; from a predictable place to an unpredictable place. You made lots of new decisions. You decided to stand up. [Points to the husband; he nods]

[To 26-year-old sister] You too. That's a big change. Mama decided to give you freedom.

[Facing Mama] That's also a big change, because you all are loyal in the family and you love each other. You did a very big piece of work and you made some new choices [to 22-year-old sister; who nods] and I am sorry I did not have much time to talk with you [34-year-old sister]. There were a lot of changes discussed and you may have felt left out. I saw your tears and I felt your sadness. I want to tell you that I worried. I asked the therapist to send you and Mama a message that we need to talk again. I hope we can look at the chaos and get some understanding, and accept the changes you want to make. That's my hope. I would like to thank you for taking the time again, and also to the group, because we are seeing a family for a second time.

[To the therapist] I also want to thank you for all the phone calls you have made.

I want to tell you that if I saw you at home or in my office, two things could have happened. Maybe we would continue; usually I would do that. In my own office I leave much time for the family, or would make another appointment. I am glad that we are here for another opportunity.

[Turns to 34-year-old sister] I know that you talked with the therapist a lot. First I want to ask you what you hoped for when you decided to come here today?

34 SISTER I've been thinking a lot in the past two days, and I went through a lot too. If I talk about what I felt yesterday, the therapist

said that you have resolved the issue for my 26-year-old sister and resolved some issues in our family. But I went through a lot yesterday and today. I discovered that I need to change lots of pieces in me so I came here for me, for my younger sister and also for my family.

MARIA Thank you. I will be back to you later, and I will ask Mama now. [Turns to Mama] Thank you for being here Mama. What could make it better for you? How are you doing?

MAMA I want to appreciate you taking so much time to help us to resolve our issues at home. This time I was not prepared for coming here. Later I still decided to come, to see if we could resolve our issue better.

MARIA Right now how do you feel being here?

MAMA Sitting here I feel grateful from my heart to all of you, and I was thinking a lot in these past two days too.

MARIA That's good that you are thinking about that.

MAMA Yes, when I was here last time I did not feel any pain, but when I got back home I felt I was quite hurt.

MARIA Could you say more about that?

MAMA Our family was already a very special family in the past. I was quite hurt when I stayed with the father of the three of them. I felt the sky was falling apart when I separated from him, because of the three children I had to sustain. I felt I had to protect the three of them, to be the father and mother at the same time. I was protecting them under my wings. I protected them in rain and wind, when there were knives and swords. Yet they still feel so hurt, and when I heard this, somehow my wound opened again. I also wanted them to support me after they grew up. I want to know that I can lean on them when I am feeling tired. They can treat me how I treated them – sometimes to be my shelter from the rain and wind. When I see them so vulnerable now, I do feel very sad. I also wish the three of them can be united together and be friendly to each other. They were like that in the past. Before the two younger ones grew up, my oldest one did help them a lot. When something happened to my youngest daughter in August, my second daughter also helped me a lot. She took lots of responsibility on my behalf. I feel grateful to them in my heart. But sometimes when I see them having an argument or attacking each other, or one of them feels hurt, I feel very sad. I hope they can be strong, and then I could lean on their shoulders when I feel tired. Thank you very much.

MARIA Thank you for sharing this, Mama. I would like to say something to you.

MAMA OK.

MARIA Last time when you were here, I did not know your family myself and I think everyone understood very clearly how much you did for your family. You said they are vulnerable. I don't look at it as a bad thing. I think that they are just being honest and sharing. I respect their vulnerability, because when we can share our vulnerable parts we can connect in the family on that level. Usually we protect our vulnerabilities, then we don't know each other. So I say the vulnerability they are sharing is a recognition and a beautiful example of how much they love you and trust you. I am very touched when my son tells me how he feels, whether it is sad or happy. I believe they are all wonderful including you.

You were talking about your first husband you divorced. I don't think that was mentioned but maybe you felt that was sort of implied. They are all grown up and they know what you did. I learned from my teacher that each of us needs a museum, and past hurts and events that we don't want to visit every day can be put into the museum. That part of your life can go into the museum. If you could do that you will feel much more peace, all of you. Maybe something sad happened, but your hard work is appreciated by everybody here. That's how I heard you and that was my impression. I think I can talk for the whole group that we respect your family so much and we are all happy to connect with you. Believe me, I am not just saying this. That comes from my heart to you. We all have past history in our lives, and some of it needs to go into the museum. I have a big museum, but I do not visit it often. I even wrote a book to let it go. I hope all of you are able to do that. We just look at the good things that happen in our life. What do you think? [Looks at the stepfather].

PAPA Very good. I agree.

MARIA Agree with what?

PAPA I agree that the history is history, and we put it into the museum. We want to look forward, not backward.

MARIA Your responsibility will be to remind Mama every day. When she thinks about bad things in the past she needs to put it into the museum.

PAPA I told her the past is over, and don't think about it again. [Points to 22-year-old sister] When we came together, she was only 8 years old. [Points to 26-year-old] She was 11 and was in grade 5. I treat them as my own children. I never beat them or scolded them either. I myself have three daughters who are all grown.

MAMA Maria, I am doing it myself too. Maybe I did not like to look back. I did not think about it often. We talked about it together yesterday, and then somehow automatically it triggered me to the past.

MARIA Today everybody will put the past into the museum.

MAMA Yes, yes.

MARIA And we celebrate the present.

MAMA I'd like to move forward, I don't like to look back. We can see hope and confidence when we look forward, then we can move forward more steadily. Thank you for all your understanding. I will do this.

MARIA Mama, I think the last session triggered in each of you some issues from the past. My approach is towards the present and the future, not the past. We can deal with the past and put it into the museum. Sometimes we need to acknowledge it first, and then put it into the museum. I believe this is what the chaos was about in last two days.

MAMA Let me say something. Because the children are feeling wounded, their hurtful feeling is related to that, and even their vulnerability is related to that. So what happened in the past came to my mind again. This is automatic.

MARIA Yes, and talking about it puts it out in the open, and will help us to put it into the museum. Just acknowledge it. As your husband said, the past belongs to history.

MAMA Thank you.

MARIA [to 22-year-old sister] How are you feeling today? What happened to you in the last two days?

22 SISTER I walked on the street with my eldest sister for a whole day, and I went to work this morning. I understand that a lot of things are happening in my eldest sister. She is stronger and wiser than I imagined. I hope that she will have more interaction with my 26-year-old sister. I am talking about interaction from heart to heart. Because they often talk about events, the more they talk about events the more hurt they feel. But those events happened out of good intentions. They were all considerate of the other person, but they didn't show their good intention. So it looks like they are blaming each other on the surface. I think we need to change our communication in this family.

MARIA You bring up a very important subject. I would like to tell all of you that we cannot change the events that happened in the past. It's already there, but we can change their impact. What we are talking about here is the impact. It's our choice whether we keep the impact of the past event to influence our present. We need to talk about it and say, "I don't allow this impact to poison my present because it's not helpful. It doesn't change the event." So you have to put the past in the museum. It seems to me you did.

22 SISTER Yes. I think I am quite positive.

MARIA Yes. I am impressed. You wish that your two sisters could communicate better. I know your wishes. [To the 34-year-old sister] I know your wishes too. [To Papa] I know Papa is supporting my idea about the museum. [Facing 26-year-old sister] When you came here today I asked you how you feel today and you said you do not feel very good. Can you say more about that?

26 SISTER Maybe I was in the chaos, like you describe. I discovered it's easy to commit but it's very hard to actualize it.

MARIA Yes. Because change is step by step and creates chaos. You know that what we discussed here is the beginning and we need to practice, practice, practice. Like you and your husband, if you want more communication with each other, if you want to be more open, remember that it will not come without any effort. I would like to know your wish and how I can help you to connect with your sister. What is the barrier between you and your sister? [Turns to 34-year-old sister] Do you know?

34 SISTER I did feel sad two days ago, because I have lots of things I need to change in myself. I did not understand why my 26-year-old sister feels so much pain, but now I can understand. I discovered that she is trying to pay a debt. Maybe that's the feeling she has. She is carrying this debt from whatever I said or other people said. I want to tell her this.

MARIA I want to ask you two to do something. Could you please move your chair here and talk to each other face to face? Otherwise it's impossible to communicate. [26-year-old sister and 34-year-old sit face to face. Maria asks 22-year-old sister to sit behind 26-year-old sister to support her. Mama sits behind the 34-year-old sister to support her.] This time I want you to be very open and congruent.

COMMENTARY *I encourage the two sisters to hear each other, and connect the two of them at a level of feeling, rather than what they believe their obligation and responsibility is to each other. Feelings have not been expressed in this family. I need to teach them step by step to hear the meaning beyond the words and the feeling behind the unspoken words.*

34 SISTER I want to tell you, what I did in the past was I tried to be responsible, and what I did was for my mother. That's all.

MARIA OK. [To 26-year-old sister] What do you hear? What did she say? I want to be sure clearly what you hear is what she said. What did you hear your sister say?

26 SISTER I heard her say ...

MARIA Please use "you said."

26 SISTER Actually I still have mixed feelings and I am still in chaos, so I was not fully present.

MARIA You didn't hear what she said. [To 34-year-old sister] Would you please say it again, because it's very important that you start hearing each other. [To 26-year-old sister] Thank you for being so honest.

34 SISTER I think what I did say was just being responsible and I did things for our mother. I hope you don't take this as your burden.

MARIA What did she say?

26 SISTER She said I just did what I should have done.

MARIA That's not what she said. I want you to hear exactly what she said because it is so important. She says it from her heart. I think you do not listen to each other. Would you tell her again?

COMMENTARY *I need to use slow motion, step by step, with patience, to teach them how to hear each other.*

34 SISTER I feel she understood me even though the words are different.

MARIA Please tell me what she said. I don't know whether she heard you.

34 SISTER I think she feels burdened about everything I did. I wish she would let go of that burden.

MARIA [to 26-year-old sister] Do you hear her? What's your response? What can help you to let go of your burden? Tell her.

34 SISTER If we talk about giving and receiving, to be honest it's not fair to either one of us. I want to say more. If we are talking about giving and receiving, I am also receiving. I know you did a lot for me and I am grateful for that. What you did for me is unique. Nobody can substitute what you did for me.

MARIA I don't know. Can you tell me what she thinks she owes you?

34 SISTER I think she felt very heavy inside because she thinks she owes me. She doesn't feel equal with me.

MARIA [looks at 26-year-old sister] Is that true?

26 SISTER [can't stop crying.]

34 SISTER I did not understand why she was feeling so hurt, but I think I can understand now.

MARIA [looks at 26-year-old sister] You don't believe her because you didn't look at her. I want you to look at your sister to see that she comes from her heart. Do you believe what she said? You don't owe her anything? What she did was coming from her heart. Would you tell her what you think you owe her? Let us talk about it openly. [Turns to 34-year-old sister] What did you do for her? What makes her think she owes you?

34 SISTER Everybody says that together with my husband I did a lot for her. I think the debt she has is that she and her husband think they should be grateful for what we have done. The other day when I said "grateful," I actually just wanted her to appreciate what she already has, but I think the word grateful is really a trigger for her.

MARIA [turns to 26-year-old sister] I would like you to take a breath. I would like you to imagine something. Would you listen to me?

26 SISTER Yes.

MARIA If you were the eldest sister in this family, and she was your younger sister, would you do the same thing that she did? What do you think? If you were in the position she was, would you do the same thing?

26 SISTER I would.

MARIA [to 26-year-old sister] I believe that you are putting a big burden on your sister. She is reaching out to you. Can you imagine accepting this? You happen to be her sister and she loves you. Did you ever tell her how you feel?

26 SISTER No.

MARIA Would you tell her now? Would you hold her hand? [34-year-old sister holds 26-year-old sister's hand.] Tell her what you never said. She really wants to connect with you. Do you believe that?

26 SISTER I feel that my emotion is taking me over and I am not well prepared. I am not ready to accept something.

MARIA That's OK. [Looks into 26-year-old sister's eyes] That's OK. I would just like you to make a decision. Get in touch with your feelings. How do you see your feelings? My feeling is purple. What colour is your emotion?

COMMENTARY *I try to get her more grounded and give her an example.*

26 SISTER Grey.

MARIA Grey. You see your grey feelings and I see my purple feelings. I am now telling you about my purple feelings. I am so grateful that I have feelings. I can laugh, I can cry, I can feel, and I am in charge. Right now I feel very sad about my purple feelings, because I see your sadness. [Standing close to 26-year-old sister, who nods] I am in charge of my feelings and I use my feelings to understand yours and respect them. You can take a big breath and know that you can be in charge of your feelings. Would you do that? [26-year-old sister takes a big breath.]

COMMENTARY *The sisters did not understand my colour metaphor, so next I ask them to externalize their feelings by using toys. Neither one of them can talk about their feelings, so I hope this process with the toys will help them become more aware of their feelings and learn how to express them.*

MARIA I'd like you to do something with these toys. Come with me. [Stands up and leads her to the toys.] We'll do something with our feelings. I choose my feelings [chooses a red toy]. Now you choose one for you, and I will invite your sister to choose one too, because I want to talk about our feelings. [26-year-old sister chooses a small grey toy.]

[Asking 34-year-old sister] What colour is yours? [34-year-old sister chooses a big white toy.] Good. [26-year-old sister chooses another big brown toy.]

[To 22-year-old sister] Do you also want to choose something for you? Let's be fair. Everyone has one feeling. Let's put words to our feelings.

[To 34-year-old sister] Ask her what she wants and what she's feeling.

34 SISTER Right now I feel quite relaxed after I went through my process.

MARIA What do you want to tell your sister? Would you remind her what you said before?

34 SISTER I want to say I believe you that you will do lots of things like I have done for you. Everything you do is so unique and nobody can be a substitute for you.

MARIA Can you give her an example of what she did so she can understand you better?

34 SISTER For example, when I went back to my hometown, she was taking care of the homework for my children. She did it very well. I can totally trust her when she does things for me.

MARIA Do you hear what your sister said? Did you do that? [26-year-old sister nods.]

MAMA I want to add something. She is doing things very well. When her 34-year-old sister gave birth to the second baby, I needed to move to her hospital to look after her. To help me, the 26-year-old sister stayed at the hospital one night on my behalf, sleeping on the floor. Just like the elder sister, she is also very caring for the younger one. [26-year-old sister keeps crying.] When the youngest one was sick, she provided care quietly. I was supposed to take over the burden, but she took everything on. I am very touched.

MARIA Did you hear what Mama said? Would you look up? You are in charge of this. There are a lot of feelings about what you did?

26 SISTER Yes.

MARIA Do they owe you? Yes or no?

26 SISTER I wish they would see this.

MARIA They do.

26 SISTER But I don't know why when we were communicating, nobody told me this.

MARIA They are telling you now.

26 SISTER That's why I was very emotional.

MARIA Would you tell them how you feel hearing from your Mama and from your sister? Do you believe that they appreciate you? I think they missed telling you at the time because they took it for granted. In your beautiful family things are taken for granted and there is no communication. It's important that people can hear each other.

Mama, can you tell her more? She and your eldest daughter need to hear this. Tell them more. This time I would ask you not to just hear but also to look at her. We know that you have feelings. Look at Mama rather than looking down.

34 SISTER I also discovered one of my issues. I like to appreciate people behind their backs. In actual fact, I was always proud of you. When you got into a famous university, when you passed the highest professional examination for English, and you earned a dual degree, all my friends knew this, and even my husband's colleagues knew this. Because I was so proud of you, so I told them all this, but I never said this to you.

MARIA Do you believe it? Do you believe her? [26-year-old sister nods.] Tell her. You people need to start talking and expressing your appreciation. I have an exercise, Mama. I would like to make sure everybody does it. Every day everyone shares one appreciation to each other, no matter how small it is. If somebody washed the dishes, if somebody drove you, if somebody just made a phone call, it is very important to appreciate it and say it. When we don't put it out in words, we feel unnoticed and not appreciated. Do you believe that?

26 SISTER Right now my feeling is, I've been waiting for this for a long time, using all my life force to wait and wait for acknowledgement from the mother and elder sister. It's so difficult, even for what happened to my younger sister on August 1st. I try to use all the energy I can, and my elder sister told me that I don't know how to be grateful.

MARIA Tell her.

26 SISTER My younger sister told me one month ago that she wanted to commit suicide. You did not know this until later. You don't know how stressful it was and how difficult it was for me. I was taking the burden all by myself. Mama and my husband made negative comments about my younger sister, which they did not dare tell her. Instead, you told me that I have to use more energy to help my younger

sister. The other day you told me that I hadn't tidied up my room and you think I am emotional. You think this will be bad modeling for my younger sister. You told me you thought you had done a lot for me, but I hadn't done the same for our younger sister. This happened more than a month ago, when the younger sister wanted to commit suicide. I already had lots of stress. At the same time, I got a phone call from you or mother. I had the impulse to cut my wrist to commit suicide. I did not want to let you know because I don't want to hurt you, so I only hurt myself. Actually for what happened to younger sister, I really was giving a lot and it was so hard. You didn't see it coming, but for me I knew it long ago. I had already talked with my husband and we were willing to pay the counselling for my younger sister. I made so much effort, from the beginning until now. None of you came to hug me and tell me that I did well. Every one of you were just telling me what I did was not good enough and you wanted me to do this and that. You want me to tidy my room. You want me to be an ideal sister or daughter.

MARIA You never got appreciation and validation for what you did. I am very proud that you finally say so. In this family you do not know how to appreciate. Now, to put it in words is very important. Would you like to respond?

34 SISTER What you just said is something I want to tell you more about. I did ask you to totally live for our younger sister. I was wrong. You have your way; I have my own way. I shouldn't ask you to use my way. Everybody saw your giving and we also felt it. Now I am clear that you are already grown up. I shouldn't have asked you to tidy up your room. That's something I need to learn. Now I totally understand what it means to let go. I won't do this in the future.

MARIA [to 26-year-old sister] Would you tell your sister what kind of relationship you want and how you want her to treat you like a grown-up person? In my eyes you just grew up, by standing up for yourself and telling her what and how you feel. Now tell her how you want to be treated. Then I will ask your elder sister to do the same. I know you both love each other, and you are both grown up.

26 SISTER I am sorry. I want to talk about one more event.

MARIA Say more. Everything has to come out, all the feelings. [Talks to 34-year-old sister] OK? [Sister nods.]

26 SISTER Thank you. [Facing sister] You hurt me most when you called me last time. [22-year-old sister put her hands on two sisters' shoulders.] I was talking with my mother, something related to my stepfather. The words I used were inappropriate. In the first call you blamed me. You called me the second time. At that time I really wanted to die. You probably don't know that all my life I wanted to protect mother because I didn't want her to be hurt. [Crying.]

After you made the phone call, you just hung up. I felt you just stuck a knife in my heart. It was too much for me. I was so furious and I felt that you neglected my feelings. I wanted to call you back to tell you about my feelings, but you did not answer, so I swallowed my feelings. I did not connect with you for a few days. I did not know how to express my feelings then, and I was not used to acknowledging my anger. Later, when I was with you, I pretended nothing happened. That event hurt me most, because you always told me that the ways I used all my life to protect others is no use, and you think I am not worthwhile. Actually, in the whole world I care most about mother. When you called me and blamed me, you said I hurt my mother. I already gave all my energy to my younger sister, but you told me how I treated her was not as good as you treated me. Then you said my younger sister didn't tidy her room because she learned that from me. I think it's ridiculous. I think my dealing with my life is also ridiculous. I don't know what I am fighting for. I don't know why it is so difficult to get validation from you and from mother. I didn't know I yearn so much for your approval.

MARIA You now know how much you did. I understand that you want their approval and I understand you want their validation. I have a suggestion for you. First of all, do you validate yourself?

26 SISTER No.

MARIA No? I feel very sad about that. Everything that you said shows how much love you have, yet there is no validation. You love these people so much. I think they know it and they just did not talk about it. Will you allow them to say it? Would you like to hear your sister share her feelings? I believe she knew what you were doing.

26 SISTER Could you give me one minute so that I can calm down and prepare myself to listen?

MARIA OK, take a breath, and let yourself be really comfortable. [26-year-old sister sits comfortably and closes her eyes] Go inside, take a big breath. I am inviting you to give yourself a big message appreciating yourself and giving yourself a hug. Value yourself for who you are in this family and how much you have done. Finally, you had the courage to tell them what you want and also that you are ready to listen to them. This is the first time you spoke up for yourself and you can make a commitment that when they forget to validate you, or forget to appreciate you, you would let them know how you feel. Today you heard them and they heard you. Today you spoke and they did also. When you are ready open your eyes and ears, and ask yourself if there is anything you want to say. Then I will ask you to listen to them and their feelings, so everybody can say what they didn't say before. Let this grey feeling become red, purple and white. When you really share your love for each other, there is nothing else left but love. Now I look at you and I see your beauty and I can feel your energy coming back. The breath from each of you will bring your energy back. I want you to feel the energy and love from everybody in the room; not only your family but the whole group. You know your loving husband is sitting behind you, and now you need to take a very big step to stand up for yourself. [The youngest sister helps the 26-year-old sister wipe her tears away.] Most important, you acknowledge how much you love these people and you don't owe anybody anything. They don't owe you either. This family is full of love. You give and receive, but no one owes. Hopefully there is no debt when you leave from here; only appreciation with everybody. I think we all feel how much you love them, but you are not accustomed to expressing it in words. I appreciate that you are taking the opportunity to talk. Are you ready to open your eyes and ears to listen to your sister, because she has a lot to say?

[26-year-old sister opens her eyes and nods.] Look at her and maybe you can hold her hands so that you can feel each other. When you look at her feel her love, both of you.

[To 34-year-old sister] Would you like to respond?

COMMENTARY *I am trying to facilitate a conversation between them so they can communicate more clearly and make new commitments by expressing themselves congruently and validating each other.*

34 SISTER I will comment to you when I see something is inadequate. I only wish you can be better. Maybe the way I have expressed myself was not correct. Maybe I should validate you first, and then tell you my comment, but I never learned anything about psychology.

MARIA What's your intention? Maybe you tell her your intentions, because I think you always have good intentions when you talk to her.

34 SISTER I want you to become better. Maybe some of my words hurt you.

MARIA [to 34-year-old] Would it be possible that whenever you tell her about something, you tell her and then you ask her, "How do you feel about this?" [26-year-old sister holds Maria's hand.] She has a lot of feelings. She thinks with her feelings, so some of your words can hurt her like an arrow piercing through her heart.

[To 26-year-old sister] Any time when you feel hurt, you tell your sister. Just say it right away. Could you accept that? Don't shoot an arrow. Just give her the information. Start communicating.

26 SISTER I did try, but...

MARIA This is a new beginning. Let's practice. [To 34-year-old sister] You say something to her.

34 SISTER Actually I feel hurt too, because some of the words you said were hurtful to me. I don't think it's so important. I knew what you did and I knew your good intention, so when you say something hurtful sometimes I would hide my feelings. Sometimes I choose to forget. Your good intentions are enough for me.

MARIA You two are different people. [To 26-year-old sister] You are talking sincerely from your heart. [To 34-year-old sister] You are talking very much from your head. You need to start talking slowly, so you can understand each other.

[To 26-year-old sister] Are you willing to do that? Meaning anytime if you feel hurt, tell her.

[To 34-year-old sister] How can she tell you, so that you can hear it and not be hurt? It's just connecting and communication. You see that's the way to communicate. Not sharing is a way to disconnect.

[To 22-year-old sister] You are included too, you know.

26 SISTER I think you must be very tired sitting like this, so I move your chair.

MARIA [to 26-year-old sister] OK. Thank you for looking after me. Thank you, I feel good about it. So what can you offer to your sister? First of all I want to make sure, I want something to represent debts. [Someone gives a big bag to Maria.] Oh, that's big enough. Is it big enough for all the debts you owe?

26 SISTER No.

COMMENTARY *I want to visually externalize the younger sister's feeling of obligation and owing to the older sister. The big bag represents the "debt."*

MARIA OK. Would you bring something else?

26 SISTER To me, it's as big as the room.

MARIA Oh, it's like the room, so you pack us together.

26 SISTER When I was sitting in front of the therapist, I felt I was just in the middle of the debt, just sitting like this [She becomes small and looks like she is carrying a heavy burden on her shoulders.] My therapist thinks I carry a lot.

MARIA I don't want you to carry anything. I just want you to let go and put it in the museum. I would like you to imagine. Close your eyes. No matter what burdens are in your package, put them in your museum one by one. OK? [Holding her hands] We'll do it together. We don't have any debts. We have paid all our mortgage. In our country when you buy a house, we take a loan from the bank, and for the rest of our life we have to pay the debt every month. If we work harder, we pay the debts earlier, and finally we are free and own the house. That's what I mean. If you think your debts are like a room, then you let go all the debts, one by one, so when you leave this room you have no debts to your sister. Is that OK?

34 SISTER I would like that to be a release for me.

MARIA When you look into your sister's eyes and do not see your debt in her eyes, you will be able to see her. When your therapist says you owe the debts tell that therapist, "You are wrong. I am not carrying any debt any more." She [34-year-old sister] gave you what she had and you gave her what you had. This is family. That's like everybody's family – to love and help each other. [Points to the bag] Can we throw whatever is in here away to the museum? Your husband will help you. [To husband] You take it away. [The husband takes two bags away.]

Now let's stand up. [Maria holds 26-year-old sister's hand and stands up, facing all the participants.] You said your debts are like this big room. In your imagination, can we let all the debts go to the museum? Close your eyes and think about your debts in your heart, and what you owe to your sister and your Mama. When you are ready tell yourself, "I gave them just as much as they gave to me. So I don't owe anybody and nobody owes me." Just take it to your heart, so you don't have go back to this. [26-year-old sister nods] When you are ready open your eyes and tell all of us, "I have no more debts to my sister or to my mother, even to myself." Ready?

26 SISTER [nods.]

MARIA Tell them first, using your words.

26 SISTER Please leave this session room, because I put this room into the museum.

MARIA And I value myself for all I did for this family. How do you feel?

26 SISTER I don't totally understand what you said.

MARIA I value myself and I love myself for what I did for my family, my sister and my Mama. Say this in your own words.

26 SISTER I've been learning how I can start loving myself and accepting myself. Maybe I've already reached grade 6. Maybe I graduated from high school now. I will continue learning to accept myself. I will put a pearl in my mind and I will tell myself I am a pearl. I deserve to be valued.

MARIA This is my homework for you. Every morning when you wake up remember what you just said. Tell your husband, so he will remember that he has a pearl. [Maria leads her to stand in front of her older sister.] What do you want to tell your sister?

26 SISTER Actually in my mind, you are just like another mother. I think maybe in your mind, I am an outstanding sister. But in my mind, you are the person I respect, and you are an authority for me, just like a mother. I never felt that you don't love me. Even when you hurt me, I still love you. That's why I feel anger. I can finally tell you this today. Now I am feeling relaxed and in my relationship with you I still feel warm. I have all my love. I will learn more about the difference between us and learn to communicate with you better.

MARIA Can you make a commitment? When you feel hurt, because she won't know it, you need to tell her, "I feel grey now." [To 34-year-old sister] That could be a signal and then you will know your sister is feeling hurt.

34 SISTER She told me in the past how hurt she was. I feel responsible and think it was my fault. But I feel I can't be responsible for all your bad feelings. When I came in this room today I felt quite relaxed already. After I heard you about your hurts, [starts crying] I feel very heavy. [26-year-old sister holds 34-year-old sister's hand.]

COMMENTARY *In this next section I encourage both sisters to let go of their "debt" to each other. It becomes a cumbersome process as we take one step forward and two steps back. Each one holds on to being a victim of obligation.*

*I suggest that by sharing their feelings they will begin to hear each other and stop protecting the other person. They try not to hurt each other, which interferes with congruent communication. As a result they hold onto unmet expectations, feel disappointed in the other, and hold onto hurt feelings, then blame themselves. I am trying to untangle this mess to help them express their feelings, as already externalized by the toys. This is a long process. A therapist needs to be very patient to allow for the extended dialogue.*

MARIA Yes. Tell her more. [34-year-old sister crying] I know you have feelings and you also feel it is hard to share them.

26 SISTER That's the reason why I don't talk. I really don't want to hurt her and I understand her pain.

MARIA She is very strong and she can cope with her feelings. This is a problem between people. We won't say something because we love them and don't share what hurts, but the outcome is that the relationship becomes more and more disconnected. Hurt feelings are human. We all hurt sometimes. When we can share in a congruent way, we become more connected. You don't have to take care of her because she is strong. [To 34-year-old sister] Would you accept her sharing her feelings? If you feel hurt you can tell her.

34 SISTER I can accept that and I find that often when she is ambiguous, I don't know whether she wants my response or not.

MARIA Can you talk to her directly, using "you" not "she?"

34 SISTER I would like to hear your feelings and your thoughts. I am also willing to hear some of your negative feelings and thoughts.

MARIA There is no "negative," just feelings, including hurt.

34 SISTER I also feel hurt sometimes but I won't allow myself to feel bad every day, or deny what you said. I think this is something you need to learn. I also had my own puzzle. It was difficult for me when I was growing up. I did not ask for help from the outside. I learned to find strength from my inside, otherwise I would repeat the same mistake, and punish myself for this.

MARIA You are both unique, different people. You dealt and coped differently when you experienced hurt. Can you accept that you are different, and respect each other for your differences? Then you can love each other, even when you have differences.

26 SISTER I am sure we need to learn how to communicate. I felt hurt and I felt being blamed, because when my sister is telling me how she handled difficulties, my understanding is that I was not good enough. I did not resolve my issues like she did, so I felt blamed.

MARIA You still put her into the judge's position and mother's position. Can you imagine that your sister disagrees and she just has a different opinion? Treat her as an equal who is no longer an authority for you. She is your elder and someone you can listen to but you can disagree or say, "I feel differently." [Asks 34-year-old sister] Is that OK?

34 SISTER Yes, I need this. I need to understand what you really meant.

MARIA [to 26-year-old] You can disagree. You are no longer a little girl, to look at her like authority. The first step is no more debts. The second step is to look at her. She is your sister, not your mother. You can disagree. You can communicate. [Asks 34-year-old sister] Is that OK with you?

34 SISTER I always thought it's OK for me.

MARIA [to 26-year-old sister] Do you believe it? When you feel blamed, you just say, "I feel blamed now."

26 SISTER [thinks for a while and nods] I really don't want my sister to feel hurt, but she does feel hurt, and I know her pain.

MARIA Her hurt is her feeling, but you cannot take care of her pain, just as she cannot take care of yours. People were telling you your sister was upset because of you. You tell the people that it's not your responsibility, and you feel sad if she feels hurt, but you won't take on this responsibility for her feelings. Who are the people who tell you these things?

26 SISTER My mother, my younger sister.

MARIA Well, ask Mama whether she thinks it is you who hurt your sister.

MAMA All three daughters are the same. Now I know where the issue is. Because my eldest one takes lots of care of the younger one, the younger sister feels she owes a debt. The elder sister is seen like a mother. After the elder sister gave birth to her children, she's not working now. Younger sister has a better job and her husband is considerate too. Elder sister thinks the younger sister is doing better and she is more outstanding than her. Both of them felt to some extent they are outstanding and in some ways they are not so good. So they couldn't communicate well. Actually this is very clear. Because both of them are already adults, I couldn't say much. I don't understand the pain of my second daughter, because in my eyes, she did so well at work, and she is very happy in her marriage. I don't know why she is feeling pain. Now I know, I learned a lot this time. I am not good at showing appreciation verbally. I like the Chinese saying that "to be quiet is more than being noisy." I think between mother and daughter we don't need to talk. We can sense our feelings between us. I like to do things rather than saying. Now I know that is something I need to learn. All my three daughters want my validation, but I blame them more than appreciate them. I thought I need to give them comments so they can do things better. In the future, since they are already grown up, I will validate them. I will learn to express myself straight and then they will have more confidence. Actually, my second daughter is very outstanding. Her elder sister and I are sure of this. I see everything she did and keep them in my mind. I just did not verbalize it. In the future I will express myself.

MARIA [to 26-year-old sister] Look at your mother when she speaks to you.

MAMA I know my three daughters love me very much. I am also aware of everything they did for me. My second daughter and her husband always feel they owe a debt to her elder sister and they want to compensate. I appreciate my eldest daughter. I hope we can communicate more in the future, especially me as a mother. When I see them do something well, I will appreciate them just like I do with my students.

MARIA Yes. Good idea, just like with your students. You know how to appreciate.

MAMA Yes, yes. Thank you.

34 SISTER I disagree with what my mother said. I don't think I am inferior because I did not go to work. I will go back to work after my children grow up.

MARIA Tell your Mama directly. [34-year-old sister turns to her mother.]

34 SISTER This is not the reason we have communication problems.

MARIA Mama, what about your youngest daughter? What do you want to tell her?

MAMA She is more open and energetic. She remembers if anybody does good things for her, but she does not think she owes any debt, like my second daughter. If people are nice to her, she feels she owes them something. I don't think she needs to do this. We are a family. We can mutually help each other. It is supposed to be like this, and it's happening naturally. So you don't need to be so heavy, especially to mother. Mothers love their children, and they love their children without being selfish. What I did for you is what I am supposed to do. You don't need to bear this as your burden. I hope you quickly grow up as an adult. I urge you to let go of this burden, and I hope in the future that you can provide for me, and I can lean on your shoulder so I can take a break. I also hope just like I said two days ago, I want to have my own freedom. I want to go through my old age with relaxation.

MARIA Can you acknowledge and appreciate what a great job you did? These are three wonderful people.

MAMA I am proud of myself inside. I am not only appreciating myself. I am proud of myself.

MARIA Good.

MAMA I have three wonderful children. They are very kind and honest. It is not only me saying this. Other people have the same feedback about them.

MARIA They are all different and unique.

MAMA Yes, yes. [Points to 34-year-old sister] This one looks like their grandma. [Points to 22-year-old sister] This one looks like their grandpa. [Points to 26-year-old sister] This one looks like me.

MARIA And … [points to 26-year-old sister] This one is full of feelings. [Points to 34-year-old sister] She represents all the thinking and wisdom.

MAMA And responsibility.

MARIA [points to 22-year-old sister] She represents all the creativity and fun. So you have all your ancestors' stories and you all have wonderful qualities.

MAMA They also have limitations. Mothers only see the positive side of their children.

MARIA I like to see their positive side.

MAMA Mother tells the children their limitations, what they need to improve, but to the outside people we say our children are wonderful and number one.

MARIA Would you also tell them?

MAMA Yes, yes. I blamed them because I want them to be more perfect. But I was wrong.

MARIA Wrong, yes wrong. I am glad you say that.

MARIA [to 22-year-old sister] You didn't say much, because you support your sister all the time. Tell us how you feel?

22 SISTER I want to say something about my eldest sister. [Faces 26-year-old sister] Eldest sister suggests you can think in another way because she thinks you will be happier if you think another way. I don't think she was blaming you. She wants you to be happy.

MARIA How do you feel? Do you think that she will give up her debts? [Puts hand on 34-year-old sister's shoulder.] And this sister feels OK that she wants to be herself.

22 SISTER I think she can put her debts aside, because she's growing every day.

MARIA [to 26-year-old sister's husband] How do you feel? What do you have to say?

HUSBAND I really feel delighted by the concept of being a grown up, since last session. It's very helpful. My wife is very responsible. Loving her mother and respect for her elder sister became her debts. It does not matter who's wrong or who's right. She can have her unique thinking. After she resolved her issue today, she can be an independent adult when we are sitting together, to communicate with each other equally. Maybe this is the issue she needs to deal with.

MARIA No, no, no more issues.

HUSBAND Yes, I agree.

MARIA Remind her. No more debts.

HUSBAND Yes, yes, yes.

MARIA Remind her every day, and remind her to value herself. You can be a big help.

HUSBAND Yes, that's the first thing. Secondly, I think the issue is their communication. I think elder sister is an outstanding person. Actually, in the past her choices changed the fate of every family member here. I want to tell the elder sister here. If we want to count your strength, we can keep talking until this course is over. Being a listener during the whole session, I think this family is quite outstanding. We moved to Shanghai and the reason we are successful is because we care for each other. Because of loving, they don't want to say something they thought may be upsetting the other person, and they don't even have arguments. I feel in the future, if we can understand this and share our happiness with each other, maybe the communication would be different in the family. There are no more big issues in this family, because that's a lot of nutrition in our soil.

MARIA I agree with you. [To the therapist] The therapist will help you to learn more about communication. [To 34-year-old sister] Is there anything unfinished for you?

34 SISTER I still have a puzzle about communication.

MARIA What is the puzzle?

34 SISTER It's so difficult for us to communicate, but I haven't figured out the reason yet.

MARIA When we try to take care of everybody's feelings, we get more disconnected and build walls between us. This is not only for your family. This is universal. "Mama, I love you and want to take care of you, so I will never tell you when something bothers me because I don't want you to be worried about me." Because you love each other you keep your pain to yourselves, but after a while you feel lonely, and you become anxious and resentful. Sometimes it is painful to tell each other something. Maybe it is painful but it might also be offering connection. Papa is the only one who is not hurting.

MARIA I suggest that when you leave today, each of you put the past events and bad feelings into your museum. The past goes to the museum. Can you imagine that, Mama?

MAMA Yes, we should put the past into the museum. We can learn from that. Rather than look into the past and contaminate our present, we should move on.

MARIA Right. We can just learn from the past. The past events we cannot change, but we can change their impact. Second, no more debts. Nobody owes anybody any debts. Everybody has paid their debt. [Points to 22-year-old sister] And you too. You all have to learn communication, because we don't learn it in school. I think you will all learn it.

Now I would like to ask you one thing before you leave here, and I hope you will do it very often at home. Each person is to give every person one appreciation. Let's sit in a circle. If you want to give more than one appreciation you are welcome. I want you to learn that. When you are all together you can do this at home. Papa will be responsible and remind you. [Papa nods.]

COMMENTARY *In order to move the conversation into a positive direction, I use part of the Temperature Reading. My hope is that sharing positives with each other will provide an opportunity to end this session on a strong note.*

MAMA My husband, even though you don't say no to me, your support is very helpful to me. My eldest daughter, you are very giving. Today's achievement is because of your effort. Thank you.

My second daughter, you did so much when your younger sister was sick. You did it on behalf of me. I knew then that it was my responsibility and you took everything on. In the beginning I did not know that she had a psychological problem. I did not understand this illness, and I was upset. I complained to you and I was a burden for you. I know all about this. But I feel touched in my heart. Thank you.

My son-in-law, my daughter has so many burdens and you were always a support for her. And when the youngest one was sick, you also made lots of effort. Thank you.

My youngest daughter, you are not independent yet. You are still living with me. I hope you can take care of us in the future. You offer lots of happiness to us when you are living with us. Thank you.

MARIA Thank you, Mama. Now, Papa.

PAPA Mama, you are the soul of this family. You always have good recommendations for all our issues. I did not take care of you a lot. I really appreciate you. I am willing to work for you. I can't do a big job but I can do a small job, because I am old. Compared to you, Maria, I am still quite young.

[To eldest daughter] The two of you are kind and very competent. Where our family is today is because of the effort you and your husband made. I sometimes don't communicate much, because your mother is my representative, so I don't talk much.

[To second daughter] You are open minded and you often are considerate for others. The three of you have different characteristics. You often feel heavy inside. After these two interviews you know you don't owe anybody. Don't carry any debts. You are also very outstanding at work and you did a lot for this family. Your mother often tells me she is proud of you three. That's true. You have no debts any more. You are not only responsible for your husband's family. You will have children. You will be a mother and you should be better than your mother. Your elder sister can totally understand your mother now.

[To son-in-law] You are better than me. You really love my daughter. I should learn from you to love my wife.

[To third daughter] You are playful and you are a character, but you still can learn, so I don't worry. But one worries that you should find a good husband in the future, then we will be happier.

MARIA Eldest daughter.

34 SISTER [to Mama\ Thank you for you doing everything for us. I also want to tell you, it's already over, whether right or wrong, it is already passed. We can leave it alone. If we can let go, we can feel more relaxed.

[To Papa] Thank you. You have given my mother a happy marriage, and thank you for giving us a family to become whole.

[To 26-year-old sister] You do a lot. I can feel and I know it. I think you are great. You can always discover your strength no matter in which stage you are. You support Mama, and you are so considerate for her. There are a lot of things I need to learn from you.

[To youngest sister] Thank you for being always with me when I need you. I think in the future, I will try to understand you more, to do something for you. After I had children, I focused on the children and I did not care for you enough.

MARIA [to 26-year-old sister] It's your turn.

26 SISTER I wanted to get the microphone earlier, because I have lots to say that I didn't have the chance to in the last session. I want to say more and maybe I want to add more later.

I want to tell my elder sister that since what happened to our youngest sister, I have recalled lots of our fun times. Even though we often had physical fights when we were young, we still had fun. You often said you hit me lighter and I hit you harder, because I was young then. When Mama was absent, I really wanted to be with you, so when you went to school, I kept looking for you. I bothered you a lot even when you closed the door, just because I wanted to be with you. Now I can recall, when you were at university, mother went back to her hometown and you took care of me. I feel in our communication, I also made some mistakes. I was the one who put you into mother's position. I was not able to communicate with you peacefully. I was seeking your validation. I became angry if you did not validate me. That's my own problem. You don't need to be responsible for my pain. What I am letting you know is that I am capable of living better. I have my own way to resolve things, and you don't need to worry for me. I know it was hard for you to come here, and you needed courage. For this last visit here, I sensed and I knew you would have some deep feelings. I wanted to respond to you with my loving and positive memory in the last interview, but because we were running out of time I could not. I am really thankful to you.

When you had your first daughter, you said I was very nice to her, and some time I even ignored you. In my mind being nice to her means I am nice to you. When you had your second child, I went to the hospital not because of mother but because of you, because I love you so much. Actually in my mind, I was not doing this because of debts, I just really wanted to be nice to you, and I know you were also very nice to me. I really love you very much. When you are feeling hurt I always feel sad for you. After we came here last time, I heard you crying in the car. I knew you were crying, but I did not know how to resolve it. I felt sad the whole evening, and I sent a message to the therapist. I even wanted to invite you to attend Maria's workshop next week. I want to use my way to let you feel better. I really love you very much and I do feel you are outstanding. I often tell my husband I was willing to marry him just because you said something good about him, and you saw his strength. You supported me to choose him. I often tell him, our life now is coming from you.

MARIA How about to Mama? Anything to appreciate?

26 SISTER After we got back from the previous interview, I realized that when I said that you control us, and blamed you for this, that was unfair. Before I got married, every night you talked to me until midnight. You told me about my work, what I should go for. It was very helpful for me. The difference is I am grown up now. I have my own family and my own ideas. I haven't learned yet how to communicate with you in this situation. So I just want to say that your controlling is not fair. I will learn how to communicate with you better. My loving towards you is far more than to myself. For a long time I felt you were just like my life, since I was very young, I wanted to protect you, and I wanted you to suffer less. Of course it's my issue, I really feel sad for the suffering you went through for so many years. That's why I became so heavy. That's my choice and my issue. I will grow and resolve these issues, so you don't need to worry for me. I am not vulnerable at all. This only happens with you. You are in the warmest place in my heart. That's why it is easy for me to feel pain. I actually can be very strong when I am feeling difficulties and pressures from the outside. I am only vulnerable in front of you. I really love you a lot and I love myself more. So don't worry for me.

Papa, I always remember – I don't know whether I was in grade 5 or grade 8 – you bought a book for me on how to write essays, and how to make fantasy. Later I wrote an essay according to the book you gave to me, and I got 100 per cent for it. That book meant to me father's love. In my mind you are my father. I love you more than I love my biological father. When you had surgery last time, I felt so sad. I cried for a long time. I wished for you to be healthy and happy with longevity, because you are so important in my mind. Like my elder sister said, because of you we have a whole family. Without you, the three of us could not have grown up so healthy. You offered much support to us. Thank you very much.

Youngest sister, when I offered my support to you, I felt very happy.

When you were feeling pain, I was even in more pain than you. To witness your growth and change, I am really happy. It's very meaningful for me because there is a lot of hope that lightens my energy. I thank for you being so courageous and so strong. I always think you are very beautiful, but when other people come over to tell me your younger sister is so beautiful, I feel jealous and don't tell you how they appreciate you. I also feel that you are the most lovable among the three of us. You are beautiful. Thank you.

MARIA To your husband.

26 SISTER Since I am married to you, I have received lots of healing. That's why I can grow. You are the most important person in my life and I am lucky that I met you. No other person could support me like you support me. You often tell me I am good. Every day you tell me how much you love me. I feel I am totally connected with you from heart to heart. When I see you every day, I can feel my loving towards you. I am so lucky that I met you. Also you are lucky finding me. I don't say it often how I love you because I think we can both sense it. I can keep telling you every day, so I won't say more here.

I have more things to say to the therapist. I am really thankful to you. You shared with me the pressure my younger sister was feeling. Without you, we could not have overcome this. Even though it was a painful journey, because of you, we could see hope and got energy to move on. I am really grateful. Thank you for everything you did. It's very meaningful for all of us. Without you, we wouldn't be here with Maria.

MARIA Let's hear your husband.

HUSBAND I want to appreciate father first. You are so happy every day. I really like to be with you because then I feel happy too.

Mama, I think you are very strong. We really respect that you are so strong and so open, and that you take such good care of all of us. You are a really considerate mother and I thank you so much for all the work you have done. I hope from now on you can do something you are happy about. If you have any dream, just fulfill your dream now.

[To elder sister] We all respect you. All the achievement and happiness in this family, often comes from you.

[To youngest sister] I think you are hopeful, because you are so intelligent, so lovable and energetic. Being in the university in Shanghai, you know lots of new stuff about Shanghai and new tech. In the future, for your life and for your work for your family, you can be happy there.

[To wife] We are very intimate. I appreciate you from my heart and words are not enough to express how I feel. I really appreciate you and love you very much. I want you to be happy and feel relaxed every day. Thank you all.

22 SISTER I want to talk to Mama first. In my mind, you have become important for me. I don't know where to start, because when I was young, I grew up with my maternal grandmother. She was important for me then. Somehow, I don't know when, you became the most important person for me. I wished you validated me, and I wanted to become a daughter you love. I apologize about the way I expressed myself. I was rebellious, because I wanted to prove myself and I wanted to prove to you that I am good enough. So if I did hurt you, I am really sorry about that.

MAMA I love you very much too. I believe I am important for you. I have no doubt about it. I also know you are very smart. I believe you are outstanding too, I am proud of you. I hope that you can really treasure yourself and value yourself. If you just value yourself it means you love us. Thank you.

I want to add more to show my appreciation for my family. I really want to appreciate my son-in-law, and the husband of my eldest daughter. He could not come here because of his busy work. He is a very competent, sincere person, and very honest. He treats this family as his own family. He shows so much caring to these two younger sisters. As a major factor, where our family is today is because of my eldest daughter's efforts and what her husband did. He offered us a lot, but he often says, he gives but he never expects us to give back. I really want to thank him. Another one I want to appreciate is Maria.

MARIA Your daughter was not finished.

22 SISTER [to Papa] To me you bear the responsibility of father. Actually, you are the father. Because of you, our family is whole. I love you very much too.

[To eldest sister] I don't think you ignored me. I totally understand the responsibility you have for your nuclear family. I am happy for the relationship and I want to continue like this.

[To elder sister] The moment I wanted to give up my life, you kept me company, and I felt you were just like a mother. I treasure my life. I will make my life beautiful. I want to show to the therapist the beauty and strength of life.

[To brother-in-law] When I observe you together with my sister, I think I want to have a marriage like yours. You are wonderful. Thank you for all you did for my sister. You offer her lots of strength. I am thankful to you.

MARIA Mama, I interrupted you before. Do you have something to say?

MAMA Yes. I want to appreciate you, Maria. You came many miles here, at your age, to help our families. I am really grateful to you. And I am also grateful to the translator. You've translated the whole afternoon. You work a lot. For our family you did a lot. And to the therapist, thank you very much. To all of you here, you all did so much for our family and spent so much time with us. Thank you all.

MARIA Thank you for trusting us by coming back. I know from the therapist that you hesitated to come. I appreciate you two decided to come finally. I feel it is a gift to meet your family. I would like to see you again and I would like you to remember three important things. One is to appreciate when you are in chaos, because out of the chaos comes new change. Secondly, remember the museum. And third, move on with your communication just as you did here. Say how you feel.

I'd like to give homework to Papa, and the therapist will follow up to see whether you did your homework or not. I suggest that you do this at least once a week when you are all together. Papa will be the chairperson. You ask them to give appreciations once a week, just like you all did here. Say to each other how you feel. Later you can do it without structure and you will do it automatically, but for now Papa will be responsible and be the chairperson. Thank you all. I am sure you will meet the therapist and you can learn more about communication.

34 SISTER Thank you very much, Maria. You really resolved the issue for our family. We also appreciate that you gave us so much time. I feel I learned a lot.

MARIA Not only me, all of us.

34 SISTER Yes thank you all.

MARIA I hope you will move on and bring about this change together. Remember to say hello to your husband. I'm sorry we did not meet him.

MAMA Yes, he is a wonderful person.

MARIA I am sure. [Maria shakes hands with everybody, and Mama gives Maria a big hug. 26-year-old sister also hugs Maria. At the end, the 34-year-old sister and Maria hug each other.]

MARIA [to the whole group] Thank you all. Is there anyone who wants to share their feelings?

COMMENTARY *I asked for participants' observations and feedback. Several participants identified with the oldest sister. Through this interview they learned more appreciation for their younger siblings. Another participant identified closely with the 26-year-old sister and the dynamics of communication in this family.*

## Evaluation notes

Following is my assessment of whether this interview utilized the goals, basic elements, and directives of the Satir Family Therapy Model as outlined earlier in this book.

### EXPERIENTIAL

In this interview I focused on educating the family members on how to communicate congruently, to share their feelings, their pains, puzzles and unfinished business. I encouraged the sisters to see each other eye to eye and to share feelings. I used toys to externalize their feelings and help them accept them. I hope that the experience of sharing will engage them in further communication.

## POSITIVELY DIRECTIONAL
Over and over again I directed them to connect. We had to surface some past painful experiences in order to let them go and to move towards self-validation in the present. Even though we talked about the past, the process was to put it all into the museum and clear the way for open communication and sharing.

## SYSTEMIC
This family is a good example of a closed system, in which painful issues are not talked about. On the surface they pretend that all is fine and great effort is made to maintain the status quo. I tried to break this rigid system and open channels for everyone to connect in a new way. The intention of the homework is to enhance and continue to build congruent communication in the family system.

## FOCUS ON CHANGE
Change is difficult for every member in this family. After the first session they experienced chaos and responded with apprehension and fear of the unknown. In addition, the parenting roles were mixed up and contributed to the confusion. My intention was to move everyone towards their third birth.

## THERAPIST'S USE OF SELF
In this interview I often felt frustrated and needed a lot of patience when we seemed to be going round in circles. As they shared more of their vulnerabilities, more fear and helplessness surfaced between the two sisters. There is an interesting process between them that repeats itself. When one offers an appreciation, the other dismisses the positive comment and immediately goes into defense. To interrupt this pattern I acknowledged that each of them is unique and have their own way of coping with hurt. I developed a close connection and trust with the 26-year-old when I respected her request for time to gain her composure, then held her hand and said "We'll do this together." I used myself in different ways, participating in choosing a stuffed toy, sharing my feelings, supporting with touch and through proximity, mediating and educating. I shared my own experiences through examples when it was appropriate.

## RAISING SELF ESTEEM
I hope that raising self-esteem was a part of each and every interven-

tion. The fact that I invited the family back for a second interview contributed to raising self-esteem for everyone, particularly the oldest sister. I recognized that the two sisters were communicating from a position of submission [26-year-old] and dominance [34-year-old]. It was important to change this submissive/dominant stance and help them to see each other as equals and value themselves as human beings. I also stressed that disagreement is not rejection. Sculpting the resources of the youngest sister was an experiential approach to raise her self-esteem and thereby contribute to the whole family's self-esteem.

## FOSTERING SELF-RESPONSIBILITY AND CHOICE MAKING
I initiated an opportunity for self-responsibility and choice making when I invited the family to return for this second interview. During this session I emphasize self-responsibility versus self-blame, placating, and covertly blaming others. With this family it was important to make the covert overt. I encouraged them to take risks and to take responsibility, to share their feelings in spite of their reluctance and intense fear of hurting one another.

## FAMILY OF ORIGIN
I did not find it relevant to ask questions about the mother's family of origin. The issues we dealt with are in this family system. It is understood that the sisters' beliefs, rules and patterns grew out of their experience in this family.

## FACILITATING CONGRUENCE
Since communication is the focus of this interview, achieving congruent communication between them is the long-term goal. The son-in-law demonstrated congruence. He specifically commented on how difficult it is in this family to have straight communication.

## Follow up (reported by Marie Lam, translator)
One year after the two interviews, Maria had a third interview with the family. The husband of the eldest sister joined the interview this time. The eldest sister did not speak as much as in the other interviews. Every other member of the family is changing and following their commitments.

Before publishing this book, there was a verifying process with each therapist and family, for them to agree to their interviews being included in this book. When the eldest sister was in the verifying process with her therapist, she expressed some resistance. She felt sad, angry and misunderstood. She was concerned about how she would be portrayed in this book. She felt vulnerable and shared her deep yearnings with the therapist to be understood and accepted. Eventually, after conversations with the therapist, the translator, and the publisher she felt understood and gave her permission for the material to be published. She requested an opportunity to add her personal interpretation, as follows.

She wanted to be acknowledged for helping the whole family move from their hometown to Shanghai and contributing generously to the family, but her family perceived her as controlling and manipulating.

As the eldest daughter she was caught in the middle between helping mother raise her younger sisters and being seen as an authority figure by them. She had difficulty protecting and expressing herself, feeling sad, angry and misunderstood since she was a young child.

In the first interview she also felt blamed and disliked by Maria, and felt she was not heard. Her intention was to cooperate but she had such a strong body reaction when practicing congruent communication that she feared her sisters would not accept her feelings. She believed that she had to sacrifice herself to be valued. She thought that her sisters were not aware of all that she had done for mother and for them.

After she verified the transcript, the eldest sister said, "I was not ready to be vulnerable in the first two interviews, even when Maria gave me a chance to express myself. Instead, I showed my strong part without awareness. I was reflecting when I read the transcript that nobody really heard me. I did not share my feelings. My body took on those feelings. I had lots of tears and chest pain. I finally allowed them to be explored because I was afraid I would become very sick if I kept my feelings inside."

Since the family had always lived together, she now realizes that she never experienced her own personal space. She feels she has too many boundaries.

Since the third interview, sadly, the stepfather drowned. The second sister got pregnant, and the youngest sister fell in love and found a new job.

Every member in the family is on a new journey, which comes with new feelings. They are showing caring and expressing feelings towards each other, cautiously. Sometimes, they are afraid about unpleasant reactions if they communicate. They are trying to be congruent, yet still have fears. However, they are growing. They are also seeking counselling from outside.

The family is OK at the beginning of 2014. They are less enmeshed and each is doing their own thing. The mother has settled after the passing of her husband. There is a good connection between the eldest sister and the youngest one. The younger sister found a job by herself. There is still distance between the oldest and the second sister. The second sister is studying psychology. The oldest sister is continuing with her own counsellor. In March 2014 in Shanghai, the youngest sister came to the book celebration. She was very happy and participated in the festive presentation. She introduced me to her boyfriend and told me that the family was doing well.

## Postscript
The three sisters have continued to attend workshops Maria has done in Shanghai or Beijing. They demonstrate a continued willingness to learn and grow.

## IN CLOSING

The project described in this book has reaffirmed for me that people and families can change. Even in the limited time I shared with the families in this book, they were clearly in transition. There is hope for all to discover a better way to live and connect within their family systems.

In each of the cases in this book, the presenting issue was something happening with a child. But, as you have learned through these families, and as Virginia taught, "the problem is not the problem." The child's behaviour is an indication that the system is dysfunctional. The parents' relationship is very important, as it relates to how the system functions and influences a child's growth and development. The parents set the tone for the whole family.

I have never been more convinced that a therapist has to see the whole family. We cannot say that only one individual is the problem. Rather, that individual is a signal that the entire family needs help.

After reading this book, I hope that you will evaluate your own family system.

If you are a parent, I hope you will recognize the tremendous responsibility you have to focus on your own relationship with your self and with your spouse.

If you are a therapist, I hope you will appreciate how your own personal development and self-awareness are the most essential tools in the therapy process.

I wish you well in your journeys!

FURTHER READING

*The New Peoplemaking*
Virginia Satir
Science and Behavior Books, 1987

*The Satir Model: Family Therapy and Beyond*
Virginia Satir, John Banmen, Jane Gerber, Maria Gomori
Hushion House, 2006

*Personal Alchemy: The Art of Satir Family Reconstruction*
Maria Gomori with Eleanor Adaskin
Hong Kong Satir Center for Human Development, 2008

*Passion for Freedom: The Life of Maria Gomori*
Maria Gomori
The Haven Institute Press, 2014


ALSO FROM THE HAVEN INSTITUTE PRESS

By Jock McKeen and Bennet Wong

*Being: A Manual for Life* (2014)
*Joining: The Relationship Garden* (2014)
*The Illuminated Heart:*
*Perspectives on East-West Psychology and Thought* (2012)
*A Book about Health and Happiness* (2007)

*A Book about Anger, Boundaries and Safety* (2006)
Joann Peterson

*A Book about Living with Passion* (2005)
David Raithby and Sandey McCartney

Made in the USA
Lexington, KY
05 June 2015